T0309816

Moderately Modern

Other Books of Interest from St. Augustine's Press

Rémi Brague, *Eccentric Culture: A Theory of Western Civilization*

Rémi Brague, *On the God of the Christians (and on one or two others)*

Rémi Brague, *Anchors in the Heavens:*
The Metaphysical Infrastructure of Human Life

Rémi, Brague, *The Legitimacy of the Human*

Stanley Rosen, *Plato's Symposium*

Klaus Vondung, *Paths to Salvation: The National Socialist Religion*

Ellis Sandoz, *The Politics of Truth and Other Untimely Essays:*
The Crisis of Civic Consciousness

Ellis Sandoz, *Give Me Liberty: Studies in Constitutionalism and Philosophy*

Pierre Manent, *Seeing Things Politically:*
Interviews with Benedicte Delorme-Montini

Daniel J. Mahoney, *The Other Solzhenitsyn:*
Telling the Truth about a Misunderstood Writer and Thinker

Peter Kreeft, *Socrates' Children: The 100 Greatest Philosophers*

Peter Augustine Lawler, *Homeless and at Home in America*

Peter Augustine Lawler, *American Heresies and Higher Education*

Roger Scruton, *The Aesthetic Understanding:*
Essays in the Philosophy of Art and Culture

Roger Scruton, *An Intelligent Person's Guide to Modern Culture*

Roger Kimball, *The Fortunes of Permanence:*
Culture and Anarchy in an Age of Amnesia

Frederic Raphael and Joseph Epstein, *Where Were We?*

Gerhart Niemeyer, *Between Nothingness and Paradise*

Josef Pieper, *What Does "Academic" Mean?:*
Two Essays on the Chances of the University Today

Josef Pieper, *Enthusiasm and Divine Madness*

Josef Pieper, *Don't Worry about Socrates*

Moderately Modern

Rémi Brague

Translated by Paul Seaton

ST. AUGUSTINE'S PRESS
South Bend, Indiana

Manufactured in the United States of America.

1 2 3 4 5 6   25 24 23 22 21 20 19

Library of Congress Cataloging in Publication Data
Names: Brague, Rémi, 1947- author.
Title: Moderately modern / Rémi Brague ; translation by Paul Seaton.
Other titles: *Modérément moderne*. English
Description: South Bend : St. Augustines Press, Inc., 2017.
Includes index.
Identifiers: LCCN 2017015747
ISBN 9781587315183 (hardcover : alk. paper)
Subjects: LCSH: Philosophy, Modern--21st century.
Civilization, Modern.
Classification: LCC B805 .B68713 2017
DDC 190--dc23
LC record available at https://lccn.loc.gov/2017015747

∞ The paper used in this publication meets the minimum requirements of the American National Standard for Information Sciences - Permanence of Paper for Printed Materials, ANSI Z39.48-1984.

St. Augustine's Press
www.staugustine.net

Table of Contents

Translator's Introduction

Paul Seaton

Moderately Modern wears its thesis on its sleeve. Modern men and women, especially thoroughgoing moderns, need to rein themselves in, they need to moderate their pace, even take in elements from outside their blinkered vision of a world thoroughly *à la mode*. Lots of facts, joined with modernity's own standards of evaluation, indicate its increasingly dire condition. Troubling demographics are one, despair among the remaining young, another, a culture that all-too-often is merely technical, or the banal display of sentimental humanitarianism, a third. One could continue, but a bill of indictment is not the purpose of the book. The examples, however, do indicate Brague's main worry: the prospect of the demise of Europe, demographically and culturally. That concern, admittedly, is not in the title.

As always, what is needed is a sober analysis of the situation in which one finds oneself and feasible prescriptions for what ails. The analysis needs a capacious framework, the prescription, norms that can address and heal. The learned Brague delivers on the former with aplomb, and his proposed norms have the merit and interest of being countercultural. The newest novelty for modernity, he argues, should be to reconnect with its premodern past.

Fear not, Brague is not a reactionary. The great prides of modern thought and society — modern science, technology, the lay State, human rights —, retain their legitimacy. However, they need to be placed within wider contexts, they need to have their limits acknowledged, and, most of all, a new foundation needs to be given to modern humanity. That foundation, as befits the depth of the problem and the character of western culture, needs to be both anthropological and ontological. What it is to be human needs to be reconceived and the "vision of the world" undergirding thought and action revised. Vis-à-vis this urgent cultural task, premodern thought becomes remarkably relevant, including its currently most scorned aspects, the biblical and the medieval. So argues Brague, scholar, philosopher, and Catholic.

Few are as capable as the polymath Brague of making that case and indicating what it entails. He is intimately familiar with the pagan Greek and Roman sources of the west, but he most impresses and surprises with his knowledge of the biblical ones, Jewish and Christian. And all that is combined in an extraordinary grasp of the nature and course of western civilization. As an added bonus, he regularly highlights the essential characteristics of the foregoing – Judaism, Christianity, the west – by comparison and contrast with Islam.

The result is fresh light on contemporary problems. But the light is not merely illuminating. Brague reprises the Augustinian distinction between the truth as *lucens* and as *redarguens*. The former allows for the appreciation of what's displayed, the latter, though, dispels shadows that the person would prefer to cover his shady motives and character. In Brague's analyses, premodern thoughts and authorities are resurrected and allowed to comment upon the world wrought by modern thought. The tables are turned and both sorts of truth are forthcoming.

But again, Brague is not a reactionary. This is done, finally, in the spirit of the Biblical God, who created the world and humankind so that they might exist and have life, even life in abundance. In fact, readopting this biblical perspective is his fundamental prescription for ailing Europe. But Brague constantly surprises with his exegesis and understanding of biblical themes, from the meaning of creation to that of man as God's image. His creator primarily wants his creatures to follow and develop their distinctive natures, and man's nature is "defined" by freedom and equipped with reason and conscience to be his own guide. According to Brague, God's commandments are more to remind than to instruct or coerce. In short, Brague's biblical faith is more philosophic than is usual, while his philosophy is marked by important biblical elements. His fidelity to the premodern tradition is thus rather creative.

If enough Europeans were to follow his lead, Europe could experience its fourth great Enlightenment, one that follows the Greek, the Christian, and the modern, but now combining them, mutually purified, exhibiting their best features. Such a Europe would be more fully itself. This is a very attractive, because very inclusive, prospect. It would be what G. K. Chesterton said about authentic tradition: democracy extended to the dead. It remains for contemporary Europeans to consider this proposition and to decide for themselves what their future will be, theirs and, perforce, that of their posterity and their estimable culture. Thanks to the writings of Rémi Brague, they will be able to choose *en pleine connaissance de cause*.

"A long book requires a short introduction." This is even truer for a long translation and a translator's introduction. I will end by reassuring the reader that the translation was done with care and vetted and approved by Professor Brague himself. I thank him for the pleasure of working with this text and his careful consideration of the translation. Once again, Bruce Fingerhut of St. Augustine's Press is to be commended and thanked for his patronage. He truly is a *servus servorum litterarum*.

Paul Seaton
St. Mary's Seminary & University
July 11, 2017
Feast of St. Benedict, Patron of Europe

Foreword

The advertisement for an eminently forgettable American film once said: "The best trilogies are in three episodes."[1] Not wanting to belie this profound apothegm, I here present the third and last volume of a trilogy whose two previous volumes are already available.

One will have no trouble in noticing that these two volumes treat in succession Antiquity, then the Middle Ages.[2] Therefore, it remains to occupy myself with Modern Times in this now become inescapable triad.

The trilogy that I finish here therefore is to a certain extent parallel to the one I began with *The Wisdom of the World*, followed by *The Law of God*, and which closed with *Le Règne de l'homme*.[3] Each of these volumes had for its center of gravity one of these periods.

However, in the present trilogy these three periods are not put on the same plane. "Antiquity" designated a period of history during which the philosophers to whom I devoted a number of essays lived. "The Middles Ages," whose thought I studied in a cross-sectional way, going beyond the boundaries of the three religious confessions in which philosophy had taken root, already appeared as a designation that one should not accept without first asking if it was justified or not.

It is the same, and *a fortiori*, for "Modern Times". For me, they do not provide a chronological framework within which authors could be

---

1   *Scary Movie 3*, by David Zucker, which came out in 2003.
2   Rémi Brague, *Introduction au monde grec. Études d'histoire de la philosophie*, Chatou, Éditions de la Transparence, 2005, and *Au moyen du Moyen Âge. Philosophies médiévales en chrétienté, judaïsme et islam*, Chatou, Éditions de la Transparence, 2006. The two have been reissued by Flammarion, "Champs", in 2008.
3   *The Wisdom of the World* (University of Chicago Press, 2004); *The Law of God* (University of Chicago Press, 2008). *Le Règne de l'homme* (Gallimard, 2015).

located. Rather, they constitute the object that I would like to problematize.

The present volume is composed of five parts, with each containing three to five chapters.

The first attempts to have Modernity appear at least as much a *problem* as the solution that it vaunts itself to be. It begins by proposing to moderate the enthusiasm of Modernity for itself by bringing to light its dark underside, which, from the name of an illness, I call "modernitis," some of whose symptoms I study. European culture, which first was ours, then invaded the globe, has, among a great number of its beneficiaries, lost confidence in itself. It is no longer capable of providing the foundation for a credible and defensible humanism. The question posed to us is whether we can give good reasons to want human life to continue.[4]

The second and longest part examines certain notions, among which are those that are the most decisive for Modernity: "reason" as the faculty by which it assures its definitive triumph; "atheism" as the attempt to finally be rid of superstition; "secularization," which leads to the expulsion of the divine; "democracy" as the final doing away with any sort of theocracy; and "progress" as the general atmosphere. Of all these, I unveil their ambiguity, even their fragility. What is more, I try to show that several of these notions harbor in themselves precisely what they were enlisted, even constructed, to do away with, and that they should not see them as enemies, but as the foundation without which they lose their meaning.

The third part isolates, in order to illumine it, one of the fundamental ideas of Modernity, that "culture" that it seeks to have triumph over savagery and barbarism. This concept has to be simultaneously enlarged and narrowed. I must also show how our concept of a profane culture which distinguishes itself from religion actually has a religious origin. And finally, I need to show to what extent the claim of truth, far from subjugating culture and depriving it of its autonomy, is indispensable to it.

The fourth part takes up the relationship to temporality presupposed by the very idea of Modernity. Modernity purports to situate itself in a long-term movement that should open to an indefinite future; but its own

---

4   See *The Legitimacy of the Human* (South Bend, IN: St. Augustine Press, 2016).

principles forbid it from doing so. "History" is the mode in which the past is represented and presented to us; one therefore must become aware of its possibilities and the weights that put a strain on it when it is viewed, as is inevitable, from the present. The future, however, does not just happen or go without saying, it depends upon us, who here-and-now prepare it, or, on the contrary, block its path.

The fifth and last part seeks points of reference that would allow the reconstruction of what Modernity threatens, while safeguarding its precious gains. It explores the agenda whose provocative slogan I characterized elsewhere as a "return to the Middle Ages."[5] It begins by recalling the troubled path that our culture has already traversed. It then sketches the program of a decidedly medieval school. Finally, it meditates on the correct way of conducting oneself vis-à-vis the past by prolonging it without embalming it, and by remaining faithful to it without being enslaved by it.

---

5   See Rémi Brague, *Le Propre de l'homme. Sur une légitimité menacée*, Paris, Flammarion, 2013, pp. 131–133.

I
MODERNITY AS A PROBLEM

Introduction

ON MODERNITIS

Readers who know my immoderate taste for puns will not be surprised by my title, *Moderately Modern*, which contains a play on words, although perhaps not a particularly good one.

The alliteration of the substantives "moderation" and "modernity" is however not without some basis. The two words have a common root, which is the Latin word *modus*, "measure."[1] On one hand, this word provided the adverb *modo*, with the meaning of "what *just* occurred." Then came the adjective *modernus*, which is first found in Cassiodorus, then passed into the Romance languages, including French.[2] The French word "mode" (fashion) came from it as well. On the other hand, the Latin *modus* gave the idea of moderation, and even of modesty.

In the Middle Ages, the adjective "modern" was perhaps understood as moderation, "in the sense of measure and equilibrium."[3]

As for the substance of my claim, the moderation I am recommending in the use of modernity is clearly opposed, even directly so, to Rimbaud's saying: "One must be absolutely modern."[4] Above all, it is opposed to the naïve enthusiasm of those who take this injunction as a slogan to be

1   For more details, see Alfred Ernout and Antoine Meillet, *Dictionnaire étymologique de la langue latine. Histoire des mots* (Paris: Klincksieck, 1939), pp. 62–24.

2   See Walter Freund, *Modernus und andere Zeitbegriffe des Mittelalters* (Cologne/Graz: Böhlau, 1957).

3   Jean Clair, *Du surréalisme considéré dans ses rapports au totalitarisme et aux tables tournantes* (Paris : Mille et une nuits, 2003), p. 104.

4   Arthur Rimbaud, *Une saison en enfer*, in R. de Reneville and J. Mouquet (dir.), *Oeuvres complètes* (Paris : Gallimard, "Bibliothèque de la Pléiade," 1954), p. 243.

constantly repeated, and who wish to be "ever more modern," "more and more modern." An example of this hollow rhetoric: "Art, true art, advances for a world ever more modern," an utterance from the mouth of a female novelist captured by Philippe Muray.[5]

This kind of utterance comes less from considered thought and more from a revealing tic, even as a symptom of a illness that I will allow myself to name by using the same procedure that André Suarès employed when he lampooned the obsession of Italian fascism with the Roman empire and "romanity," by means of the term "romanitis." I can do the same thing with "modernity," simply by changing two letters: "modernitis." Now, let's try to describe the symptoms.

The present at the center of everything

The first of these symptoms was observed in connection with the political regime that characterizes Modernity, democracy, of which it is quite proud, and not without reason. Democratic life concentrates human consciousness on the present and causes it to disinterest itself in the future. Now, since the future does not arrive all by itself, but results from the constant action of men to maintain and prolong humanity, in the long term democracy must end with the end of humanity. This question is almost as old as the birth of modern democracy in Europe with the French revolution.

In the strongly critical judgments he made about events in France as early as 1790, Edmund Burke wrote: "People will not look forward to posterity, who never look backward to their ancestors."[6] Half a century later, Tocqueville, who unlike Burke was a considered partisan of the New Regime, reprised the rhythm of the sentence, and even deepened it, in his famous chapter on individualism, where he wrote: "Not only does democracy cause each man to forget his ancestors, but it also hides his descendants from him."[7]

5   Marie Darrieussecq, interview in Carole Bachelot and Adrien Taquet, *La Politique et moi. Jeunes artistes en quête de politique* (Paris : Fondation Jean Jaurès/Plon, 2005), p. 62; Philippe Muray, in *Le Point*, 24 November 2005.

6   Edmund Burke, *Reflections on the Revolution in France*, J. G. A. Pocock (ed.), (Indianapolis, IN: Hackett, 1987), p. 29. See also p. 83. And see below, pp. 184–185.

7   Alexis de Tocqueville, *De la démocratie en Amérique*, II, ii, 2, in A. Jardin (dir), *Oeuvres* (Paris: Gallimard, "Biblothèque de la Pléiade," 1992, t. 2, p. 614.

In fifty years, the frightened prediction of the Irishman, who wrote in view of the future, had become an observation expressed in the present tense by the Normand aristocrat. As for the content, one should note an important nuance. Tocqueville juxtaposed the two attitudes and introduced a gradation, while Burke suggested a causal connection between them. For him, it is *because* we do not look toward the past that we also no longer look toward the future.

To name our current chronological consciousness, I would propose the inelegant neologism, "parontocentrism."[8] It names the fact that our experience of time, and of our existence in time, is centered on the present. How is this new? That the present is the center and the other two dimensions, the past and the future, are the periphery, this is an image that is not simply recent. When he wanted to oppose the "now" to these two other dimensions, Aristotle called them "the time that surrounds" (*perix*).[9] Moreover, that the present is the time of action, the only one of which we can make use, this too is an observation that goes back to Antiquity. A famous fragment of Aristippus of Cyrene already recalled it: "Only the present belongs to us, and not what came before us, nor what awaits us: one has disappeared, and the other, it is uncertain that it will be."[10] Stoics such as Seneca and Marcus Aurelius left us similar observations. However, for the Ancients it was a matter of muzzling an excessive interest in the past or for the future, objects of nostalgia or anticipation, in order to return to the demands of action. Our problem however is the opposite: disinterest, lack of interest, for the past as well as the future.

Some may be tempted at this point to offer a double objection. On one hand, Modern Times have seen an unprecedented increase in historical

---

8   Elsewhere, I proposed "semerocentrism," even less felicitous; see my "Élargir le passé, approfondir le présent," Le Débat, 1994, p. 32. Since then I learned that P.-H. Taguieff proposed the term "presentism" and has given much thought to the subject. See Pierre-André Taguieff, *L'Effacement de l'avenir* (Paris : Gallimard, "Débats," 2000), in particular p. 98.

9   Aristotle, *On Interpretation*, 3, 15b18.

10 Aristippus of Cyrene, cited by Aelian, *Variae historiae*, XIV, 7, in Heinrich Ritter and Ludwig Preller, *Historia philosophiae graecae* (Gotha: Perthes, 1888 (7th edition), p. 210. See also Seneca, *Letters to Lucilius*, 74, 34; Marcus Aurelius, *Meditations*, III, 10, 1.

knowledge; on the other, the birth of the literary genre of utopia. Don't they witness to a passionate interest in the past and the future?

Nothing of the sort. The *objectification* of the past which history presupposes, and in turn produces, prevents it from being an awareness of this sort. On the contrary, it is a distancing and even an unmooring vis-à-vis the past. It is part of a system constructed by the project of progress. The past has to be fixed so that one can measure the progress made. Distance remains exclusively what *separates* the past from the present. One cannot let it flow from the present into the future.

On the other hand, a utopia that anticipates the future is the opposite of an apocalyptic *expectation* of the future. It is a systematization of the way in which the present advances towards the future, and it never ceases being connected with it. At the limit, it testifies to an impatience: the future must become the present even more quickly.

This haste began with the desire to make the past a *tabula rasa*. "Let's forget the past," we hear people say, "and turn resolutely toward the future." This proposition can have great value when, for example, it is a matter of making the coexistence of citizens possible on the basis of mutual forgiveness. Thus, the edict of Nantes imposed something of a duty of not-remembering on the events of the wars of religion. Perhaps our current societies, gnawed by self-hatred, would do well to follow their lead.

But that sort of thing doesn't touch the level I consider here. In order to concern ourselves with the future, we must know that there will be one. Now, how do we know there will be a future? That which, by definition, does not yet exist, we have no experience of it. The response to this conundrum is found in another: we know that we have a future because we have a past. The past once had to face the future and make it real. What we are today will tomorrow be a past. We know that there will be a future because we are able to operate a "shift in the distances." We can cause the distance that separates us from the past to shift, by taking ourselves and our present experience as the point of departure. In the same way that "today" followed a "yesterday," which today, yesterday was a "next day," in the same way our today will be the "yesterday" of a "tomorrow." Concretely, we discover ourselves capable of future projects when we become aware that our present state is the result of our past action.

French has found a word to designate activity which is related to what is present as such, and only to it. The word "action" isn't appropriate, because action necessarily impinges on the future. Another word was necessary therefore. We invented the word "manage" (French: gérer) and the substantive that corresponds to it, "management." According to Littré this is a recent word, which only gives examples from the nineteenth century and distinguishes it from "régir." "To manage current affairs" is almost a tautology. We live in a world where management tends to replace action. Ordinarily this rise in "management" is attributed to economics taking over politics, which above all is action. I wonder if it is not the reverse. The hegemony of the model of managing the present would call for the mode of economic reason, as being the best suited to deal with a world that presents itself as to be managed.

The fidelity of the parasite

Modern Times distinguish themselves from the historical periods that preceded by defining themselves by a break, a rupture effected vis-à-vis what came before, and for which it invented a name: "the Middle Ages."[11] Now, the rather complacent picture that Modernity has formed of itself hides a less pleasant fact, which is that Modernity lives off of the past, as Tocqueville, perhaps the first, noted. As he put it, democracy is not viable unless citizens are animated by virtues that do not have a democratic origin, but which it inherits from older periods.

The distinctive character of a parasite is not that it nourishes itself on something other than itself. That is what every living thing does. And civilizations themselves are living things, which constantly draw technologies, knowledge, and even words from outside themselves. But the parasite lives from what it kills, and to the extent that it kills it. The death of the victim entails that of the guilty party with it. Sometimes, too, the parasite is aware that it is caught in a self-destructive dialectic.

Thus, if Modernity lives by the past, at the same time it does its best to repudiate it, even to destroy it. This fact was seen very clearly at the beginning of the twentieth century, and even earlier by Nietzsche, if one can

---

11   This is what Hans Blumenberg shows very clearly, *Die Legitimität der Neuzeit*, (Frankfurt: Suhrkamp, 1988, 2nd ed.), p. 543.

interpret an obscure fragment in this sense: "We have ceased to accumulate, we spend the capital of our ancestors, even in the way we know."[12]

Here I will limit myself to citing two authors. First Charles Péguy, who is the first that I have been able to find who explicitly mentions the idea of parasitism. And parasitism of the most radical sort, even if death prevented him from drawing the consequences of his intuition. Péguy formulated the notion of parasitism in the context of a meditation on historical science, writing in 1907:

> In reality, with imperturbable aplomb, and what is perhaps its only invention and all that is *its* in the entirety of the movement, the <modern world> lives almost entirely on past humanities, which it disdains, which it pretends to ignore, whose essential realities it truly is ignorant of, while it does not ignore the commodities, usages, even abuses and other utilizations of the same. The sole fidelity of the modern world is the fidelity of parasitism.[13]

In 1914, shortly before being killed at the beginning of the Great War, the writer expressed himself even more forthrightly:

> The modern world is, also, essentially parasitical. It does not derive its strength, or its appearance of strength, except from the regimes it fights, the worlds that it aims to do away with.[14]

The second author is the Englishman, G. K. Chesterton. In a text from between the two wars, he is even more precise:

---

12 Friedrich Nietzsche, fragment 14 [226], Spring 1888, in G. Colli and M. Montinari (dir.), *Kritische Studienausgabe* [KSA] (Berlin: De Gruyter, 1980), t. 13, p. 398 = *Der Wille zur Macht*, #68b.

13 Charles Péguy, "De la situation faite au parti intellectuel dans le monde moderne devant les accidents de la gloire temporelle" [October 6, 1907], in R. Burac (dir.), *Oeuvres en prose*, Paris, Gallimard, "Bibliothèque de la Pléiade," t. 2, 1988, p. 725.

14 Charles Péguy, "Note conjointe sur M. Descartes et la philosophie cartésienne" [1914], in M. Péguy (dir.), *Oeuvres en prose* (Paris: Gallimard, "Bibliothèque de la Pléiade," 1961) p. 1512.

The fact is this: that the modern world, with its modern movements, is living on its Catholic capital. It is using, and using up,
the truths that remain to it out of the old treasury of Christendom; including, of course, many truths known to pagan antiquity but crystallized in Christendom. But it is not really starting
new enthusiasms of its own. The novelty is a matter of names
and labels, like modern advertisement; in almost every other
way the novelty is merely negative. It is not starting fresh things
that can really carry on far into the future. On the contrary, it
is picking up old things that it cannot carry on at all. For these
are the two marks of modern moral ideals. First, that they were
borrowed or snatched out of ancient or mediaeval hands. Second, that they wither very quickly in modern hands.[15]

One could apply the same concept of parasitism to "modernism" in the aesthetic domain. In order to give itself the leading role of *enfant terrible*, even
victim, modernism presupposes the existence of a norm that it claims it
has to transgress, but which it secretly needs.[16]

One has to ask: Is Modernity capable of reproducing its own conditions
of existence? To the contrary, does it not ceaselessly destroy them? Doesn't
it need to borrow from elsewhere what it lives off of? Even supposing, as
it claims, that it is superior to the ancient world, one must ask with Stanley
Rosen if it is capable of offering criteria for this superiority that it did not
derive from the ancient world itself?[17] The same suspicion is found in other
contemporary philosophers, who also note that Modernity consumes meanings without creating any. Thus Charles Taylor speaks of "parasitism" in
connection with certain theories of moral philosophy, but as we have seen,
one can ask if Modernity might not be a parasite from one end to the other,

15 Gilbert K. Chesterton, "Is Humanism a Religion?," in *The Thing* [1929] (Lon-
    don: Sheed & Ward, 1946), pp. 16–17.
16 See Roger Shattuck, "The Poverty of Modernism," in *The Innocent Eye. On
    Modern Literature & the Arts* (New York: Washington Square Press, "Pocket
    Books," 1986), pp. 395–409, esp. p. 403.
17 See Stanley Rosen, "A Modest Proposal to Rethink Enlightenment," in *An-
    cients and Moderns. Rethinking Modernity* (New Haven/London: Yale University
    Press, 1989), pp. 1–21, esp. p. 19.

and at least one passage in Taylor seems to generalize the idea.[18] The political aspects of this dialectic are put in relief in the famous thesis (in Germany at least) of the jurist Ernst-Wolfgang Böckenförde: "The State devoted to freedom, the secularized State, lives from presuppositions that it itself is incapable of guaranteeing."[19]

Would not Modernity be the expenditure of an accumulation of energy by the Middle Ages?[20] From the perspective of material history, this is not lacking in plausibility. Historians recall the importance of the medieval agrarian and technical revolutions, of demographic growth, of urbanization, or even the very idea of civil society, which seems to be a European particularity.[21] As for the "history of mentalities," the idea and reality of a separation of powers, temporal and spiritual, or the conception of a person having liberties, are medieval.

Modernity worked at applying these "values" and gave them the character of self-evident premises. But has it created new ones? Is it capable of giving them a foundation?

The difficult birth of modern man

Modern ideas are premodern ideas. Only the name is new. Modernity puts to work a strategy in which negation or denial is indispensable. The choice of a new designation corresponds to the need to conceal the origin of what one has borrowed, like a receiver forges a new brand for stolen merchandise. This is how the first theological virtue, charity, has become "compassion," and the second, hope, has become "optimism." The very name of "Europe,"

---

18 Charles Taylor, *Sources of the Self. The Making of the Modern Identity* (Cambridge, MA: Harvard University Press, 1989), pp. 20, 339–40, and 517.

19 Ernst-Wolfgang Böckenförde, "Die Entstehung des Staates als Vorgang der Säkularisation" [1967], in *Recht, Staat, Freiheit. Studien zur Rechtsphilosophie, Staatstheorie und Verfassungsgeschichte* (Frankfurt: Suhrkamp, 1991), p. 11.

20 Here I reprise, although in an exaggerated form, an idea that, after the fact, I saw was implicit in my *Excentric Culture* (South Bend, IN: St. Augustine Press, 2002), chapters 7 & 8.

21 See, for example, Jenó Szúcs, *Les Trois Europes*, trans. from the Hungarian by V. Charaire, G. Klahiczay and P. Thureau-Dangin (Paris: L'Harmattan, 1985), chapter II.

used to designate not a direction or a specific geographical region but a civilization, allows one to dispense with speaking of "Christendom."

As the key example, one could cite the "rights of man" which are so much extolled these days. The behaviors that violate these purported "rights" and which, consequently, are severely and rightly condemned are, as for their content, exactly the same that are condemned by the Decalogue or even the pagan moral teachers of all the schools of Antiquity. The sole difference relates to the fact that these contents, whose origin was previously sought in God or Nature, are henceforth referred to "man" as sovereign.

This man who has these rights and who is conscious of having them is therefore "modern man," who is also constantly spoken of, to the point, sometimes, of making him the standard of judgment. There are things, we are told, that modern man can no longer accept—for example, miracles. Isn't there some presumption there? The sophist Protagoras once made man in general (*anthrōpos*) the "measure of all things."[22] However, does not the modern version of man, restricted to the last three centuries and to the Western world, does it not place him on even more of a pedestal? Does it not allow this late-comer to appoint himself the judge of all the millennia covered by human history?

Even beyond the ridicule I just allowed myself, one can ask quite seriously if the expression "modern man" doesn't mask a contradiction. Can Modernity actually say what man is insofar as he is human?[23] To be sure, ancient and medieval thought did not ask the question of what man is as a central question. It came up rarely.[24] But the answer to what specified man was basically fairly easy: he was an embodied soul, or an animated body. Or again: he was a living thing that distinguished itself among the animals by reason, and among pure spirits by the flesh that made him mortal. Neither angel nor beast, therefore. Or yet again: he was the sole creature made in the image and likeness of God, the sole among whom, and for the salvation of whom, the Word was incarnate.

---

22 Protagoras, n. 80 in Diels-Kranz, *Presocratics*, fragment B 1.
23 See Pierre Manent, *The City of Man* (Princeton: 1998), especially Chapter 4, "The Hidden Man."
24 See, for example, Plato, *Theatetus*, 174b4.

For us, the task of defining man is more difficult. Premodern humanism, be it "pagan" or Christian, based human dignity on an external reference. Modernity purports to do without any such reference. To indicate or represent the problem, I propose the following very simple table:

Epoch	Figure of the subject	Reference
Antiquity	Soul	Nature
Christianity	Person	God
Modernity	I (self)	?

The last question mark is perhaps the defining problem of Modernity. From where does the man of modern humanism derive his legitimacy?

The ballast of the past

At this point I would like to meditate on a brief reflection of a philosopher, and borrow an image from him, or rather a counter-image. This reflection comes from the French mathematician, economist, and philosopher Antoine-Augustin Cournot (d. 1877) who, in the introduction to his voluminous considerations on universal history, which he published in 1872, treated, very briefly, the idea of private property. It was in this context that he wrote:

> As a matter of fact, hardly anything more than that [idea] remains from the medieval system; but it still serves as ballast for modern European societies in their hazardous voyage towards unknown regions. The day when this ballast is thrown overboard, one can foresee that, despite all sorts of protests to the contrary, the rule of law will have ended.[25]

I will leave to one side Cournot's argument in favor of private property (which is not without interest) in order to concentrate on the image he

25 Antoine-Augustin Cournot, *Considérations sur la marche des idées et des événements dans les Temps modernes* [1872], A. Robinet (ed.) (Paris: Vrin, 1973), p. 67.

uses. Modernity is compared to a ship. This is an apt comparison, since Modern Times are connected with the great discoveries and circumnavigation of the globe. This ship is launched on an adventurous crossing, "hazardous" says Cournot. The adjective first of all means "risky," but the French word also connotes "luck" or "chance." We travel towards unknown waters, without being sure that they are bound by a shore. Here too the image is full of meaning. When Cournot wrote these lines, Rimbaud had just composed his *Bateau ivre* (Drunken Ship) (1871). And ten years later, Nietzsche was to generalize the image of having cast off and wandering in infinite space that had to follow the "death of God" that he announced in trembling. Now, what is the role of the Middle Ages in this vessel of Modern Times? The role is neither that of a home port nor the goal of the voyage. By this very fact, the symmetrical dreams of Progress, dear to the Enlightenment, and of Reaction, dear to certain Romantics, find themselves implicitly denied. For Cournot, the Middle Ages remain as it were *aboard* Modern Times and constitute an integral part of them. They too share the journey. But they are not a compass. Rather, they are ballast. Now, ballast can be experienced as a burden, in such a way that there is a temptation to do without it by throwing it overboard. But the consequence would be that the ship would go down with everything, and everyone, aboard.

A failure?

One can therefore ask if the modern project has not *already* failed, at least to the extent that "modern man" proposes to reject every extrinsic foundation in order to rest only on himself, and where the rhetoric of Modernity loves nothing more than to speak of "adventure," "essay," "attempt," or "experiment." However, an experiment is not necessarily conclusive, it can fail. Who in fact can guarantee its success? It has often been noted that the history of Modernity, even in its happiest period, is always the implicit history of its failure, and that the possibility of failure is the very heart of Modernity.

In the famous monologue of Ulysses in Shakespeare's *Troilus and Cressida*, the praise of hierarchy ("degree") ends with an evocation of the disastrous consequences of its neglect: "Appetite . . . must make perforce an universal prey, And last eat up himself."[26] For us, the hierarchical vision of the world expressed by the word "degree" is irrevocably lost[27]; but the danger of self-destruction is always there. Do we have the means to avert it?

26 William Shakespeare, *The Wisdom of the World*, I, 3. v. 124.
27 See my *La Sagesse du monde, op. cit.*

1
CAN EUROPE SURVIVE MODERNITY?

Modernity appeared in Europe. Elsewhere I have sought to characterize European culture, and I believe I identified some concepts that allow one to recognize and comprehend its singularity. For me, it was not a purely academic exercise, but was born of a certain apprehension before what I believed threatened a culture to which I am very much indebted, and which I was not sure would survive. I therefore ended with an apprehensive question. Does Europe still have what it needs to continue its cultural adventure in the time of late modernity? Is the wellspring that gave it life and motion still functioning?[1] Here I wish to pursue that investigation.

I will begin with a portrait of one of the former presidents of the French Republic which I deem very revealing, and which I have from one of my oldest friends. His participation in European affairs led him to rub shoulders with the president almost every day, and allowed him to have a thousand conversations with him. My friend confided to me in private one day: "He's a bastard." The word was harsh but the explanation came immediately afterwards: "He doesn't believe in anything." He meant by that a total lack of convictions, be they political, moral, or religious; the rejection of everything conveyed by the Latin word *fides*: a perfect lack of scruples, a total disdain for keeping his word or promises, and even more for those who considered themselves so bound. Then, after a brief silence my friend added: "He doesn't believe in anything, except for Europe."

---

1   See *The Eccentric Culture: A Theory of Western Civilization* (St. Augustine Press, 2009), Chapter IX.

Europe and nihilism

The anecdote allows me to pose a question here: what is the relationship between the two beliefs or, in the case that occupies us here, the belief and unbelief invoked here? The friend who offered this judgment is a convinced Europeanist because he is an incorruptible servant of the common good, and in his eyes the common good requires the European construction. For the president, "to believe in Europe" is a concession, a nuance he thought he needed to bring to the too-abrupt formula, "believing in nothing." Now, I sometimes wonder, and not without real anguish, if "believing in Europe," rather than a concession or qualification, would not be the most perfect expression of absolute unbelief, and if Europe would not be the home of nihilism.

"Believing in nothing" is the way contemporary language formulates what we call "nihilism." The term dates from the beginning of the nineteenth century,[2] but it received its title of nobility from Nietzsche, who saw in it a European-wide phenomenon, but by "Europe" he did not merely mean a little cape of Asia, but modern humanity. The editors of the fragments collected under the title *The Will to Power* gave the title "European Nihilism" to the first subdivision of the compilation. And in his courses on Nietzsche dating from the 1930s, Heidegger placed this same notion at the center of his reflections.[3]

In this context, the adjective "European" is more than a geographical designation, which would give the real or supposed origin of a pathology, similar to the way people speak of the "French disease" or the "Spanish flu." It suggests that it was not by chance that nihilism appeared in Europe. Europe constituted a favorable terrain for the infection. It so happens that certain parasites receive their name from their hosts, for example, people speak of *wheat* rust. It is in this sense that they speak of European nihilism.

Nietzsche did not particularly thematize the connection between nihilism and Europeanness, but that is because it was so ubiquitous. However, he did pose a fundamental question, whose relevance is more and more

---

2   For the history of the term, see Franco Volpi, *Il Nichilismo* (Bari: Laterza, 1996), p. 151.

3   Martin Heidegger, *Nietzsche* (Pfullingen: Neske, 1961), t. 2, pp. 31–256.

evident. It was formulated in a fragment he entitled "the hammer," in which the philosopher wrote: "To summon a terrible decision, to place Europe before the consequence of knowing if its will wills [its own] disappearance."[4]

We are tempted to dispel this nightmare of the disappearance of Europe by opposing the splendid reality of the construction of the European Union. Isn't this project the antidote to nihilism? In Brussels milieus we hear that this is one of the few enterprises still capable of interesting a young high-ranking official who wants to do something worthwhile. Recall the felicitous formulation by which Jean-François Lyotard characterized the so-called postmodern era: it is the end of "grand narratives."[5] These were ways of ordering history so as to give it a meaning, thus rendering intelligible the practice of those who lived, by allowing them to situate themselves in history and giving them to believe that they were contributing. This was true of the history of salvation according to Christianity, or what were different secularized versions thereof: the myth of Progress according to the Enlightenment, or the Marxist doctrine of History. The formation of Europe would be the last of these "grand narratives."

I too will begin with a narrative concerning Europe. This will be my own "grand narrative," for which I will base myself upon the characterization of European culture that I developed elsewhere.[6] In a word, the cultural identity of Europe is "eccentric". It is characterized by a double secondarity vis-à-vis its ancient and biblical sources. Earlier, I studied this culture as a quasi-essence that I could grasp in a synchronic fashion; now I am going to retrace its diachronic development.

The European dynamism and its wellspring

The elements of European grandeur were acquired in the Middle Ages. To show this historically, one must step back a thousand years and establish a

---

4   Friedrich Nietzsche, fragment 2 [131], Autumn 1885–Autumn 1886, t. 12, p. 133 = *Wille zur Macht*, #1054.
5   Jean-Francois Lyotard, *La Condition postmoderne* (Paris: Minuit, 1979), esp. pp. 7, 31, and 63.
6   See *Eccentric Culture, op. cit.*

millennial balance sheet, as well as distinguish the project from its realization. The project is even older, since it dates from the idea of a Western empire found perhaps with Charlemagne (800), but in any case with the Ottonians (962); its realization was necessarily a very long-term process. The turning point that leads to it and was, as it were, the parting of the waters in European history seems to me the eleventh century, for it was at this period that the mechanisms were put in place that led to the establishment of Europe as a civilization.

For greater clarity, one can distinguish three aspects, even if in actual history they mutually conditioned one another:

At the beginning of the eleventh century, the list of peoples present in the area of Europe became complete and definitive. This completion corresponded to the end of a millennial movement, the migrations of populations that the Roman ruling class called by the pejorative term the "barbarian invasions," an appellation that has lasted. From the first Germans, the Cimbri and the Teutoni slaughtered by Marius, to the Hungarians, nomadic tribes from Asia constantly advanced towards the west and the south. They were pushed closer together by their neighbors, with the invisible prime mover being perhaps the expansion of the Chinese Empire and civilization. In the same way, it could be that the end of the long-term movement was connected to the crisis of the Chinese Empire that began in the eighth century. As the Turks established themselves in Islamic lands and the Bulgarians in Byzantine regions, the Poles and the Czechs converted to Catholic Christianity: the Czechs in 863, the Hungarians in 985, the Poles in 966. The new arrivals acquired their ecclesiastical independence around the year 1000, in particular thanks to Pope Sylvester II. He granted them their own bishops, independent of those of the Holy Empire, with which they were not obliged to associate themselves.

In the middle of the eleventh century, Europe completed its self-definition in the most concrete sense of the term, by distinguishing itself from what it was not. It had already separated itself from Islam ever since the Arab conquest of the south of the Mediterranean in the seventh century. In 1054, with the mutual excommunications of the Latins and the Byzantines, the two halves of the northern part of Christendom (let's not forget to their south the Ethiopians and the Christians living in Muslim lands) separated. Henceforth there was a Latin Christianity that was really distinct from that of Greek culture. A few years later, the battle of Mantzikert (1071) signaled the entrance on the scene of the Turkish power, which will be the gravedigger of the Byzantine Empire.

Finally, towards the end of the eleventh century Europe filled itself in, by making its culture coincide more and more perfectly with its geographic definition. It reconquered Spain from Islam, in a movement that was pan-European, since the Christian kingdoms of the north of the Spanish penin-sula received the aid of mercenaries come from France, Normandy, and even Germany. In 1085 the Castilians took Toledo. It was also during the second half of the eleventh century that the Normans put an end to the Byzantine domination of the south of Italy, as well as the Muslim control of Sicily, by taking Messina (1061), then Palermo (1072).

Within this henceforth closed area, Europe worked on itself, it inten-sified its life.[7] Europe saw a significant demographic growth, to the point where it became able to feed a more numerous population, thanks to an economic revolution marked by the extension of cultivated lands which had been wrested from forests, the introduction of new crops, and the improve-ment of agricultural techniques, such as crop rotation, harnesses, and plows. It doesn't really matter whether these technical advances were first discov-ered in Europe or elsewhere, for example in China, because it was in Eu-rope that they were applied and generalized.

The European model of development

Medieval Europe was characterized by a crisscrossing structure in which this internal elaboration made common cause with external borrowing, in such a way that, in two words, the *resources* were within, while the *sources* were without. Europe drew from itself the real, i.e., its population and the wherewithal to feed itself; on the other hand, it imported from without what pertained to the symbolic, because its reference points were Christi-anity, a religion come from the Middle East, and the Greek literature and Roman law of Antiquity. It was by rediscovering and systematizing the

---

7   See Marcel Gauchet, *Le Desenchantement du monde. Une histoire politique de la religion* (Paris: Gallimard, 1985), pp. 115–17.

latter that the legal revolution of the eleventh century launched Christianity on the enterprise of reforming the world.[8]

Moreover, the internal elaboration preceded and made possible the external borrowing. This can serve as a law of the dynamism of Europe. People speak of "European imperialism," and by that one designates a real phenomenon, or one that was. But the expression hides the fundamental fact, the one that made possible the overseas interventions, which is that Europe is a civilization that is not founded on external, but on *internal conquest*. Europe is founded on self-development, and it began by deeply exploiting the resources available in itself, before borrowing them from elsewhere.

This is true first of all on the material level. Thus the Crusades were made possible by the demographic development within the European space, and served as an outlet for the younger sons of noble families. The discovery of the New World was made possible by the invention of the rudder. But the same law is verified in the cultural domain. Europe knew how to open itself to the outside because, if one can put it this way, it already had an exterior within itself. The culture of Europe was founded on nostalgia for the "elsewheres," real or imagined, of Athens and of Jerusalem. The study of oriental cultures by Europeans, far from being, as many believe, a consequence of colonization, actually situates itself in the wake of the humanist movement of return to classical sources. The European Arabists were originally Hebraists and Biblicists; Sanskrit was studied in the group of classical languages, in order to discover their ancestor.

People have emphasized forever the borrowing from without of European thought, and underscored that scholasticism would have been completely different without the contributions of Jewish thinkers and Muslims who wrote in Arabic. One is completely right to recall that Thomas Aquinas, Duns Scotus, Meister Eckhart, and so many others constructed their systems by drawing from Avicenna, Averroes, and Maimonides. But one forgets that in order to borrow, one has to feel the need to do so. One has to explain the demand. In other words, why did the West feel the need for more refined intellectual instruments? The West first worked on what

8   See Harold J. Berman, *Law and Revolution. The Formation of the Western Legal Tradition* (Cambridge, MA: Harvard University Press, 1983).

it had at its disposition before importing; it began by exploiting to the highest degree the rudimentary instruments it possessed.[9] Great minds like St. Anselm (d. 1109) or Abelard (d. 1142) had to content themselves with working with St. Augustine and the available portions of Aristotle. Without them, though, Europe would not have felt the need to look elsewhere for what it lacked of Aristotle.

Islam as counter example

The Islamic world represents an interesting counterexample. Curiously, this world also took on a new orientation in the eleventh century, but one that was asymmetrical to Europe's. When Europe intensified internally, Islam expanded; while Europe set about borrowing from without, Islam henceforth contented itself with the meaning it produced itself.

Islam had begun with a century of conquests. It then remained more or less stable after the set-backs which, as it were, bookended the next century (in the west, the failure of the siege of Byzantium in 718 and the skirmish of Poitiers in 732, and in the east, the battle of Talas against the first Chinese advances in 751). The eleventh century was for Islam the time of the relaunch of external expansion. Earlier, I indicated the importance of the battle of Mantzikert in the direction of the west. Towards the east, it was in 1020 that Mahmud of Ghazni sent pillaging expeditions towards the Punjab, thus opening the way to India.

As for culture, the contrary movement, that of retreat, was the case. A symbolic date is the death of Avicenna in 1037, who is the first philosopher writing in Arabic not to have published a commentary on Aristotle, and whose philosophy is like a declaration of independence vis-à-vis Greece, once Aristotelianism had been entirely absorbed.[10] The Islamic world which had translated an enormous amount in a movement that had its peak in the ninth century, ceased to do so in the eleventh. Islamic thought was

9   See Kristell Trego, *L'Essence de la liberté. La refondation de l'éthique dans l'oeuvre de saint Anselme de Cantorbéry* (Paris: Vrin, 2010), p. 271.

10   For more details, see my "Inclusion et digestion. Deux modèles d'appropriation culturelle," in *Au moyen du Moyen Âge. Philosophies médiévales en chrétienté, judaisme et islam* (Chatou: La Transparence, 2006), pp. 187–204.

henceforth self-sufficient. And perhaps it was, since philosophers, astronomers, and physicians felt strong enough to doubt the results obtained by the Greeks.[11] In the same eleventh century, Islam as a religious system perceived itself as having obtained such a fullness that any novelty could only detract from the perfection already obtained.[12]

The modern inversion

One could ask, although not without a certain exaggeration, if modern Europe, insofar as it is modern, would not rest on the exact opposite of the model described above which brought about the success of the Middle Ages. And whether, therefore, one must not distinguish, with the German sociologist Niklas Luhmann, the "old-european" civilization (*alteuropäisch*) from the Modernity in which we live. In that way, Europe would never have been so much itself as during the premodern period, and, on the other hand, Modernity would be essentially post-european.

Let's begin with a paradox. The use of the word "Europe" in its current meaning is essentially a recent usage. To be sure, the word itself is very old. But it was from Modern Times that people began using it more and more frequently, and as the substitute destined to replace the word "Christendom." Europe was supposed to be the stage on which the drama of civilization took place. It also was to be the subconscious, or superego, which was to judge men and deeds according to their conformity with the Enlightenment project. The period was rife with these words which signified nothing new, but which had the advantage of relegating to oblivion notions that designated Christian realities, such as (to use an example given above) "compassion" allows one to avoid "charity." In this way, the expression "modern Europe" is almost a pleonasm.

But the fact that then, as well as now, one speaks so much about Europe has nothing to do with the vitality of the latter. It would even be interesting

---

11 See Dimitri Gutas, *Greek Thought, Arabic Culture. The Graeco-Arabic Translation Movement in Baghdad and Early Abbasid Society (2nd–4th/8th–10th centuries)* (London/New York: Routledge, 1998), p. 152 ff.

12 See Tilman Nagel, *Die Festung des Glaubens. Triumph und Scheitern des islamischen Rationalismus im 11. Jahrhundert* (Munich: Beck, 1988), p. 13.

to see if the reality would not be in inverse proportion to the use of words, and if Europe had not entered into a self-destructive pattern at the very moment when the word took on the character of a slogan. What as far as the expression is concerned was a quasi-pleonasm, perhaps for the thing itself is an oxymoron.

The modern inversion, therefore, like the medieval model that it overturns, was put in place by a long-term process. Medieval Europe, as we saw, exploited its inner resources and imported from without its cultural sources. Now, everything occurs as if Modernity had reversed this relationship. Europe set about exploiting resources from abroad, at least raw materials: economically, Modern Times began with the importing of precious metals from the New World; today its material civilization depends upon oil from the Middle East or uranium from Africa.

On the other hand, modern Europe is more and more content with its own resources in the domain of culture. A long-term Quarrel of the Ancients and the Moderns was engaged. The polemics between intellectuals in the Paris of 1687-88 which gave birth to the expression were only a symptom.[13] It has ended with the victory of the Moderns, for whose sake one could do without, in fact, one did without, the ancient authors. In contemporary Europe, the detachment from Greek and biblical roots grows apace, to the point of being a deliberate ignorance which sometimes takes on a horrifying aspect. It is still too early to know if the current vogue of Buddhism represents a true borrowing of meaning from the East, or the projection on an imaginary "Other" of purely Western temptations or thoughts.

Premodern anthropology

Without wanting to explain anything, I propose to reflect on a parallel. What is true at the collective level of civilizations is verified on the individual level. The structure that I observed above is found in the anthropology that corresponds to it. Medieval man, as well as ancient man, felt himself engaged in a double relationship: to himself and the exterior. His relationship to

---

13   See Anne-Marie Lecoq (ed.), *La Querelle des Anciens et des Modernes. XVIIieme-XVIIIieme siècles* (Gallimard, "Folio," 2001).

himself presupposed a need to work on himself that received different names, such as the *epimeleia sautou* of the Greeks, the *cura animi* of the Romans, or Christian asceticism, but which in each case consisted in introducing within oneself a model that came from without and above. The image of the statue that each one receives to sculpt, which is currently en vogue, actually comes from Plotinus, for whom it wasn't a matter of sculpting an image that we created, but on the contrary, to sculpt ourselves on the model of the gods.[14] In his relationship to the external world, man knew himself to be ordained to a *kosmos* which was a source of meaning for him and which he experienced as superior.

Medieval man conceived himself by means of schemas that came to him from these two sources, the Greek and the biblical. No matter how different they were, the Greek and the biblical anthropologies shared certain traits that oppose both to the modern vision of the world. They have in common the same basic structure concerning the relationship between being and ought-to be, between what man is and what he is called to be, between his nature and his destiny. Both are thoughts focused on dependency and flourishing. Man is given to himself by a power that rules him and which invests him with a mission, which is to carry to perfection the gift that makes him what he is.

For ancient man, this power is nature. Thus, Aristotle underscores that politics doesn't fabricate men; it receives them already made by nature.[15] Ancient man understands himself as a natural being among others, even the most natural being of all. What elevates him above the other natural beings is not that he separates himself from nature, but that he realizes more fully what one can call (Nature being quasi-personified) her intention. It is in man that nature best arrives at her ends. From the beginning, man is the animal most conformed to the universe.[16] And he has the mission of making this conformity more perfect by imitating what's most beautiful and ordered in nature.[17]

---

14   Plotinus, *Enneads*, I, 6 [1], 9, 13.
15   Aristotle, *Politics*, I, 10, 1258a21–23.
16   See my *Aristote et la question du monde. Essai sur le contexte cosmologique et anthropologique de l'ontologie* (Paris: Cerf, 2009), p. 234 ff.
17   See my *The Wisdom of the World, op. cit.*, chap. X.

The man of Judaism and Christianity understands himself as "created in the image of God" (*Genesis*, 1, 26). The formulation has two sides that complete and correct one another: man shares his creaturely status with the rest of what is; but he distinguishes himself from the other creatures by his status as the image of God.

In Christianity, the second anthropological model did not simply replace the former, which would have been relegated to the sidelines. Nature is itself the object of divine creation. This metaphysical decision allowed two series of consequences. Positively, it rendered possible the reprise of the cosmology of Plato's *Timaeus* by the School of Chartres and the idea according to which Nature is the intermediary of the Creator. A century later, it will entail Thomas Aquinas's rejection, following Maimonides' lead, of the vision of the world of the Islamic kalâm, a vision of radical discontinuity, according to which things are made up of atoms and time made up of instants, which are only maintained by the habit that God has of creating them together.

The two models have in common a certain limitation of man. The ancient model situated man among the natural beings, like the animals, and even the gods who, in a certain sense, are also natural beings. Man has a nature that opens possibilities to him, but also imposes limits on him. Ancient wisdom consisted in man remaining aware of what separated him from the gods. This is the meaning of the precept of Apollo at the Delphic oracle: "Know thyself." Man without doubt was the most perfect animal, but he was not the most perfect being, because the celestial bodies looked down on him in their splendor.[18]

The biblical model, for its part, made man the image of God. This assured him an incomparable dignity. But it also assigned him tasks and duties. Here too, man was just below divine beings (*elohim*), but still below them, as the Psalmist sang (Ps. VIII, 6).

This image of man was easily transposed at the level of culture into an acceptance of dependency or "secondarity" vis-à-vis earlier sources.

The modern non-anthropology

This double relationship to the self and to the other is inverted by modern thought. Modern man no longer has to work on himself. He is deemed to

---

18   Aristotle, *Nicomachean Ethics*, VI, 7, 1141a18–b3; for the context, see my *Aristote et la question du monde, op. cit.*, pp. 205–12.

be a primary given. He has become, perhaps even more radically than with Protagoras, the measure of all things. It is he who has rights; it is from him that people expect meaning to come.

For modern man, conversely, the exterior is no longer a place of meaning, a fact tied to the rise to authority of the sciences of nature, which was already the decisive argument of the Moderns in their quarrel with the adherents of the Ancients. Since then the sciences of nature have become the capstone of material civilization by means of the technologies they make possible. But, whatever might be their value in the production of truth, they are not a source of culture. Indeed, if they place man in the demanding school of radical exteriority, at the same time they place him before a brute fact which in no way can guide the human search for meaning.[19]

Here too, an entire anthropology is at stake. Pierre Manent has characterized Modernity as the attempt to sever all relations with both pagan Antiquity and Christianity, by playing one off against the other.[20] This is what it also does with the two anthropological models that came before it. Against Christianity, Modernity invokes naturalism. According to it, man is a pure product of nature. This allows it to reject divine authority. But at the same time, against paganism modern man continues to claim the biblical heritage, for example the mission to subdue and dominate the earth. To do that, he must take himself to be more than one of nature's beings. Modern man feels himself to be more than a part of nature, but not to have received from without characteristics that would make him who he is. In a word, he claims *to be* natural, without, however, *to have* a nature.

Nothing puts him in being, nothing affirms him in his legitimacy, except he himself, which means: nothing does. "I based my cause on nothing," this phrase, which the German philosopher Max Stirner (d. 1856) borrowed from Goethe, could serve as modern man's motto.[21] This modern man populates Europe today, or at least provides its cultural tone. It is he who holds the levers of power, in the economy as well as national or European politics.

---

19   See my "La physique est-elle intéressante?," in *Au moyen du Moyen Âge, op. cit.*, pp. 97–118.

20   Pierre Manent, *The City of Man, op. cit.*

21   Max Stirner, *Der Einzige und sein Eigentum* [1842], first and second sentence: "Ich hab' mein' Sach' auf Nichts gestellt."

It is he who, without always knowing it, controls the consciousness of European peoples by making them see the world through his own categories.

The impasse

A new fact, however, characterizes the contemporary period, a fact that situates itself in the straight line of the modern history of Europe, but which still represents a decisive turning point. The product to be imported is less and less raw materials, and more and more human material, as a consequence of the demographic crisis that has been in place for a long while, to different degrees in different places, but beginning with France in the middle of the eighteenth century, and which has taken on a particularly dramatic aspect since the 1960s. The media's awareness of this crisis has only dawned the past ten years or so. The earlier fantasy of overpopulation no longer survives except among a few holdouts. Those who much earlier had sounded the alarm and were insulted for their pains, or at least ridiculed, now appear to be prescient.

Today there are statistics that cause worry about the very survival of humanity. As for Europe, the Commission in Brussels ventured the idea that massive immigration is necessary to maintain Europe's current level of living. More and more, Europe is called to live by infusion. And be it noted, this is the infusion of peoples who retain premodern beliefs and practices. Europe therefore will not be able to survive unless the rest of humanity does not adopt its ways. At the end of the Second World War, the Frankfort School philosophers spoke of the "dialectic of Enlightenment."[22] Here it finds a concrete realization. The hope for the continuation of the modern mode of life resides in the failure of its project, which is to raise the entirety of humanity to its own level.

It is under this same angle that one must see the entrance of new countries into the European community. That a political entity is formed, then grows by entirely peaceful means, this is an unprecedented novelty in human history, about which one can congratulate oneself. But we must not be naïfs, and we should know how to perceive behind the "Hymn to Joy"

---

22   See Max Horkheimer and Theodor W. Adorno, *Dialektik der Aufklärung. Philosophische Fragmente* [1944] (Frankfor: Fischer, 1989).

the cold calculations of decision-makers; the enlargement of the Community has something predatory about it. The advanced economies hope to exploit the reserves of cheap labor found there.

Not having any competence in demography, nor the means of surveying all the domains of knowledge implicated in the problems of population, which is to say, almost all those that have something to say about man, from depth psychology to sociology, while passing through economics and politics,[23] I will ignore these countless contributions and reflections to go straight to what seems to me the essential, and which relates precisely to the anthropological deficit to which I drew attention earlier. There is one thing, and perhaps only one thing, that Modernity cannot do. Despite its undeniable successes, it does not have the means of responding to the question of the *legitimacy of the human*.[24] Modernity has made itself capable of producing prosperity, justice, and spreading culture, in this way giving a practical answer to the question of the good life, or at least "the good life" we hear about in commercials; in contrast, though, it has become incapable of saying why it is good that there are men to live such a life.

Let's end on a less somber note. It is not impossible that in Central and Eastern Europe, or elsewhere in the world, that there are still available reserves of human material. But one can also hope that somewhere there is what is even more precious: reserves, not only of humans, but of what makes human beings human, *new deposits of meaning*. We need them, because merely "believing in Europe" does not suffice. In fact, as I feared at the beginning of this chapter, that could be the height of nihilism. One still needs to believe properly in Europe. But that isn't possible if one *only* believes in Europe.

---

23 See below, "The Conditions of a Future," Chapter 13.
24 I began to pose this question in *The Wisdom of the World, op. cit.*

2
FROM ONE TRANSCENDENTAL
TO ANOTHER

To see more clearly *the* problem posed to European culture in late-modern times, or those that have felt its influence (which would mean, almost all), I need to put in place a rather simple structure, in which three pairs of fundamental concepts are opposed. For philosophers, I could use the name that medieval philosophy gave to this sort of concept: the "transcendentals." But even if this technical term is appropriate, it is not indispensable. I therefore will write them simply as follows:

Good/Evil

Truth / Falsity

Being / Nothing

It was not by chance that I sketched the three pairs in a way to form a sort of pyramid. For indeed, the question of good and evil is founded on that of the true and the false; and the question of the true and the false is founded in its turn on that of being and nothing. That evil is founded on the lie, we know since Augustine. For him, sin consists in not living in the way for which one was made, in betraying one's vocation, and thus lying. St. Augustine concludes that "it's not in vain that one could say that every sin is a lie."[1] And the lie in turn is founded on the love of nothing, because to lie is to prefer what is *not* to what is.

---

1   St. Augustine, *De civitate Dei*, XIV, iv, 1, C. J. Perl (ed.) (Paderborn: Schoningh, 1979), t. 1, p. 918.

Historical recall: where is the fundamental question?

Now I would like to propose an historical hypothesis. It is a crude schema, a caricature, to which one would need to add a thousand nuances. But I want to go straight to the essential. I therefore propose to characterize each of the last centuries by a dominant problem, which each time is a transcendental. The nineteenth century was that of the Good; the twentieth, that of the True; and I ask, whether the twenty-first century will be the century of Being?

The question that dominated the nineteenth century was the social question. This question was not only posed within Europe, but also in the regions where it had taken its colonial adventures. In the European space and in its overseas prolongations (the United States, for example), the capitalist economy, which no legislation had yet come to counterbalance, had created structures that were easily seen to be unjust because they produced a class that was exiled from society. The social question in the West was the demand of justice for those disadvantaged by competition; it was imperative to reintegrate into society the class that was excluded. Evil was exploitation, poverty, exclusion. In the colonies, this question was posed in the form of the huge differences that separated the colonial powers and their subject colonies.

In the twentieth century, a new transcendental entered the scene, adding itself to the Good that was already present: the True, with its contrary the False, but under the species of the Lie.[2]

The question that dominated this century was the emergence of ideological regimes, Leninism and National Socialism, both rendered possible by the new form that Truth took in Modern Times, to wit: scientific truth. Not the truths of the sciences, which are always partial and provisional, but "the Truth" with a capital "T" of "Science" with a capital "S," as they were imagined by those who weren't really scientists. Ideology was impossible without the scientism that dominated the end of the nineteenth century.

These two ideologies each claimed an incontestable truth. National

---

2   Here, as well as in several other passages later in this chapter, I am inspired by the thought of Alain Besançon, in particular his reflections on the notion of ideology.

Socialism presented itself as a coldly scientific vision of the world, founded on biology and "racial science"; Leninism presented itself as based on economic science and on the new science of the evolution of societies established by Marx.

In this context, the lie took on a new form. What one could call the "classical lie," that of the hypocrite or the politician, about which La Rochefoucauld or Machiavelli had theorized, masked the truth; the ideological lie claimed to unveil it.

The battle against the ideological regime, whether in its Nazi version or even more clearly in the Leninist version that represented its most perfect form, did not situate itself on the plane of good and evil. It was not, finally, comprehensible except as a struggle between the true and the false, more exactly: between the truth and the lie. The objection that needed to be made to "socialism" was not of a moral nature. It consisted in observing that the claim that "real socialism" existed was quite simply a lie, and that this "socialism," which perhaps was perfect in theory, had the defect of not existing. As Solzhenitsyn said, the worst suffering caused by the ideological regime, worse than poverty or oppression (although both were quite real), was obliging those who were subject to it to lie; and on the other hand, the first condition of liberating oneself from ideological oppression was to refuse to be complicit in this lie.[3]

The twenty-first century and Being?

The already-begun twenty-first century will be dominated, it seems to me, by another major transcendental, Being.

To be sure, the concern for the good, the duty to speak the truth, are far from being irrelevant or useless. They will continue as long as there are evil and lies in the world, hence to the last day. The social question has not been definitively resolved, but it has calmed down in the West; and while the ideological temptation has not disappeared, it no longer has the support of powerfully armed States. However, at the present time, another dimension has been added to the older problems. It is not a matter

---

3   Alexandre Soljenitsyn, *Lettre aux dirigeants de l'Union soviétique*, 6 (Paris: Seuil, 1974), p. 36.

of an additional floor, though, but rather, as my initial sketch indicated, of the foundation.

What are the fundamental problems of this century that, henceforth, is ours? Without claiming to give an exhaustive catalogue, I first will name the central problem, before enumerating various versions thereof. This central problem is nothing less than the very existence of man on this earth; its manifestations occurred more or less suddenly: the environment; the atomic bomb; demography; biology. Let's examine them one at a time.

Since the beginnings of the industrial era, humanity produces wastes that the planet has a hard time eliminating and which compromise its own well-being, perhaps its very survival. It destroys natural protections without being able to replace them, thus threatening the regularity of the climate. It consumes non-renewable energy sources and depletes them.

Since the 1940s, with atomic weapons and their successive improvements, humanity has the capacity to destroy itself completely in a spectacular conflagration, merely by pushing a button.

Since the 1960s, with the progress in artificial contraception, whether instruments or chemicals, humanity has the capacity to extinguish itself gradually, passively, discretely, without even particularly noticing, by simply ceasing to reproduce.

It is an ancient dream of humanity to take control of itself as a biological species, not only eliminating individuals it considers to be "defective," but by redefining itself according to some global project. Now, since the 1980s it attempts to give itself the technological means of realizing this project; those more learned than I in these areas will have to say whether it is technically feasible or not.

The question of nihilism

Thus, in our century the fundamental question is not that of Good and Evil, nor of Truth and Falsity; it is the question of Being and Nothing. I am not the first to put forth this view. At bottom, it is rather obvious.

Nietzsche, from the 1880s, predicted that the major problem of the following centuries would be what he, following others, called nihilism. In fact, in speaking of nihilism, what he recounted was "the history of the next two centuries."[4] I, however, will not define nihilism in the same way as Nietzsche, rather I will try to define its central question. To do so, it is necessary to recall an older question, posed at the beginning of the eighteenth century, more precisely in 1714, by Leibniz: "Why is there something rather than nothing?" This is a strange question. The German philosopher explained it as follows: "Because nothing is simpler and easier than something."[5] Leibniz, however, did not feel the need to compare the claims of the two possibilities and to compare the rights or advantages of "nothing" to those of "something." For him, it went without saying that Being was worth more than Nothing.

This conviction went back more than two millennia, since it was found in the two sources of European culture, in ancient Greece as well as the Bible, even if its explicit formulation only rarely appeared. This is the case with the most fundamental presuppositions of a culture, which have such a blinding evidence that one hesitates to state them explicitly. In any event, one does encounter the equation two or three times among the Greek philosophers, ventured with more or less discretion: Being is good; even: it is identical to the Good;[6] or an inequation: Being is better than Nothing.[7] In the Bible, the same affirmation is implicit in the admiration that the Creator expresses for his work once it is finished, according to the first creation-account. What God just created, and which was already "good" when taken piece-by-piece, is, once seen in its entirety, "very good," which also means "very beautiful" (*tōv me'od*) (*Genesis*, I, 31). In the Middle Ages, the identification of Being and the Good was taken up by the thinkers of the three religions.[8] In the Latin West, it was even formalized in the doctrine

---

4   Friedrich Nietzsche, fragment 11 [119], November 1887–March 1888, *KSA*, t. 13, p. 57. On the history of the word, see the synthesis of Franco Volpi, *Il Nichilismo, op. cit.*

5   Gottfried W. Leibniz, *Principes de la nature et de la grâce*, #7, A. Robinet (ed.) (Paris: PUF, 1954), p. 45.

6   Theophrastus, *Metaphysics*, IX, #32, 11a26; Plotinus, *Enneads*, V, 5 [32], 9, 37–38; V, 8 [31], 9, 40–41.

7   Aristotle, *On the generation of animals*, II, 1, 731b30.

8   Avicenna, *Shifā'*, *Metaphysics*, VIII, 6, G. C. Anawati (ed.) (Cairo: Organisation générale des imprimeries gouvernementales, 1960), p. 355, 14–16; Maimonides, *Guide des égarés*, III, 10, I. Joël (ed.) (Jerusalem: Junovitch, 1929), pp., 317, 5–6.

of the transcendentals, to which I alluded at the beginning. According to the technical term, these transcendentals are said to be "convertible". every thing that is, insofar as it is, is good.[9] This greater value of Being counterbalances what Leibniz called the "facility" of Nothing.

Now, today it appears that this evidence has abandoned us. Our question, the nihilistic question, is no longer, "Why is there something rather than nothing?" It has become: "Why should there be something rather than nothing?" Or, if one prefers: "Everything taken into account, is it really necessary that there be something rather than nothing?"

Being is no longer considered as something that is good, but at most as a neutral fact, even in certain extreme cases, as bad.[10] Nihilism draws the consequences from this and aims at the destruction of what it considers unworthy of being.

It spares the present, but only because it harbors the agent of the destruction. It seeks to destroy everything except the present. That means the past and the future. The logic of nihilism is therefore what one could call an absolute "presentism." It aims at the destruction of the past and the future.

The destruction of the past

The past is manifest under two forms: nature's past and the historical past. But it is one and the same thing that presentism reproaches to both: not to be well and truly past, and thus to encroach upon the present. We therefore have an ambivalent attitude toward the past, quite comparable to what Augustine unmasked about our attitude toward the truth: "They love the truth when it shines and illumines (*lucens*); they hate it when it turns to them, refutes and convicts them (*redarguens*)."[11] One can show this in both cases, the natural as well as the historical past. Let's consider them one after the other, while underlining the parallel between them.

---

9 St. Augustine, *De diversis quaestionibus LXXXIII*, #24 (Bibliothèque Augustinienne [*BA*] (Paris: Desclée de Brouwer), t. 10, p. 74; St. Thomas Aquinas, *Summa contra gentiles*, II, 41 (Rome: Leonina manualis, 1934), p. 131b.

10 For some of the reasons that lead to the axiological neutralization of Being, even to its negative valuation, see my *The Wisdom of the World, op. cit.*

11 St. Augustine, *Confessiones*, X, xxiii, 34, *BA*, t. 14, p. 202.

We love and defend nature to the extent that it constitutes a controllable domain that we can enjoy: as a reality, we take pleasure in nature mastered or set aside for our leisure, a place to stroll, under the rubric of "landscape"[12]; as a concept, we use nature as a reservoir of facts destined to relativize everything that is human, deemed to be purely "cultural." On the other hand, we hate nature to the extent that we sense its presence within each of us, as what imposes its own rules on us. For that nature we have found a name designed to devalue it, "biological." We represent "culture" not as the development and flowering of nature (as in "agri-culture"), but as a "wrenching" or "wresting" from it.

We love the historical past to the extent that it is held at a distance for us by a historical science that "prepares" it for us (like a butcher prepares a cow), and reduces it to the status of an object of knowledge. The past thus becomes what is other than us. It constitutes a kind of temporal landscape in which we can stroll in our imagination. A formulation of Nietzsche highlights this parallel without thematizing it: a certain sort of history consists in making "a spoiled stroller in the *garden* of knowledge."[13] As with the natural past, we willingly use the historical past like a supermarket of outmoded anthropological models that nourish our relativism. On the other hand, we distrust the historical past to the extent that we feel in ourselves the presence of something that more or less consciously determines us to a particular behavior; here too we have found a pejorative term and we speak of "traditional." We thus represent historical development not as a creative extension of the past, but as an *overcoming* of it that should be continued.

Professional historians have remained seekers who attempt to reconstruct what really happened, and all honor to them. But let us also look at the affective dispositions that pervade the enterprise to recount the past. The great historians methodically control these affects; but popularizers gain their livelihood by stirring all sorts of emotions in their readers:

12 Joachim Ritter, "Landschaft. Zur Funktion des Ästhetischen in der modernen Gesellschaft," in *Subjektivität. Sechs Aufsätze* (Frankfurt: Suhrkamp, 1974), pp. 141–63.
13 Friedrich Nietzsche, *Unzeitgemäße Betrachtungen, II: Vom Nutzen und Nachteil der Historie für das Leben*, Preface, KSA, t. 1, p. 245. (My italics.)

nostalgia; horror; curiosity; a taste for the exotic. The most characteristic is the intermediary level, however. Between the experts and the vulgarizers an entire literary genre develops, sometimes written by competent men, but at the use of the "educated public" and of intellectuals who are not historians. This history seeks to show that the past is a succession of arbitrary constructions, of artificial objects whose mode of fabrication is recounted. Correlatively, though, history is increasingly attributed a kind of culpability. The past of the West in particular has been reread in this dark way. The horrors that it contains, which were quite real, are rehearsed *ad nauseam*. This past becomes the object of a sort of confession, but without absolution.

The Catholic church is especially accused. That does not come from the fact that it is more culpable than any other institution, but that it is more accusable. Indeed, it is the only one that can still lend itself easily to an accusation. For, to do this two things are required: to have been there at the time of the (mis)deeds, in order to be able to be culpable; but also to be here today, at the time when one seeks someone responsible to accuse. Now, the majority of the institutions that one could accuse are gone; the Ancien Régime, feudalism, certain "mentalities," no longer exist. There are only two groups of humans who claim a continuity that coincides with the entire trajectory of Western history: the Jewish people and the Church. The first has already paid, and how much! The second, at least for the moment and in Europe, only pays a little, as the favorite target of the media's mockery.

The destruction of the future

Our attitude towards the future is the same as our attitude toward the past. We love the future as long as it is truly future: far away, utopian, the "rosy future." In contrast, we hate it when it encroaches on our present, because we have to prepare it, starting today. To assemble the conditions for a livable future, or even a merely viable one, imposes upon us, starting now, the duty of taking certain measures of prudence or foresight.

One can see this in connection with two groups of questions: demographic and ecological.[14] Both crises have been foreseen for decades. Rachel

14 On demography, see "The Conditions of a Future," Chapter 13 below.

Carson's book against pesticides, *Silent Spring*, which was to lead to an ecological awareness of vast extent and at the highest levels, dates from 1962. That of Adolphe Landry, *La Révolution démographique*, dates from 1934 and led French governments of all stripes, from the Popular Front to post-war Gaullism, to react in the form of "pro-family policies."[15] Moreover, the demographic decline of Europe was predicted from the beginning of the 1970s by the historian Pierre Chaunu.

However, today the future is the object of an obstinate desire *not* to know. The "long term" which, as long as it bears upon the past was dear to historians of a certain stripe, as soon as it concerns the future has become a taboo which determines what is acceptable or not in academe. One of the towering figures of this world, Lord Keynes, famously declared the concern for the long run to be otiose. In a passage that is constantly cited, but very rarely referenced, the famous economist wrote thus: "This long run is a misleading guide to current affairs. *In the long run* we are all dead."[16] To halt all speculation that risks being misdirected to the long term, the average decision-maker, whether a high official, a media personality or a politician, is always ready to bring up the quotation.

Let's take a closer look at the formulation, however (and pretend not to see its humor). The truism is undeniable, because it is certain that in the long run we will all be dead. But everything depends on the way in which one understands the pronoun "we." If one understands by that living persons, it is a tautology, and this is probably what Lord John meant to say, as one can guess if one pays attention to his use of the present tense, "we are," instead of "we shall be." If one envisages the totality of the human race it is equally true, but we have greater leeway, since the biologists give us a few hundred thousand years before the species exhausts the possibilities it contains. The real question, however, is to know if we can overcome the limits of the present ego, for example in the direction of our descendants. For Keynes who was a homosexual and had no children, the question was

---

15   Rachel L. Carson, *Silent Spring* (Boston: Houghton Mifflin, 1962); Adolphe Landry, *La Révolution démographique. Études et essais sur les problèmes de la population* (Paris: Sirey, 1934).

16   John M. Keynes, *A Tract on Monetary Reform* (London: Macmillan, 1924), chap. 3.

hardly relevant. But for us, his formulation has become a comfortable excuse, which spares us any thought about what *we* could do *now* so that *others besides us* could *later* live well, or, even before that, live at all.

We live in an "enlightened" and "disbelieving" age, for which every "superstition" is not only an error but an unforgiveable lack of taste, at least in intellectual milieus. In any case, this is what we imagine about ourselves. But what we say is belied by what we do. For in reality, our practices clearly show that with us "adults," people "who are nobody's fool," we entertain the same illusions as children. We believe wholehearted in those little elves who at night clean up the natural world that our factories have poisoned during the day; we believe wholeheartedly in the stork that will bring us the babies that we have kept from being born.

The superdetermination of the transcendentals

I cannot pretend to give concrete suggestions for ways to confront what I just described. However, I would like to sketch, if not a strategy, at least the cartography of the battlefield. I will pose as a general rule the following: the entrance on the scene of another transcendental further determines the one, or those, to which it was just added. This phenomenon is verified each time. Thus, the question of the Good was further determined by that of the True. The social question, which was and remains real, whether in the form of the workers' condition or the colonies, was the real support that the lying ideology of Leninism chose as its host and then poisoned.

In a similar way, today the question of Good and Evil is modified by that of Being and Nothing. The intrinsic goodness of Being loses its evidence, it is even directly called in doubt; while Nothing becomes the object of a troubling fascination, even a temptation. A diffuse but widespread sense of culpability in Western societies, even more than in what was recently called—another lie—"the East," feeds a more or less acknowledged desire for death. Having committed evil (from which no individual or collective can claim to be innocent) becomes so intolerable that the only way of forgetting would be to totally disappear.

Let's point to a symptom of this repression of the question of Good and Evil by that of Being and Nothing. A strange adjective has appeared the past few years, "societal." Dictionaries don't have it, it sounds strange, it runs counter to the genius of the French language. However, it survives, it has a function. What is its purpose then? It qualifies what are called "the problems of society," which means something quite different from "social problems." The latter concern an evil to repair, a good to reestablish, since it is a matter of becoming aware of the injustices of the present distribution of material or moral (honor) goods within society, in order to better distribute them and thus to build a better order. The "problems of society," however, even though they claim to repair injustices, concern the very foundations of the State, i.e., of human life and what makes "social life" to begin with, above all, marriage, family, education. Now, it is with surprise that one observes the Left in advanced societies stepping back from "social problems" for the sake of "societal problems." To be sure, they speak about them, but they do very little to improve the lot of certain social strata. They prefer to occupy themselves with same-sex marriage or euthanasia.[17]

The existence of man as a problem

What I called the superdetermination of the Good by Being presents an opportunity, however. Why? How? With the emphasis placed on the "problems of society," the fundamental presupposition of modern political thought comes to the fore, and allows us to see what is problematic in it. The model upon which the Moderns based themselves to conceive the city of man is that of a contract established by, and among, members of a group. Concerning this group, one knows at least three things: (a) it already exists, its members are alive; (b) it is constituted of men, living beings who possess intellectual faculties, i.e., reason and will, which allow them to contract; (c) in order to do so, the group must already exist as such, its members must already be together.

Now, this is a fiction that abstracts from the concrete nature of man as a biological species. To be sure, the philosophers who proposed this model of the ideal genesis of society were perfectly aware of the fictive character of the "social contract." But they could allow themselves to pose this explanatory fiction as long as the survival of the species was assured by

---

17 I owe this observation to Roland Hureaux, *Pour en finir avec la droite* (Paris: Gallimard, 1998), pp. 135–38.

instinct. However, today this survival is in the hands of its various sorts of leaders – scientific, economic, political, media. Hence, the very existence of man becomes a problem, and humanity is obliged to reflect on the basic presuppositions of Modernity. In order to do that, one needs to have the courage to open one's eyes.

The center, or the basis, of the problem, however, is in the process of relocating to a "metaphysical" domain. The term "metaphysical" ought not cause fear or lead to the charge of "too abstract!" On the contrary, metaphysics too is in the process of descending from the ethereal heights where it was customarily put, in order to take on an extraordinarily concrete form. The tradition saw in metaphysics one of those sciences in which one considered the things that could not be altered by human intervention. The Greeks coined the term "theory" for this sort of knowledge. Aristotle thus classified it as "first philosophy," which dealt with the highest things, and for this reason "divine," along with mathematics and natural philosophy in the theoretical sciences.[18] In contrast, the direction of our life, with the choice between good and evil that it implies, pertains to "practice" or the practical sciences.

However, at this time we are witnessing a conceptual revolution which leads to the following paradox: metaphysics is becoming a practical science and thus competes with the discipline that until now was the practical science par excellence, moral science. Traditionally, the latter dealt with the relations that needed to be established among human subjects who already exist, and who seek to make their relationships as harmonious as possible; at the limit, it dealt with the way in which they should deal with themselves as individuals, but still as already existing. In contrast, moral science was and had to remain silent when it came to the question of the entrance into the human community of members who did not yet exist.

The necessity of metaphysics

Can't we do without all this "metaphysics," though? To reprise a phrase probably coined by the Italian philosopher Augusto Del Noce, why can't we imagine a "gay nihilism"? Our motto would then be: "There's nothing,

18 Aristotle, *Metaphysics*, E, 1, 1026a18–20.

but that's nothing to worry about!" This would be an Epicurean attitude, in the strict sense of the term. I am willing to grant that that would be well and fine, as long as we attach ourselves solely to the present. Since we already exist, since we already are part of the Great Whole, why not try to make our stay as comfortable as possible? To do that, to arrange a peaceful life, even a just life, we only need a bit of practical wisdom, but absolutely no metaphysics. However, to the contrary, we need to pay attention to Nietzsche's perceptive remark. The very fact that we say that life has meaning, which is the central affirmation of all metaphysics, presupposes that life needs something other than itself, and superior to it, to justify itself. As a consequence, while believing one was rendering a service to life, one only devalues it vis-à-vis the "meaning" that one would like to ascribe to it; at the extreme, one condemns life in the name of that meaning.[19]

I will first respond with a play on words: the word "meaning" (*sens*) has several meanings. One of these is "signification," which is the case here, but others include "perception" (the sense of sight) and "direction" (the course of a river). Now, life does not only consist in being alive (in Greek: zôè); it also means to lead a life, to have a history, a *bios*, the root of our word "biography." Life is a kind of movement. It evolves from an elementary level of organization to another, one that is more complex. It passes from an individual belonging to a given species to its descendants. Among human beings, it accumulates its own distinctive experience thanks to individual and social memory (language, writing) and grows like a snowball.

Now, even if one admits for the sake of argument that life doesn't have any meaning in the sense of significance, the question still remains to know if we can do without "sense" in the sense of "sense of direction." Such a sense, we don't grasp it by rising high above the concrete realities, but on the contrary, by inserting ourselves in their current, or, to borrow an image from Plotinus, by dancing to their rhythm.[20]

We are asked to accept life as it is, without asking if it measures up to some criterion that exists outside it. That's fine. But I ask: Do we really *love* that life, life as such? Love of life can mean two very different things.

---

19 Friedrich Nietzsche, fragment 10 [192], Autumn 1887, *KSA*, t. 12, p. 571; then 10 [152], *ibid.*, p. 541.

20 Plotinus, *Enneads*, VI, 9 [8], 8, 36–37.

There is one expressed by the wonderful Homeric phrase: "to live and to see the light of the sun."[21] This can be interpreted: to live is to bathe and to be bathed in the light of the presence. Here, we naively love *our* life, such as we can experience it. We love to be alive because it allows us to produce and experience agreeable sensations, from the crudest pleasures to the most sublime and worthy of man. But to what extent do we love life *as such*? If we love our life, that means that we love ourselves. But we cannot be sure that we love life as such unless we look favorably upon life outside of ourselves. This difficulty is at its peak when it is a question of not merely continuing one's own life, but of transmitting life, thus "creating" a life that does not yet exist, in this way having the future encroach on the present, as we said earlier.

To play our role well on the stage of the world, that is within our competence, at the very least because we have to. The difficulty begins when the question is to know if we have the right to bring new actors on the stage. Are we authorized to inflict life on others whose consent we, obviously, cannot solicit? We do not have the right to do so unless we are convinced that life is a gift, that it is intrinsically good. If we do not wholeheartedly believe in life's goodness, to take Buddha or Schopenhauer seriously becomes not only possible but the most sacred of duties. However, if we believe life is good, one can ask if we can do so without something like an implicit or even explicit faith in some transcendence.

Opportunities for Christianity

Not without some surprise, I would observe that Christianity and the Christian churches are fairly well placed to respond to the challenges faced by humanity. With respect to the most recent, that of Being and Nothing, the Church is perhaps, and paradoxically so, better placed than for the first two. In order to show this, I need to pass in review once again the three centuries and the three transcendentals that correspond to them. I do this because the situation has changed.

Earlier, when it was a question of Good and Evil the Church was not alone. In principle, even if his conscience is wounded and darkened by

---

21 Homer, *Iliad*, 24, 558; *Odyssey*, 4, 540 ff.

original sin, man can know what is good, even if he isn't strong enough to do it. In fact, the struggle for social justice was led by agents, many of whom were from outside of Christianity, and who had various sorts of relations with it, according to individual, country and period. But for the essential, the Church and the workers' movement, as it was expressed in social democracy, pulled in the same direction. Contrary to what one would have us believe today, the Church need not be embarrassed by its previous attitude. To be sure, often this alliance was not understood, or was poorly understood, by the two parties; it nonetheless existed.

When the opposition was between the True and the False, the Church was not alone either. Against the Nazi and Leninist ideologies, the Church and "secular" liberalism pulled in the same direction. Here, too, the alliance was not always understood. Liberals often saw in the two ideologies "secular religions," which needed to be rejected at the same time as real religions. For its part, the Church had the tendency to bring together secularism on one hand, Hitler and Lenin's totalitarianisms on the other, by putting them under the same heading of "atheism" or "materialism."

How are things today in connection with the third front, Being and Nothing? Again, the Church has objective allies. First of all, we discover in ourselves certain emotions that probably correspond to biological regulations aimed at assuring the preservation of the species. They cause us repugnance before what detracts from the honor of our forebears; and by awakening various affects (fear, shame, disgust), they prompt us to defend life in the face of death and behaviors that lead to it. But today nothing is easier than discrediting these sentiments by calling them "prejudices" and mere "taboos," and the human sciences, powerfully aided by the medias, constantly employ these terms.

On the other hand, the awareness of many "secular" people of the cultural value of Christianity is a positive sign. A while ago I had the occasion to express myself concerning "Christianists," an inelegant term that I may have been the first to use.[22] I meant by it those who recognize the positive contributions of Christianity and are favorable to it, without believing in Christ. They should not be discounted, rather the hand that they extend to

22 See my *Europe, la voie romaine, op. cit.*, p. 182, and my interview with G. Valente, "Cristiani e 'cristianisti,'" *30Giorni*, October 2004, pp. 40–44.

us should be welcomed. But we should not separate this gratitude from an invitation to these well-disposed souls to recognize the true source of this "Christian civilization," and to let them know they too can drink from it.

From this point of view, one can note the astonishing contemporary relevance of Augustine's *City of God*. What he said about the pagan gods recognized by the Roman Empire can be applied to what is said today about the "values" on which the Western empire is said to rest. The rapprochement is even closer when one recognizes that certain of the pagan gods bore the names of what we today call "values." This was already the case in Hesiod's *Theogony*; it was also the case with Rome. Among all the pagan divinities Augustine accepts only one, *Felicitas*, "Happiness," but he adds a decisive qualification: it is not a goddess, but a gift of God.[23] Let us transpose this into more modern terms: *"values" are impotent to cause life; they themselves presuppose Life.*

Against nihilism, therefore, the Church is not entirely alone, at least at the start. On the other hand, it is by itself in the final analysis. This is because it is at the forefront, because it alone is capable of going to the very end and employing the trump cards that it alone possesses.

To support this, let's first note a circumstantial fact. In this area, it took the first step, it was the first *to name* the adversary, to recognize that it was the adversary. This is new. For a long time it had difficulty in calling ideology by its name, especially under its Leninist form, and it too often took refuge behind a vague formulation, one employing the plural: "ideologies." Today, I am glad that the highest authority, the papacy, dared to name "the culture of death."[24] To be sure, at bottom this formulation is an oxymoron, because culture is essentially the cultivation of life. But the oxymoron accurately names the perversion by which what should serve the growth and flowering of life turns against it, and against itself.

Moreover, the Church possesses precious antidotes to the nihilistic double destruction of everything that is not the present. As for the rela-

23   St. Augustine, *De civitate Dei*, IV, xxi, *op. cit.*, t. 1, p. 254; the idea was suggested to me by don Giacomo Tantardini, Invito alla lettura di sant'Agostino. Appunti dalle lezioni de don G. Tantardini alla Libera Universita San Pio V di Roma, anno 2000–2001 (Rome: San Gabriele, 2003), p. 14.

24   St. John Paul II, encyclical *Evangelium Vitae*, 25 March 1995, #12 and *passim*.

tionship to the past, it perhaps is the sole institution that can speak with authority of pardon, thus avoiding the trap of imprisoning oneself in a confession of one's faults but without the hope of absolution. In fact, pardon is not a moral notion but a purely religious one. Morality as such knows what is a moral law and it knows what a transgression is; but it can only acknowledge this transgression. It does not know and cannot know what pardon is.[25]

As for the relationship to the future, the Church is perhaps the sole institution to be able to defend life in a responsible manner. To do so, one must dare to affirm that life, in and of itself, is good. Not that it is pleasant (which I don't deny), but that it is good in the weightiest sense of the term, that it represents a good such that it is not only enjoyable for me but that it merits being transmitted to others. The Church confesses that the world is created by a good God, a "generous" God, that it is the object of a providence that does not deny liberty but gives each creature what it needs to freely seek its good, and in particular that man's freedom, wounded by sin, has been redeemed by a God of love. In that way, the Church is perhaps the sole institution that possesses, both theoretically and practically, what is metaphysically needed by man so that he can survive nihilism.

25   See my *On the God of the Christians (and on one or two others)* (South Bend, IN: St. Augustine Press, 2013), Chapter 7: "A God who forgives sins, " pp. 139–54.

II
SACRED COWS OR MAD COWS?

3

TO GROUND REASON

Modern Times understand themselves as the age of reason. In the image of the ages of humanity that it is particular fond of, and whose irresistible succession is parallel to an individual's stages of development, they see an "age of reason" succeeding an ancient infancy, innocent but quite naïve, then a tormented medieval adolescence. This reason had to affirm itself against those it considered its enemies, among which religious faith was seen to be the most dangerous. During the French revolution, as is well known, the goddess Reason was celebrated on November 10, 1793, in a ceremony held at Notre Dame de Paris.

On its side, faith sought to defend itself, to present its "apology," not in today's sense of a "mea culpa," but in the original sense of "defense," as in Plato's *Apology of Socrates*. Reconnecting with a literary genre that went back to the age of persecutions in the Roman empire, religion surrounded itself with an "apologetics" that conceived its role to be a defense of the faith against the pretensions of an arrogant reason.

Today things are quite different. It is no longer a question of rebuffing the assaults of reason by showing that it is unaware of its own limits. On the contrary, it is reason itself that needs to be defended against its own demons.

In what follows I will present a typology of the dangers that threaten reason. Then, I will recall the rational, even rationalistic, nature of Christianity, and symmetrically, the Christian nature of rationality. One can venture a diagnosis of the current illness of reason from several points of view. Some are traditional, others more original.

The traditional reproaches made to reason

Classical reason was to shed light and itself be a light that could never grow dim. Its demons were external enemies. For example, they were the faculties of the soul different from it, considered as inferior to it: the senses, as in Plato's *Phaedo* and the entire Platonic tradition, or the passions and imagination, as with the Stoics or, much later, Spinoza. One could put these enemies in a sort of developmental schema: the movement of the education of man, whether of the individual or the human race, went towards reason and distanced itself from an initial darkness. What one could blame, what one could claim bore the responsibility, belonged to the past, which only survived in anachronistic holdovers. Thus, we had "prejudices," which could be, as with Descartes,[1] those of the infancy of each individual, or the prejudices of the collective infancy of the human race, what the rhetoric of the Enlightenment called "the powers of darkness."

Reason too, however, knew its errors and aberrations. It could do too much, but also too little, it could sin by excess as well as by defect. In the first case, it was a matter of philosophical pride. Curiously, the expression is found, doubtless for the first time, uttered by a self-proclaimed *philosophe* of the eighteenth century, Voltaire, who wrote: "[...] philosophical pride/sours the irenic sweetness of our days."[2] Reason must take care not to overestimate itself, and an extensive school of apologetics took this wise recommendation as its point of departure. It was a matter of humbling reason by means of the instruments of skepticism, in order to clear a space for faith. This was the way Montaigne's endeavor is to be understood, as building on the foundation of Christian skepticism.[3] Pascal flirted with it, as when he wrote: "Humiliate yourself, impotent reason."[4] And even Kant alluded to this procedure in his famous formulation: "I had to limit reason in order to make room for faith."[5]

Conversely, reason sins by defect when, without yielding to the blows of its enemies, it withdraws itself from the game. One can illustrate this idea by means of an image involving fatigue and sleep. In a famous lecture

---

1   Descartes, *Principia philosophiae*, I, #71, in C. Adam and P. Tannery (dir.), *Oeuvres* [abbreviated as *AT*], t. VIII, pp. 35–36.

2   Voltaire, *À Horace*, 1772.

3   See in particular Richard Popkin's works.

4   Blaise Pascal, *Pensées*, n. 434, ed. L. Brunschvicg (Paris: Hachette, 1925), t. 2, p. 347, and see also n. 282, ibid., p. 205.

5   Emmanuel Kant, *Kritik der reinen Vernunft*, Preface to the Second Edition, B XXX.

given in 1935 at Vienna, Husserl explained that the principal danger for Europe—by which he meant not a continent but "an internal teleology of reason"—was nothing other than lassitude.[6] A further step was taken with the "temptation to despair," to employ an expression coined by the French novelist George Bernanos.[7] Despair is more than simple fatigue. It has a temporal dimension. Postmodern man despairs because he has abandoned the idea of progress that found its source in Enlightenment reason.

It therefore seems that the danger today is less pride than the opposite vice, an excessive humility, which one could name "pusillanimity." This term is very old, since it is a vice described by Aristotle under the name *mikropsukhia*, and which Descartes called "baseness" or "vicious humility."[8] What is new is its application to intellectual endeavors, which was hardly prefigured in antiquity, except for Socrates' rejection of the temptation to "misology" (hatred of reason), depicted by Plato as analogous to the misanthropy that assails the one who, having put too much confidence in an individual who betrayed him, henceforth distrusts all men.[9] The "dare to know!" (*sapere aude*) that Kant made the motto of Enlightenment, if it is still uttered today, is much less practiced that it might appear.[10]

The positivistic spirit represents a synthesis of pride and humility, where reason no longer looks up, but rejects all transcendence, becoming a "bent over reason," to adapt a phrase of St. Bernard of Clairvaux, who spoke of a "bent over soul" (*anima incurvata*).[11] Positivism, however, does not only turn away from a transcendent divine. With its founder Auguste Comte, it initially meant the renunciation of seeking the ultimate causes of phenomena,

---

6   Edmund Husserl, "Die Krisis des europäischen Menschentums und die Philosophie," in W. Biemel (ed.), *Die Krisis der europäischen Wissenschaften und die transzendentale Phänomenologie* (The Hague: Nijhoff, 1962), Husserliana, t. 6, p. 348.

7   Georges Bernanos, *Sous le soleil de Satan* [1926], title of the first part.

8   Aristotle, *Nicomachean Ethics*, IV, 3, 1129b9–11; 1125a19–27; Descartes, *Traité des passions*, III, # 159, AT, t. 11, p. 450.

9   Plato, *Phaedo*, 89c-d.

10   Emmanuel Kant, *Was ist Aufklärung?*, first paragraph.

11   The original source is the Latin poet Persus, *Saturae*, II, 61; St. Bernard of Clairvaux, *On the Song of Songs*, XXIV, II, 6–7, Patrologia Latina [abbreviated as *PL*], 183, 897 ad.

and resigning oneself to only writing their laws. However, behind all this one glimpses the temptation that man experiences to consider himself as self-sufficient, what has been called "exclusive humanism." In fact, there is no contradiction between excessive pride and excessive humility; on the contrary, they go together well. To claim to be capable of determining by oneself one's limits has nothing humble about it; in reality it is the height of pride.

Internal enemies

It could be—the hypothesis has certainly been put forth—, that the crisis of the ancient world was also a crisis of reason, more precisely a "disillusionment" (*desengaño*) vis-à-vis the latter. Socially speaking, it corresponded to an "impotence of philosophy" to go beyond an elite in which it was confined, in order to propose to the masses ways of escaping from despair.[12] But it is in modern times that something like the suicide of reason took on a rather concrete form.

The idea according to which reason can put itself in danger received powerful development with Kant, in the transcendental dialectic of the first *Critique*. Reason can be caught in a net of its own making and be trapped in antinomies, when it ceases being guided by sensibility. The Kantian revolution thus overturns the classical hierarchy of the faculties of the soul, recalled above. The latter devalued the faculties of the soul said to be inferior, such as, to begin with, perception, or the imagination. Kant rehabilitates them and even offered an energetic plea in favor of the senses.[13] The inferior faculties are no longer considered as chains or snares for reason. On the contrary, they constitute very useful guard rails, which allow it to avoid being its own victim. The notion of "fidelity to the earth" in Nietzsche is a sort of long-term consequence of the defense of sensibility by Kant, whom he, nonetheless, constantly attacked.[14]

12   Maria Zambrano, *La agonía de Europa* [1945] (Madrid: Mondadori, 1988), pp. 52–53.

13   Emmanuel Kant, *Anthropologie in pragmatischer Hinsicht*, # 8–10, in *Werke*, Ed. W. Weischedel (Darmstadt: Wissenschaftliche Buchgesellschaft, 1960), t. 6, pp. 432–36.

14   Friedrich Nietzsche, *Also sprach Zarathustra*, Preface, 3, *KSA*, t. 4, p. 15; I, *Von der schenkenden Tugend*, 2, *ibid.*, p. 99.

The idea of a self-destructive dialectic of Enlightenment received its first expression in the famous work of Max Horkheimer and Theodor Adorno bearing that title.[15] One can understand it as the historicized version of Kant's transcendental dialectic. Now, if reason undermines its own foundations, the historical project of the Enlightenment, i.e., the complete rationalization of life, is condemned to failure. Modernity, which embarked on its journey to realize this project, and which from the beginning understood itself as just such an effort, thus cannot fulfill its promises. Like a parasite, it feeds on what it cannot reproduce (the idea, we saw earlier, is found in Charles Péguy).[16]

Let us look at a famous etching by a man of the Enlightenment, the Spanish painter Goya (1746–1826). A man is seated at a table sleeping, propped up by his elbow. Found in the background are strange animals. A creature looking like a cat is seated behind the chair, another is just behind the back of the sleeper. Flying creatures that could be vampires or birds cover him with their shadow. The birds evoke birds of prey. One of these birds of prey is about to land on the shoulder of the sleeper. The epigram declares: "The sleep (*sueño*) of reason produces monsters."[17] From the painting itself we have no indication of what could have caused reason to sleep or have nightmares.

However, the image is more complex that appears at first glance. On one hand, the sleeper could very well be the painter himself. On the table are found sheets of paper and what seems to be the brush of a painter. The sleeper is not some animal, but a fully human being, of the masculine sex, an adult, white, civilized, clothed in very proper apparel. On the other hand, the birds of the nightmare that assail him resemble owls, the bird that is the symbol of Minerva, who is the goddess of reason. And the title itself is ambiguous. The Castilian *sueño*, which I initially translated as "sleep," can equally mean "dream," an ambiguity founded on the inseparability of the two phenomena, which can be found in other languages, for example

15 Theodor W. Adorno and Max Horkheimer, *Dialektik der Aufklärung. Philosophische Fragmente, op. cit.*

16 Charles Péguy, "De la situation faite au parti intellectuel dans le monde modern devant les accidents de la gloire temporelle", in *op. cit.*, p. 725.

17 Goya, *Los Caprichos*, n. 43 (around 1799).

Russian. We don't know if one should seek the danger in the fact that reason sleeps, or in the impossibility it experiences of totally losing consciousness. The dreams that thus emerge are much more dangerous as they are those of reason itself, in such a way that man is then going "to dream according to principles, to be delirious with reason."[18]

The irrationalism of rationalism

Those whose reason ought to pray the most to God that he protects them are, as the well-known joke has it, his friends, not his enemies. Those who today claim to be "rationalists" aren't really. For them, reason is something secondary. Reason comes from the irrational. Reason is explained, for example, as an instrument in the struggle for existence, in keeping with the criterion of the survival of the fittest: a being endowed with reason has more trumps to play in the contest of this sort.

The intelligibility of what is, is often taken to be obvious, in no need of being made intelligible in its turn. The greatest thinkers however dared to acknowledge its enigmatic character, for example Einstein: "The eternal mystery of the world is its comprehensibility."[19] We therefore need a contemporary version of the "philosophy of nature" already sought by German idealism and romanticism, then by English and French thinkers, who at least were able to give an account of the very rationality of nature, who gave, as it were, a *logos* of its *logos*.[20]

For the adherents of the two biblical religions, Jewish or Christian, on the other hand, all these phenomena, or to put it better: these hypotheses, come *after logos*. Only the *logos* is at the beginning, it alone is the principle. The English physicist Fred Hoyle mocked the hypothesis of the priest Georges Lemaître about the expansion of the universe by speaking of a Big

18   E. Kant, *Kritik der Urteilskraft*, "Allgemeine Anmerkung zur Exposition der ästhetischen Urteile", K. Vorländer (ed.) (Hamburg: Meiner, 1963), p. 123; see also *Anthropologie in pragmatischer Hinsicht*, # 40, in Werke, t. 6, p. 510.

19   A. Einstein, "Physik und Realität," *Journal of the Franklin Institute*, 221–23, March 1936, pp. 313–47, citation on p. 315.

20   See in this sense Bertrand Saint-Sernin, "Y a-t-il place, aujourd'hui, pour une philosophie de la nature?," *Bulletin de la Société française de philosophie*, 93rd yr., n. 1, January–March 1999.

Bang, a phrase that has since been accepted and has lost its initial pejorative connotation. But this image of a beginning of everything also suggests a noise devoid of meaning, not an ultimate principle accessible to reason.

Here, however, one must be clear. Biblical faith does not at all claim to refute any of the scientific hypotheses about the origin of reason to which I just alluded. Even less does it claim to replace them by others that would be better. Nor does it seek to furnish the philosophy of nature that we need. None of these tasks pertains to it. The affirmation that, in the last instance, Being has a rational character provides no answer to the questions that science poses, to which it seeks to find answers. But faith does provide the ground on which science moves and which, for that very reason, it cannot see and should not see.

Nietzsche perfectly understood that this supposition is a belief that finds its origin in the Bible. For the German philosopher, even if we are the fiercest partisans of Enlightenment, "we are still pious," because our belief in reason is still a "metaphysical faith," a long-term consequence of choices that were made in Greek philosophy and Christianity, our lights are the flicker of a fire lit by Plato.[21] Nietzsche wanted us to discard the last vestiges that still connect us to this belief. But can we? And should we?

To defend reason is therefore not a merely strategic tactic on the part of Christians. This defense is part of the very essence of Christianity. Chesterton has his priest-detective, Fr. Brown, when a false cleric whom he just unmasked asks him how he could have seen through him, say: "You attacked reason, which is bad theology."[22] Jews and Christians are, as such, rationalists. In their eyes, "at the beginning," the principle of all things, there was and still is *logos*. The first words of the fourth Gospel: "In the beginning was the Word" (*logos*) echo the first words of *Genesis*, which opens the entire Bible. God himself is also rational, and perhaps even a rationalist.

This is even more important to recall today as an opposition between

---

21 Friedrich Nietzsche, *Die fröhliche Wissenschaft*, V, # 344, *KSA*, t. 3, pp. 574–77. See Henri Birault, "En quoi, nous aussi, nous sommes encore pieux (Nietzsche)," *Revue de métaphysique et de morale*, 67-61, 1962, pp. 25–64.

22 G. K. Chesterton, *The Blue Cross*, in *Father Brown. Selected Stories* (London: Collector's Library, 2003), p. 33.

Athens and Jerusalem, between the Greek heritage and the biblical message, has become current, not to say, a commonplace.[23] It is too often cast as a conflict between Greco-pagan reason and Israel's faith. As if rationality were the monopoly of Greece, while the rest of the world, including Israel, would have been plunged into the irrational.

In this connection, some have assumed the habit of constructing the historiographical hypothesis of an "Hellenization" of Christianity, which leads, by means of a reaction, to the call for a (re)judaization as an antidote. It would be good therefore to show how rationality is as present on the Jewish side of things as the Greek, even if it is found in another form in Israel. I would even venture to say that biblical rationality contains elements that its Greek sister had not fully developed, but which can be very precious for treating our contemporary illnesses.

This case, however, presupposes that one does not treat "Jewish" as an eternal category, which too often is the case, but that one considers it by turning to the texts and concrete events of the Jewish tradition in its biblical origins. This tradition is complex and is not unified within itself. The point where its different elements converge is not in it, but outside of it. In any case, one also finds in the Bible passages, in particular those revolving around the image of a potter and the clay that he forms as he will, in which the creature addressing God is presented as impious, and even as absurd.[24] But other sorts of passages can be found.

Reason as nature and as conscience

As everyone grants, the Bible does not contain concepts; those are and remain the monopoly of philosophy, which is of Greek origin. The Bible proceeds by narratives. But it succeeds in presenting the fundamental dimensions of reason in this narrative style.

First of all, the idea of nature, on which the entire philosophical enterprise depends. To be sure, the word is found nowhere in the Bible, and the Talmudic term, medieval and modern, that designates it (*teva'*) only appears later in the Mishnah and signifies less birth and growth (*physis*),

---

23 See my *Europe, la voie romaine, op. cit.*, p. 38.
24 *Isaiah*, XXIX, 16; XLV, 9; *Wisdom*, XII, 12; *Romans*, IX, 20.

than the mark or character that gives form.[25] However, the concept is implicit from the first creation-narrative. Each thing is created "according to its kind [or species]" (*Genesis* I, 12, 21, 24–25), not as a chaos of elements or properties. Each creature possesses its internal characteristics and deploys itself in being by remaining faithful to them. Thus, reproduction occurs "according to the species" of what reproduces. Aristotle would have seen in this a poetic way of expressing the formula that he repeats apropos to nature: "a man engenders man."

The connection between the idea of a creation by speech and the fact that the creative act establishes in being a system of carefully distinguished natures seems clear to me. The created world forms a sentence whose words are distinct, with each having its meaning. This determines the relationship of the Creator to the created. God can only expect each thing to produce the effects that express its nature and its internal logic. This is teaching of the parable of the vineyard in Isaiah (V, 1–7): the wine-presser must await the vine to produce its grapes.[26] In this way, one has the first presence of reason.

A second presence is that of conscience. *Logos* is not solely theoretical, it is also practical. And according to Kant and his "primacy of practical reason," it would be more itself in the practical domain than the theoretical domain.[27] In any case, Greek *logos* possessed this ethical dimension. According to Aristotle, each virtue is given its rule or measure by *logos*.[28] Now, the knowledge of what he must do and must avoid was already granted to man. And not necessarily by the teaching of Moses, but from time immemorial, as the prophet Micah suggests: "It has been said (*huggad*) to you, mortal, what is good, what YHWH demands of you: nothing other than to do justice, to love tenderly, and to walk humbly with your God" (VI, 8).

The reading I prefer here, which is that supposed by the Septuagint translation, has the advantage of leaving in the dark the subject of "to say"

---

25 See Ernest Klein, *A Comprehensive Etymological Dictionary of the Hebrew Language for the Readers of English* (New York: Macmillan, 1987), pp. 239–40.

26 See my interpretation of the passage in *On the God of the Christians, op. cit.*, pp. 123–24.

27 E. Kant, *Kritik der praktischen Vernunft*, K. Vorländer (ed.) (Hamburg: Meiner, 1967), pp. 138–40.

28 Aristotle, *Nicomachean Ethics*, II, 6, 1106b36–1107a2 (*hōrismenē logō*).

(more precisely: "to recount"): earlier prophets? Moses? God? In any case, it is interesting to note that the presence of conscience in the heart appears as something "said," as a linguistic item, thus prefiguring what will later be called the "voice" of conscience.

Pleas and negotiations

When men do not listen to what their conscience dictates to them, God reproaches his people for their faults, in the form of a legal proceeding that he himself initiates. Since the article of the South African exegete, Berend Gemser, which has become classic, scholars have identified and isolated what is called the "model of legal proceedings" (*rib-pattern*) in the prophets. Here are two examples:

> Hear the word of YHWH, children of Israel, for YHWH has begun legal proceedings (*rīv*) with the inhabitants of the country; there is neither sincerity nor love, nor knowledge of God in the country, but perjury and lying, assassination and theft, adultery and violence, murder upon murder (Hosea IV, 1-2).

> YHWH goes to his tribunal (*la-rīv*), he stands to commence a process (*la-dīn*) against his people. YHWH brings to justice (*mišpat*) the aged and the princes of his people. "It is you who devastate the vine and conceal the remains of the poor. With what right do you crush my people and grind the face of the poor? Oracle of the Lord YHWH Sabaoth" (Isaiah III, 13–14).

It is quite remarkable that the chief accusation that leads God to complain is not an offense against God himself, such as the neglect of his cultic precepts, the abuse of ritual, or an injustice committed against his priests, like that which raised the ire of Apollo at the beginning of the *Iliad*, and which has equivalents in the Old Testament. Here, it is solely a matter of faults that concern the human domain. God has no personal interest to protect. In contrast, he feels directly offended by the fact that men kill themselves, steal from one another, lie to each other, and take their wives. Even the "knowledge of God" which is lacking concerns the divine in general (*elohīm*), not the God of Israel, and it only designates the rules of elementary justice, such as Abraham expected that he would not find among the Amalekites (*Genesis* XX, 11).

Micah adds an important detail:

> Hear therefore the word that YHWH speaks: Rise up! Enter into legal proceedings (*rīv*) before the mountains, and let the hills hear your voice! Hear, o mountains, the legal proceeding (*rīv*) of YHWH, lend your ear, foundations of the earth, for YHWH is at trial (*rīv*) with his people, he argues against Israel. My people, what have I done to you? How have I exhausted you? (Micah, VI, 1–5)

The passage begins by invoking witnesses belonging to natural realities, mountains and hills (as other verses call upon heaven and earth as witnesses).[29] It is clear that a pre-scientific vision of the world is here expressed, even a mythological one, since the natural things are endowed with the power of hearing. But the essential thing is that a third party appears between God and the people he accuses. Its presence allows them to leave the sphere of relations of mere force to enter into that of juridical discussion by means of *logos*. The presence of a neutral third party constitutes the foundation of law.[30]

With a God who speaks, one can speak. This God can also—this is unheard of—agree to learn something from his creature, as when he waits to learn what name Adam will give to the animals (*Genesis* II, 19).[31] His waiting, his silence, and his listening are the conditions that make dialogue possible. With this God, one can therefore dispute and negotiate. In a famous scene of *Genesis*, Abraham negotiates with God and makes him lower his price (*Genesis* XVIII, 22–32). The principal argument of Abraham is that a certain behavior would not be worthy of God, that it would contradict his essence. The just God cannot act unjustly (XVIII, 25). In this way, man appeals from

---

29 *Isaiah*, I, 2; *Deuteronomy*, IV, 26; XXX, 19; XXXI, 28; see also XXXII, 1.
30 See Alexandre Kojève, *Esquisse d'une phénoménologie du droit. Exposé provisoire* (Paris: Gallimard, 1981), # 7, p. 24; #14, pp. 73–75.
31 See my *Europe, la voie romaine, op. cit.*, pp. 152–53.

God to the concept of God,[32] in this case from his power to his goodness. This movement is found from one end of the book of Job to the other.

Here, it is already the idea of God's nature that is rationally graspable which makes itself seen. As action expresses the inner nature of the acting subject, according to the scholastic formula, *operari sequitur esse*, it suffices to know how God is made, to be able to divine his actions. A God who acts justly, a God who finds injustice repugnant, for Whom it is even absurd, must have a particularly close relationship with justice, to the point of coinciding with his essence.

The reflective awareness of rationality

It is not only in the form of narratives that rationality is manifest in the biblical writings. One also encounters traces of moments of reflection on the rational dimension of the relationship of God to man.

From the time of the Ancient Alliance, the content of the revelation made to Israel was highlighted by comparison with other possibilities. Thus, *Deuteronomy* invites the comparison by asking: What God has ever made himself so close (*qarōv*) to his people? (IV, 7). This proximity is not without a connection to the proximity (*qarōv*) of the word, which is a presence in the mouth and in the heart (XXX, 14). What is found in the mouth and in the "heart" (as the term was understood in ancient Israel) is what the Stoics formulated much later in terms of the double aspect of *logos*: the spoken word and interior reason.

It is a question that one perhaps can understand as a reflection on the fact that the event of salvation, God coming to seek his people to liberate it from captivity, has the character of a word: "Was there ever a word (*davar*) so august?" (IV, 32).[33] But, since the Hebrew word *davar* can also signify "thing" or "event" as well as "word," the interpretation of the passage remains uncertain.

The Commandments are a wisdom (*hohmah*, *bīnah*) that other nations will be obliged to admire (IV, 6, 8). Now, such a comparison is not possible

---

32   See Robert Spaemann, "Die Frage nach der Bedeutung des Wortes 'Gott,'" in *Einsprüche. Christliche Reden* (Einsiedeln: Johannes, 1977), p. 26.

33   The Targum *ad loc.* translates by *pitgam*, "dict."

unless there is a certain common ground between Israel and the neighboring peoples. This common ground is humanity, pure and simple, as well as *logos*, which makes communication possible, and hence comparison.

This idea is found throughout the Bible, but it becomes explicit from time to time, as in a brief passage of the second part of the book of *Isaiah*. It merits some attention, because it contains several dimensions of what will appear later as reason, and in a combination rich with significance. The text dates from the period that followed the Babylonian exile. Israel's elite, deported to Mesopotamia as hostages and having undergone the influence of the Babylonian cultural milieu, was forced to think anew about the content of the traditional religion in order to resist the challenge of the ambient ideas. The prophet has the God of Israel say:

> For this is the word of the Lord, who created the heavens—He is God!—who formed the earth and made it; He established it solidly; He didn't create it as a chaos (*tohu*), He formed it to be inhabited: "I am the Lord, and there is no other. I have never spoken in secret, in some spot in the land of shadows; I have never said to the children of Israel: 'Seek me in the void (*tohu*).' I, the Lord, I say the truth (*dôbèr tsédèq*), I declare what is right (*maggid meysharim*)."[34]

We have here what one could call the *triangle of rationalities*. Reason is manifest under three aspects: as the well-ordered, intelligible character of the created world, in opposition to the primordial chaos; as the clarity of verbal expression, in opposition to the discordant notes of occult experiences; as the rectitude of conduct, in opposition to perverse ways. God presents himself as speaking Subject and as Creator. But he does not thereby raise the claim of dominion, rather he specifies the way he is going

---

34 *Isaiah*, XLV, 19–20. See my *The Wisdom of the World, op. cit.* Among the commentaries on the passage from Isaiah: Klaus Baltzer, *Deutero-Jesaja* (KAT 10, 2) (Gütersloh: Gütersloher Verlagshaus, 1999), pp. 316–20; Hans-Jürgen Hermisson, *Deuterojesaja, 2. Teilband, Jesaja 45*, 8–49, 13 (BKAT, XI/2) (Neukirchen-Vluyn: Neukirchener-Verlag, 2003), pp. 62–68; Ulrich Berges, *Jesaja 40-48*, Übersetzt und ausgelegt von Ulrich Berges (HthKAT) (Freiburg: Herder, 2008), pp. 427–31.

to speak. In the same way that he solidly established the earth, one can base oneself on his word. In the same way that he created it inhabitable rather than void, his affirmations display order and meaning. They are even vivifying, as an order that makes it possible for an association of men to live together; in short: civilization. God does not speak in secret (see also XLVIII, 16). Revelation took place in a public space, one that was open, not in some lost corner. No doubt the allusion is to the event at Sinai, which would have transpired before the entirety of the assembled People, a theme that Jewish apologetics will take up. Even more important is the rejection of a purely private experience which would be ineffable, whose content would be incapable of being expressed. The revealed content is open to examination. Justice is at one and the same time the content of the commandments and a characteristic of the way that God expresses himself. The order of creation, the clarity of linguistic communication, the justice and appropriateness of what is communicated, all mutually reinforce one another. These three elements form a triangle in which God shows himself to be a friend of reason.

The Bible and the Quran on logos

The notion of the Word of God (*logos*) is quite clear in the New Testament, where the Greek word figures in all the epistles, especially the writings of John. To bring in this second part of the Bible also obliges one to bring to the fore a comparison between Christianity and Islam, which can lead, and has led, to misunderstandings. To prevent these errors, it perhaps would be smarter to place oneself beyond the separation between Judaism and Christianity, and a fortiori, between Christianity and Islam. One therefore could compare the Hebrew Bible with the Quran, and in that way compare the biblical model with the Quranic model of Revelation.[35]

Many elements are common to the two books, including the representation of creation by a single word. It sufficed for God to say, "Be!" for

---

35 One can find precious assistance in the voluminous work, almost an exhaustive dossier, by the author of a translation of the Quran: Danielle Masson, *Monothéisme coranique et monothéisme biblique. Doctrines comparées* (Paris: Desclée de Brouwer, 1976).

something to come to be. The idea is often found in the Quran, where it is a question of creation (XVI, 40; XXXVI, 82 *et al.*), such as, in an interesting way, when it is a matter of explaining the creation (which is not a generation) of Jesus (XIX, 35). While Christian thinkers identify the Word with the second hypostasis of the Blessed Trinity, the Quran considers Jesus as a creature brought into being by a divine word, even though one isolated passage calls Jesus the "word of God" itself (IV, 171). A number of thinkers in Islam have taken the representation of a creative word (*kalimah*) of God as the point of departure for their reflections and have developed it further, not without letting themselves be influenced by ideas that had a Greek origin, such as the Neoplatonic concept of the intellect (*nūs*).

Apart from that, one hardly finds in the Quran any counterpart to the passages from the Old Testament that I cited above. There is the interesting exception of the verses on the proximity of God, which have their equivalents in the Quran in the context of prayer and the way in which God hears it: God is "near" (*qarīb*) to him who invokes him (II, 186; XI, 61 *et al.*).[36] In other cases, though, the biblical and quranic texts are almost opposed. This is obviously true of the New Testament, and above all for the verse I cited above concerning the creation of Jesus, with which we touch upon the most manifest difference between Islam and Christianity. But one could also take an example from the Old Testament, such as the scene I already invoked, where Abraham negotiates with God over the fate of Sodom. The parallel passage in the Quran is very instructive. There, one only finds a brief allusion to the scene, and God abruptly rejects Abraham's intercession: it is in vain, because the decision to destroy the city has already been made (XI, 74).

If the Quran places itself in the train of the Bible in what concerns the imperative and creative nature of the divine word, it departs when it is a question of a dialogic dimension.

Creation in the Word

The biblical *logos* distinguishes itself from the Greek *logos* in that the latter remains within an intra-human sphere. It is human beings who engage in

36 *Ibid.*, pp. 50–51.

discussions of a political nature or, as with those involving Socrates, a philosophical one. To be sure, the gods speak to men, but they express themselves by oracles, which are always obscure and ambiguous, but above all in monologues. When they are represented as fabricating the world, the gods do not do so by an act of speech, even if they can address themselves to those they have created.[37]

In their turn, these attitudes are not possible unless *what is* represents more than what *de facto* is, the "that's just how it is" before which one can only humble oneself, like the young Hegel before the Alps; nor if *what is* only represents what one is able to accept because one has to in keeping with intellectual honesty, of the sort that Nietzsche praised as "our last virtue,"[38] but which one cannot truly love, simply because it's not loveable. Can *what is*, as such, become the object of love? From what point of view can it appear as worthy of being loved?

In connection with this question the biblical doctrine of creation by the Word of God (*davar, logos, verbum*) takes on new relevance, even urgent contemporaneity.

The representation of a creative command has deep roots which go back to the ancient Middle East. W. F. Albright drew attention to what is undoubtedly the oldest attestation, the Sumerian concept of ENEM, in Akkadian, *awatu*.[39] Be that as it may, here I would like to draw attention to a point that concerns content. Since the world was created by *logos*, it is as it were imbued with *logos*. In this way, the object of respect is nothing other than *logos* itself, this *logos* which arrives at its conscious and voluntary expression in man. The respect of man for *what is*, is nothing other than *logos*'s respect for itself. It is the moment of truth that contains all the idealism of an Hegelian sort.

---

37   Plato, *Timaeus*, 41a–d.

38   Hegel, extracts from the Diary of a tour in the Alps around Bern, in E. Moldenhauer and K. M. Michel (ed.), *Werke in zwanzig Banden* (Frankfurt: Suhrkamp, 1971), t. 1, p. 618; Friedrich Nietzsche, *Morgenröte*, V, # 456, *KSA*, t. 3, p. 275; fragment 1 [145], August 1885–Spring 1886, in *ibid.*, t. 12, p. 44. See also my "Possiamo amare la verità?," *Philosophical News*, 2, *La verità*, March 2011, pp. 48–52.

39   William F. Albright, *From the Stone Age to Christianity. Monotheism and the Historical Process* (New York: Doubleday, 1957), p. 195.

To the nature of such a God who creates by *logos* corresponds the attitude one must have towards him. There's nothing surprising therefore that the response of man should be a "sacrifice of the intellect," a phrase that does not mean (despite widespread misinterpretations) that one must sacrifice one's intellect, but on the contrary, that reason is worthy of being the subject of supreme worship, that it alone is fit to do so. The sacrifice offered by the intellect is a "rational worship" (*logikē latreia*) (*Romans* XII, 1).

Those who believe in such a God are not only rationalists, they are without doubt the only ones to be so, or, at the least, they're the only ones who do so in a coherent way. Once again I would like to cite Chesterton's character, Fr. Brown: "I know very well that men accuse the Church of degrading reason, but it is really quite the contrary. Alone on the earth, the Church makes reason something that is truly supreme. Alone on the earth, it affirms that God himself is bound by reason."[40]

Thus, as the Bible presents it, reason has this peculiarity, especially vis-à-vis Greek understandings of reason, that it is rooted in the most high, i.e., in God himself. Reason is not a strange quirk of man, but a fundamental trait of the Creator, and therefore of his creation. The portrait of the divine presented to us by biblical religions is not solely that of a God who commands, but of a God who agrees to discuss with the creature that he sovereignly called into existence. Reason thus constitutes a common ground between the Creator and creatures, and above all that of the creatures who have an active relationship with reason, who can discover it in *what is* and give it a verbal expression. The legitimacy of reason thus finds itself grounded in the most high, anchored in the heavens.

40   G. K. Chesterton, *The Blue Cross, op. cit.*, p. 28.

4
ATHEISM OR SUPERSTITION?

In 1873, Ignaz Goldziher left Budapest for the Middle East. The young man, then twenty-three years old, who was to become the greatest scholar of Islam of all time,[1] encountered a group of Turks in Istanbul when it was quarantined. He quickly was on good terms with all, with the exception of one person, "the most fanatical among them," as he puts it. The latter explained to him that unbelievers, who were lacking the distinctive characteristic of humanity, that is, reason as the faculty that allows one to know God, were not humans, but animals in human form.[2] Here we have a revealing archetypal scene. The Western scholar, who had a friendly, even admiring, attitude towards Islam, had an already prepared category to designate this sort: a "fanatic." For his part, the Turk considered himself to be a pious believer, who merely knew his Quran. He therefore saw in Goldziher, who was quite attached to his Judaism, one of those atheists who, because they lack the true religion, had fallen from the human estate and become "the worst of animals" (Quran VIII, 22).

Unfortunately, this scene has lost none of its contemporary relevance, even with the progress of Modernity. Except that it does not always take place between the same protagonists. Hereditary enemies are wont to change places. A few years ago, the "wicked" was the "atheistic Communist," and we, who were the good guys, formed "the Christian West." Today,

---

1 See my introduction to Ignace Goldziher, *Sur l'islam. Origines de la théologie musulmane* (Paris: Desclée de Brouwer, 2003), choice of texts and introduction: "Ignace Goldziher (1850–1921)," pp. 7–36.

2 Raphael Patai, *Ignaz Goldziher and His Oriental Diary. A Translation and Psychological Portrait* (Detroit: Wayne State University Press, 1987), 23 September 1873, pp. 89 & 92.

for our most decided adversaries we are "Godless," while for us they are "fundamentalists" subject to the greatest superstition. And everyone from whom we so carefully distinguish ourselves are put in the same camp or category, whether they come from Saudi Arabia or from Texas: they all are "fanatics."

Let's seek some critical distance on the contemporary scene by clarifying the basic concepts that we employ with such assurance. This is not the first time that someone has opposed atheism, superstition, and fanaticism, with, perhaps, religion being somewhere between the extremes. On the contrary, the question is very old: which is better, unbelief or superstition?

I will begin by briefly recounting the history of the comparison between superstition and atheism. However, since several concepts overlap, it is appropriate to make a list of the three aspects under which this comparison is drawn. First of all, a psychological question is raised: Is it more pleasant to be superstitious than atheistic? Then there is a theological question: Which of the two attitudes constitutes the greatest blasphemy against the divinity? Finally, the political question: Of the two human types, which forms the more irenic, the more peaceful, citizen?

Superstition as atheism

The first two questions were already posed in classical Antiquity. They therefore are not totally original.

The idea of superstition appeared as a subspecies of atheism, and not as its opposite. Plato distinguishes three sorts of atheists. The first do not believe at all that there are gods; the second freely admit the existence of gods, but do not believe that they concern themselves with human affairs; the third believe in the existence of gods and their providence, but they imagine that the gods allow themselves to be bribed by men and close their eyes to their transgressions, the currency being prayers or sacrifices.[3] The latter are the superstitious.

According to Epicurus, who belonged to the second of the categories that Plato distinguished, one must consider an atheist the one who has the same idea of the gods as the vulgar: the "impious (*asebès*) is not the one

---

3   Plato, *Laws*, X, 888c.

who denies the gods of the crowd, but he who attributes the conjectures of the crowd to the gods."[4] Plato and Epicurus, to be sure, form a strange pair. However, their conceptions of atheism are similar, to the point that Neoplatonists could cite Epicurus's sentence.[5] However, while the superstitious person is for Plato one type of atheist among others, for Epicurus he is the atheist *par excellence*.

This argument remained alive among the Church Fathers. This is the case with Arnobius, who, at the beginning of the fourth century, brought together all sorts of arguments against the pagan gods in order to use them in favor of Christianity. Why, he asked, did the pagans treat as "atheists" those who either deny the existence of the gods or call them into doubt, or even those who, like Euhemerus, make them the divinized benefactors of humanity? They themselves ought to be called atheists, because they attribute to their gods all sorts of misdeeds unworthy of them.[6]

Plutarch: atheism or superstition?

Plutarch (45–120 A. D.) is the first author who considered atheism and superstition, in order to compare them, as two diametrically opposed attitudes. An entire treatise, *On superstition*, is given over to a systematic, if brief, comparison.[7] The little work exerted a great influence on all of Europe, above all thanks to translations of the Greek original that was printed for the first time in 1509 by Aldus Manutius in Venice, in the context of a complete edition of the *Moralia*. In fact, these essays had already been translated in Latin in 1471. The French translation of Jacques Amyot (1572) constitutes a masterpiece of the French language in its own right and achieved great success even outside of France.

The terms that Plutarch uses are themselves quite interesting. The historian hardly speaks of "atheism" in the sense of a theory of the existence, or rather nonexistence, of the divine, but rather as an attitude towards it.

---

4   Epicurus, *Letter to Menoeceus*, # 123.

5   Porphyry, *Letter to Marcella*, # 17, E. des Places (ed.) (Paris: Les Belles Lettres, 1982), p. 116.

6   Arnobius, *Adversus Gentes*, V, 30, 1–2, *PL*, 5, 1145ab.

7   Plutarch, *De superstitione* (*Peri deisidaimonias*), in *Moralia*, 164E–171F.

The Greek word that he uses in this sense is *atheotès*. The word that designates superstition, *deisidaimonia*, does not contain the idea of "faith" at all, itself an idea that very imperfectly conveys the Greek religious attitude, but rather signifies fear before the divine.

According to Plutarch, one must prefer atheism to superstition. But for him, a pious man who was a priest of Apollo at Delphi, atheism cannot be anything but a second best. The best attitude, whose mention closes the little treatise, is an enlightened piety which constitutes the golden mean between the two extremes.[8] The object whose existence the religious man affirms, which the atheist denies, is not so much the gods as "the divine," in the neuter. The atheist is the one who imagines "that there exists nothing that is blessed and incorruptible." Atheism is a decision of reason; superstition, a passion. Atheism is an insensibility to the divine, which imagines that the Good does not exist; superstition is an excess of passion, which suspects the Good of being bad.[9]

Atheism does not attribute anything bad or evil to the gods. In contrast, superstition constitutes a blasphemy. It does more honor to the gods to say that they do not exist than to present them as thieves, vindictive, and adulterous. Plutarch himself would not be offended by someone who would deny his existence. And he would even prefer that men imagined that Plutarch did not exist, than to believe that he devoured his children as soon as they were born, which the poets do in connection with Chronos.[10]

Superstition is essentially a fear, and this is why it has such a paralyzing power over spirits. As a passion, it deprives the soul of everything that prompts it to act. It ends in an extreme fatalism: the sick superstitious person is not going to seek the doctor. God, says Plutarch in a magnificent formulation, ought to be the hope of virtue, not the pretext for sloth. Atheism is not the only form of impiety; superstition too merits being stigmatized as impious. The superstitious man represents the rule of the gods as a tyranny. He secretly wishes that the gods did not exist. He even envies the atheists, who are free from fear. In this way, superstition is a lazy or inconsistent atheism.[11]

---

8   *Ibid.*, 14, 171F.
9   *Ibid.*, 2, 165AB; 165C; 6, 167E.
10   *Ibid.*, 10, 169F–170A.
11   *Ibid.*, 3, 165C; 7, 168C; 8, 169C; 10, 169F; 4, 166D; 11, 170E.

Among the Fathers of the Church, some associated themselves with Plutarch's way of looking at things, such as Hilary, the Bishop of Poitiers in the fourth century, who wrote that a complete ignorance on the subject of God was better than an erroneous faith. With a smile that one can hardly fail to detect, the Scottish historian Gibbon remarked that on this score the bishop would be on the side of Bayle and Plutarch.[12] The idea was long-lasting and recurred numerous times. Thus, shortly after the middle of the nineteenth century, the Goncourt brothers wrote in their journal: "If there is a God, atheism must seem to him less of an injury than religion."[13]

However, not everyone grants atheism the advantage over superstition. One finds defenders of the opposite view. Thus Jean Bodin, in his Latin treatise on the method of historiography (1571). In it he invokes historians like Livy, who reported unbelievable miracles, then Polybius, who mocked this sort of narrative. He then wrote that he would more willingly pardon the former, the superstitious, than hardened skeptics. In fact, superstition is better than impiety, and it is better to have a false religion than none at all.[14]

The majority of authors, however, try like Plutarch to find a happy middle, i.e., piety or religion. Pierre Charron (1541–1603) thus distinguishes between religion and superstition.[15] He does not take quite seriously the third possibility, theoretical atheism. According to him, the criterion of religion is of a moral nature, it is probity, "preud'hommie," which ought to be the consequence of piety.[16] Piety without probity is superstition; probity without piety is atheism.[17]

---

12 Edward Gibbon, *The History of the Decline and Fall of the Roman Empire*, II, chap. XXI, n. 65.

13 Edmond and Jules de Goncourt, *Journal*, 24 January 1868 (Paris: Robert Laffont, 1989), t. 2, p. 129.

14 Jean Bodin, *Methodus*, IV, P. Mesnard (ed.) (Paris: PUF), p. 130a; French trans. p. 301a; Bodin ventures a similar judgment in *Les Six Livres de la République* [1583], IV, 7 (Aalen: Scientia, 1961), p. 655; the discussion is pursued in the posthumous *Colloquium Heptaplomeres de rerum sublimium arcanis abditis*, L. Noack (ed.) (Schwerin: Friedrich Wilhelm Bärensprung, 1857), chap. V, pp. 182-84.

15 Pierre Charron, *De la Sagesse*, II, 5 (Paris: Fayard, 1986), p. 455; (Genève: Slatkine, 1968) p. 134.

16 *Ibid.*, p. 148.

17 *Ibid.*, p. 150.

Francis Bacon and the possibility of an atheistic morality

With the beginning of Modern Times, the question took a turn in the work of Francis Bacon. The second edition of the *Essays* (1612) of the English chancellor begins the essay on superstition with the already cited passage from Plutarch: it is better to believe that a man named Plutarch does not exist, than imagine that he is a criminal. His essay was translated into Latin and thus became accessible to the educated public of Europe. Bacon however began where Plutarch left off.

In the same way that the blasphemy is greater in superstition than in atheism, so too the danger for man is greater. Here, Bacon examines an aspect of the question that the Ancients had neglected or that they only touched upon, i.e., the social and political consequences of religious views. Atheism leaves good sense in men, philosophy, natural piety, the sentiment of honor, everything that can aid man to adopt a correct attitude, at least externally. At the time of Bacon the impious was often presented as a scoundrel, and atheism was equivalent to moral libertinage. According to Schopenhauer this confusion of concepts was the product of priests, and allowed for the birth of the "frightful monster" of fanaticism.[18]

Superstition, on the contrary, removes all inhibitions and "establishes an absolute monarchy in the spirit of people." The metaphor became the source of an authentically political reflection. Atheism has never ruined a State, because it has for consequence that men act prudently, because they limit their views to the present. That's why we observe that the periods when there is a tendency to atheism were also periods of civilization. Bacon cites the example of the time of Augustus. In contrast, superstition entailed the loss of several States. As is often the case, Bacon ends with an image: superstition introduces a new first mobile that moves all the spheres of government.[19] The meaning of the image is not totally clear. Obviously, the context is the ancient and medieval representation of the universe, a world with concentric heavenly spheres. But Bacon does not speak of a new prime

18   Arthur Schopenhauer, *Die Welt als Wille und Vorstellung*, E. Lohneysen (ed.) (Darmstadt, Wissenschaftliche Buchgesellschaft, 1982), t. 1, p. 493, n. 1.
19   Francis Bacon, *Essays, XVII, Of Superstition*.

mover, but rather a first mobile, i.e., a new sphere of fixed stars.[20] Be that as it may, the passage was favorably cited by several free thinkers, including the learned La Mothe Le Vayer.[21]

Already with Bacon, it is clear that an atheist can conduct himself as a honorable man. However, according to other things that Bacon says, all that remains illusory, and the comparison in its entirety must necessarily fail. He also composed an essay on atheism, and placed it just before the one on superstition. This new essay advances the idea that atheism as a theoretical position is not possible. It is only the cloak under which the corrupt seeks to dissemble his hunger for the basest pleasures. The so-called atheist is certainly capable of professing his unbelief with his lips, but he cannot think it coherently.

Bacon does not clarify with an example the way in which superstition causes States to falter. But the background of his thought allows itself to be easily reconstructed: it was the religious rupture of Europe brought on by the Reformation. This in fact was the first time that a religious revolt was supported by the political power of States, a support that led to wars undertaken in the name of religion. It was to have even worse consequences in the Thirty Years War which began in Bacon's lifetime, less than ten years after his essay appeared. Bacon attempts to found civic peace on the mutual tolerance of the confessions. In this way he places himself in a tradition that includes, before him, Erasmus, and many after him, Locke and Leibniz, for example.

The capital point is that the idea of the adversary is no longer the same as it was in Antiquity. The superstitious of Plutarch was the same whom Theophrastus caricatured in his *Characters*, basing himself on the definition of superstition as cravenness toward the divine.[22] For Antiquity, the superstitious man was ridiculous. One could bemoan him, one could mock him, but one could not fear him. Modern Times repeat the story, but this time

---

20   For the context, see *ibid., XV, Of Seditions and Troubles.*

21   La Mothe Le Vayer, *Dialogue d'Horatius Tubero* [1630?], "La Divinité," 6, *Dialogues faits à l'imitation des Anciens* (Paris: Fayard, "Corpus des œuvres de philosophie en langue française," 1988, p. 213, cited in Antoine Adam, *Les Libertins au XVII siècle* (Paris: Buchet-Chastel, 1964), p. 136.

22   Theophrastus, *Characters*, # 16.

what began with comedy ends in tragedy. Superstition became dangerous. In this way we observe the birth of a concept that would provide Enlightenment with its preferred nightmare: "fanaticism."

Pierre Bayle and the possibility of a society of atheists

The seventies and eighties of the seventeenth century are today held to represent a parting of the water in the intellectual history of Europe. With Spinoza's *Theological-Political Treatise* (1670), the Quarrel of the Ancients and Moderns in Paris (1687–88), Newton's *Mathematical Principles of Natural Philosophy* (also in 1688), and Locke's *Letter on Toleration* (1689), begins what has been called "the crisis of European consciousness".[23]

In his *Various thoughts on the comet*, which appeared in this context in 1682, Pierre Bayle treated our theme in such a penetrating way that his argument remained determinative for the entire eighteenth century.[24] On the occasion of the appearance of a comet, he attempts to show that this celestial phenomenon is not a miracle and foretells nothing. He then asks what a miracle of this sort could in principle have demonstrated, and who would have an interest in seeing in it a sign? The appearance of a comet would be more advantageous to superstition than to atheism. In a word: "There has never been a misfortune less to fear than atheism."[25] The devil prefers idolatry to atheism. In fact, atheists do not honor him at all. In contrast, a part of the worship rendered to false gods redounds to the demon. Bayle maintains an opinion which he explicitly characterizes as a paradox: "atheism is not a greater evil than idolatry." And in this context, he cites the principal argument of Plutarch.[26]

According to the Fathers of the Church, he continues, idolatry is the worst of all crimes. Idolaters were the true atheists, because to represent God as a plurality indicates they do not know him at all. The knowledge of God they may have only renders the crimes of idolaters more serious.

23   Paul Hazard, *La Crise de la conscience européenne* (Paris: Boivin, 1935).
24   Pierre Bayle, *Pensées diverses sur la comète*, A. Prat and P. Rétat (ed.) (Paris: Société des textes français modernes, 1994), # 113-132, t. 1, pp. 301–50.
25   *Ibid.*, # 105, t. 1, p. 288.
26   *Ibid.*, # 114, t. 1, p. 303f; # 115, t. 1, p. 307F.

Idolaters are more difficult to convert than atheists. Atheists cannot commit crimes that are more serious than idolaters. The greatest evil-doers of Antiquity were not atheists. A bit later in fact, Bayle invokes some virtuous atheists.[27] The knowledge of God, if one does not take into account grace, is too weak against the passions. In order to establish society, atheists, like idolaters, need a more powerful brake than religion, in other words, human laws.[28]

A bit later in Bayle's work, the paradox takes on even greater sharpness: a society of atheists would be, as far as mores and social actions, entirely similar to a society of idolaters. Such a society would impose "civil and moral actions" as effectively as others, as long as it severely punished crimes and attached honor and shame to certain actions. In fact, among men certain representations of honor exist that are the work of nature alone, that is to say, of general providence.[29]

Thus with Bayle we take another step. To be sure, the question of the political effects of religion and atheism had been posed before him. But atheism only concerned individuals or small circles. In any event, it was a private matter. The Greek historian Polybius (200–120 B. C. E.) had indicated that a society of wise men would not need religion. But since the vulgar remained blind and superstitious, it was necessary to hold them in check by means of the fears that religion inspired.[30]

Bayle therefore assessed the possibility of a society of atheists. His response is surprising: a society of atheists would not only be possible, but it would be even easier to direct than a society of fanatics. In this way, atheism attains the status of a theoretical possibility and a viable attitude. Behind Bayle's reflections lies the new political philosophy of Thomas Hobbes, according to whom it is the fear of death, the greatest evil, that constitutes the most powerful wellspring of human activity.[31] It is only on this basis and not, for example, on the search for the supreme Good, that one can

---

27 *Ibid.*, # 130, t. 1, p. 338-341; # 174, t. 2, pp. 107–14.
28 *Ibid.*, # 131, t. 1, p. 342.
29 *Ibid.*, # 161, t. 2, p. 77; # 172, t. 2, pp. 102–03, 105.
30 Polybius, VI, 56, 10-12, L. Dindorf and T. Büttner-Wobst (ed.) (Leipzig: Teubner, 1889), t. 2, pp. 306–07.
31 See Leo Strauss, *Natural Right and History* (Chicago: The University of Chicago Press, 1953), p. 198.

found society as the mutual guarantee against violence. If there are more frightening objects than death – hell, for example – all the social edifice would be threatened. As a consequence, society must unencumber itself of these chimeras, by promoting "enlightenment" in matter of religion.

We don't know the final core of Bayle's thought, but the importance of his work was recognized by subsequent authors. Edward Gibbon (d. 1794) remarks in his posthumous autobiography that Bayle did nothing more than reprise the old paradox of Plutarch, but that he gave it a force ten times greater by painting it with the colors of his spirit and sharpening it with the rigor of his logic.[32] Vico explicitly names Bayle in the context of the discussion of one of his principles, according to which all peoples believed in a divinity and its providence.[33] According to Bayle, however, there are people lacking in the knowledge of God, and who nonetheless are capable of living according to justice, a position that Vico compares to the much earlier dream of Polybius, a society of philosophers. Finally, in 1845 Karl Marx will see in Bayle the prophet of a new form of society: "[Bayle] announced the atheistic society, which was soon to begin to exist, by demonstrating that a society entirely constituted by atheists could exist, that an atheist could be a honorable man, that man does not degrade himself by atheism, but by superstition and idolatry."[34]

Montesquieu: the utility of religion

The century of Enlightenment took different positions on the paradox proposed by Bayle, according to which atheism was better than superstition.

Certain authors attempted to show that the quarrel was vain. Thus Mendelssohn, in his *Jerusalem* (1783), sought to define and limit the task: atheism and fanaticism are two evils, and neither should be tolerated. Which of the two constitutes the greatest evil is, in the final analysis, rather

---

32 Edward Gibbon, *Autobiography* [1796] (London: Oxford University Press, s.d.,), p. 53.
33 Giambattista Vico, *Princìpi di scienza nuova* [1744], v. I, III, in A. Battistini (ed.), Opere (Milan: Mondadori, 1990), t. 1, p. 543.
34 Karl Marx, *Heilige Familie* [1845], in *Die Frühschriften*, ed. S. Landshut, 7th ed. (Stuttgart: Kröner, 2004), p. 391.

otiose.[35] Others expressed themselves in favor of atheism. First of all, in a discreet way, and between the lines; then more frankly after the 1760s, when one sees a general change of climate in favor of "philosophy," as Voltaire wrote in a letter to Helvetius.[36] D'Holbach and others allowed themselves to plead openly in favor of atheism. Superstition, on the other hand, as one could expect, found no defender.

In his *Spirit of the Laws* (1748), Montesquieu addressed Bayle's paradox in two chapters. In the first, he reprised Plutarch's theological argument. According to him, it is a sophism that evaporates once one also brings into the equation the social utility of religion. That one believes that a man named Plutarch exists is perfectly indifferent to the human race. But, on the other hand, for Montesquieu it is of the highest utility to believe that a God exists, because from the idea that there is no God results the idea of our independence; or, in the case when we aren't capable of grasping that idea, the consequence of atheism is mere revolt. Religion exists to repress. In a way that we today find counter-intuitive, Montesquieu here uses a political term, "repression," that the Romantic Prometheanism of the following century will put back in the saddle, but reversing its meaning. Religion must play the role of a power that constrains, and its abuse is not so great an evil as its complete absence.[37]

In the second chapter, Montesquieu takes up the claim that authentic Christians could not form a State capable of surviving. Montesquieu in contrast affirms that such citizens would know very well their duties, and fulfill them with the greatest zeal, because what they owe to religion they also owe to the fatherland. The principles of Christianity would be stronger than those of the three types of government, to wit: honor, virtue, and fear. Bayle was mistaken, because he failed to distinguish commands that oblige from the evangelical counsels that are optional.[38]

---

35 Moses Mendelssohn, *Jerusalem*, I. M. Albrecht (ed.) (Hamburg: Meiner, 2005), p. 64.

36 Voltaire, to Claude Adrien Helvetius, 26 June [1765], D 12660, in T. Besterman et al. (ed.), *Complete Works, 113, Correspondence and Related Documents*, XXIX (Oxford: Voltaire Foundation, 1973), p. 139.

37 Montesquieu, *De l'esprit des lois* [1748] [V], XXIV, 2, in R. Caillois (dir.), *Oeuvres complètes* (Paris: Gallimard, "Bibliothèque de la Pléiade," 1951), t. 2, p. 715.

38 *Ibid.*, 6, p. 719.

Voltaire: a religion for the people

In 1763, Voltaire published his *Treatise on toleration*. At the beginning of chapter XX, the writer compares superstition and atheism. His point of departure is pessimistic: the human race is so weak and so perverse that it needs a "brake." A belief, whatever it may be, is therefore better than atheism. An atheist who would be calculating, violent, and powerful would be a calamity as devastating as a superstitious person hungry for blood. Everywhere there is a society, religion is needed; laws take care of manifest crimes, religion observes secret ones. Voltaire here makes a distinction: as long as men do not have a healthy conception of the divinity, they need superstition as a surrogate. But once they have arrived at adopting a pure and holy religion, superstition becomes not only useless, but extremely dangerous. Voltaire ends with an image: superstition is to religion what astrology is to astronomy.[39]

Seven years later, Voltaire returned to the same question and treated it in greater detail. In the second edition of the *Philosophical Dictionary*, published in 1770, Voltaire devotes a rather extensive chapter to our question, whose title alone testifies to the fact that it had become classic: "On the comparison so often made between atheism and idolatry." Plutarch's argument, according to which it would be less serious to say that something doesn't exist than to calumniate it by attributing to it all sorts of crimes, is not tenable. The question whether God is more offended when one denies his existence than when one affirms false and unfitting things about him is, at bottom, otiose. Without a revelation, we cannot know how God reacts. And everything that one can say about God's anger, his jealousy, his desire for vengeance, is pure metaphor. The true question, "the interesting object for the entire universe," is to know if it is not better for the good of all men to admit "a God who rewards and revenges," and thus a God who would reward hidden good actions and punish secret crimes, rather than no God at all. Voltaire then sketches an interesting rehabilitation of paganism. He distinguishes between the mythology of the Ancients, which represents the gods as adulterous and thieves, and their "true religion," according to which, for example, Jupiter punishes perjurers with Hades.

---

39   Voltaire, *Traité sur la tolérance*, chap. XX, beginning.

A people of atheists, could it survive? Voltaire distinguishes between "the people" in the proper sense of the term and a community of philosophers, who would be above the people. In all countries, "the populace" has need of the "greatest brake." If Bayle had to govern five or six hundred peasants, he would have preached to them a god who rewards and punishes. In contrast, there would be no need to proclaim a god of this sort to the disciples of Epicurus. They were wealthy, peaceful, they practiced the social virtues, in particular friendship, and they avoided getting mixed up in politics. The witness of "people who are entirely primitive" means nothing. They are situated well before the choice between atheism and theism. To be sure, they live in society. But is it a genuine society, or rather "a band of wolves"?

The idea that superstition is not something that needs to be suppressed without further ado also appears in Kant. In his book on religion, which appeared in 1793, he warned against putting in danger "the faith of the people." It would not be judicious to "efface" it, because, he writes, "an atheism yet more dangerous to the State" could emerge.[40] After the French Revolution and the wars of the Empire, Joseph de Maistre expressed himself in a similar way in his *Saint Petersburg Dialogues*, which appeared posthumously in 1821. One of the characters of the philosophical dialogue, an officer, employs a military image: "Superstition is the advanced bastion of religion. No one has the right to destroy it. Without it, the enemy could approach too close to the true fortification."[41]

Thus, in the majority of its moderate representatives, the century of Enlightenment remained faithful to Plutarch's solution and rejected the two extremes in favor of a "purified religion." As a consequence, they attacked Bayle's arguments in favor of the superiority of atheism.

Rousseau: the advantages of fanaticism

With Rousseau a new point of view emerged, which consists of two original propositions. In the *Social Contract* (1762), the philosopher mentions yet

40   E. Kant, *Die Religion innerhalb der Grenzen der bloš en Vernunft*, III, 6, in W. Weischedel (ed.), *Werke* (Darmstadt: Wissenschaftliche Buchgesellschaft, 1960), t. 4, p. 772.

41   Joseph de Maistre, *Les Soirées de Saint-Pétersbourg*, 7th conversation (Paris: Garnier, s.d.), p. 264f.

again Bayle's paradox and distinguishes between two sorts of religion. Concrete Christianity has ruinous consequences for the constitution of the State; but the possibility remains open for a religion that could not have any negative consequences, the "civil religion" whose main features he presents, among which one finds the interdiction of all claims of exclusive truth.[42]

In a second text, Rousseau posed a new question. Until then, atheism was opposed to superstition, which was also called idolatry. The contrast was made in favor of atheism, or in favor of religion as the golden mean between the two. In certain cases, however, one could also be better disposed in favor of superstition. The one who wanted to defend superstition must show that a religion, even one that is rudimentary and semi-magical, could be advantageous for social life. Superstition is a harmless naiveté, and presents no danger. The danger is violence, "fanaticism." No one would have the audacity to defend this scarecrow. The opponents of Enlightenment were accused by its propagandists of being "fanatics," but they themselves considered themselves to be pious, to be sincere believers. In neither case could "fanaticism" serve as one's self-designation. For example, when the Catalan priest Jaime Balmes (d. 1848) attempted to demonstrate the superiority of Catholicism to Protestantism, he made the latter simultaneously responsible for "fanaticism" and its reverse, "indifferentism."[43]

With Rousseau, new arguments in favor of fanaticism come into play, at the same time that the possibility of an atheistic society is radically called into question. In his famous "Profession of Faith of the Savoyard Curate," published in 1762 as a part of his pedagogical treatise, *Emile or On Education*, Rousseau summarizes his teaching on religion. Toward the end of this profession of faith, he adds a long note in which he directly confronts our problem. But with this capital difference, that he opposes, not atheism to superstition or idolatry, but atheism to fanaticism. The philosopher begins by a critique of fanaticism that barely goes beyond the commonplaces of the Enlightenment. Then he continues: Bayle demonstrated irrefutably

---

42 Jean-Jacques Rousseau, *Du contract social*, IV, 8, in B. Gagnebin and M. Raymond (ed.), *Oeuvres complètes* (Paris: Gallimard, "Bibliothèque de la Pléiade," 1964), t. 3, p. 464.

43 Jaime Balmes, *El protestantismo comparado con el catolicismo*, chap. VII–IX, in P. Casanovas (ed.), Obras completes (Madrid: *BAC*, 1967), t. 4, pp. 67–92.

that fanaticism is more pernicious than atheism. But he neglected another truth. Fanaticism, as bloody and cruel as it might be, is "a great and strong passion" which elevates the heart of man, which makes him despise death, which gives him an astonishing source of motivation. Better guided, one would derive from it the most sublime virtues.

This idea of Rousseau's, however, and the laudative sense of "fanaticism," did not, to my knowledge at least, gain many followers. I only know two examples: Auguste Comte, who in a letter speaks of "the current need of a worthy fanaticism," because "dedication must replace devotion," and André Breton.[44]

The new element here is that fanaticism appears as something that gives life. It constitutes an active passion. This distinguishes it from superstition. For Plutarch, as we have seen, superstition was essentially a fear, and that is why it exercises a paralyzing action over spirits. Fanaticism, for its part, neutralizes the fear of death. And with it, the greatest of fears, every other fear finds itself overcome. Rousseau commences from an idea that was already quite old at the time, that of a creative enthusiasm. However, he also inaugurates a theme to which subsequent thinkers will devote considerable attention: it is only in the light of some belief, even an illusory one, that one can create.

In contrast to this, it is important to recognize that "irreligion, and in general the calculating and philosophic spirit, attaches itself to [mere] life, renders souls effeminate and vile, concentrates all the passions in the baseness of self-interest, in the abjection of the human person, and thus saps the true foundations of all society, because what particular interests have in common is such a small thing that it will never match what opposes them." The phrase Rousseau uses to describe the negative consequences is "render effeminate." In this way he returns, perhaps quite consciously, to the objection Machiavelli had raised against Christianity, which would have "rendered the world effeminate and disarmed Heaven."[45] Next, Rousseau pens a decisive paragraph:

44 Auguste Comte, Letter DCLV to A. Leblais, 15 of Moses 63 [1851], in P. E. de Berrêdo (ed.), *Correspondance générale et confessions* (Paris: EHESS/Vrin), t. 6, p. 11; André Breton, "Trois interventions à *Contre-Attaque*," III, 8 December 1935, in M. Bonner *et al.* (ed.), *Oeuvres complètes* (Paris: Gallimard, "Bibliothèque de la Pléiade," t. 2, 1992) p. 609.
45 Machiavelli, *Discorsi sopra la prima deca di Tito Livio*, II, 2, in F. Flora and C. Cordie (ed.), *Opere* (Milan: Mondadori, 1949), t. 1, p. 238.

If atheism does not cause the shedding of human blood, it is less because of love for peace than by indifference for the good: [...] *Its principles do not cause men to be killed, but they prevent them from being born*, by destroying the mores that multiply them, by detaching them from their species, by reducing all their affections to a secret egoism as disastrous to population as to virtue. Philosophical indifference resembles the tranquility of the State under despotism; it is the tranquility of death, even more destructive than war itself.

Rousseau alludes to a theme that began to attract attention for the first time: contraception. Contraceptive practices had begun to spread among the lower classes of the French population around 1750, such that France would have begun its demographic revolution a century earlier than the rest of Europe. Rousseau concludes: "Thus, fanaticism, although more injurious in its immediate effects than what is called today 'the philosophic spirit,' is much less so in its consequences."[46] Fanaticism kills, but it causes one to live. Perhaps in this way it is closer to the way that life itself, understood in the most banal biological sense, proceeds vis-à-vis its creatures, whom it makes compete with one another, even eat each other.

Our situation today

How does the problem pose itself today? In Europe, the great Churches lose their influence, but does that touch upon "religion" as a whole? One can doubt this. To be sure, a European or North American intellectual can travel across the world and remain within walls impermeable to religious phenomena, and therefore not see the vitality of new movements or non-Christian religions. As for superstition, no one acknowledges professing it. But the practices that we enlightened ones stigmatize as superstitions have not thereby disappeared. To the contrary, they persist, even grow.

---

46   J-J. Rousseau, "La profession de foi du vicaire savoyard," in *Émile*, IV, in B. Gagnebin and M. Raymond (ed.), *Oeuvres complètes* (Paris: Gallimard, "Bibliothèque de la Pléide") t. 4, pp. 632–33. (My italics.)

Atheism is no longer regarded with suspicion, it has become entirely respectable. What previously was an insult is today accepted as a "profession of faith" that is entirely unobjectionable. Moreover, atheism has succeeded in demonstrating in practice that not only can there be perfectly honorable atheists, but also that a State can be neutral in matters of religion. The French Revolution showed that secularized societies are possible, or at least, real. Throughout the West, atheism has even lost its polemical connotation, as the success of the more modest term, "agnosticism," created by the biologist Thomas Huxley, the famous "bull-dog of Darwin," during a memorable session of the *Metaphysical Society* testifies.[47]

Can religions with chastened claims conclude peace with an atheism that itself has put some water in its wine? Would my question, therefore, have been totally superseded, perhaps even less relevant than I thought? Let's cast a glance over the arguments that I have examined and ask, what is their contemporary relevance?

The fanaticism with which we have to do today rests squarely on the foundation that Hobbes wanted to eliminate.[48] Our democracies implicitly suppose that it is enough to threaten our enemies with death. But the authors of suicide attacks do not fear death, and disdain those among them for whom death remains "the last enemy." Against men who are thoroughly convinced of the existence of a paradise and of hell, our democracies are disarmed.

Voltaire feared "the calculating atheist."[49] Now, this has become an historical figure, one even capable of making history: to wit, the ideologue, with Lenin being the best example. Entire countries have been subject to an atheism that claimed to be "scientifically founded" and was imposed by the power of the State. These regimes left far behind the records of religious fanaticism, even if one accepts the count of victims of the Inquisition or Crusades as they were inflated by the historiography of the Enlightenment. When one compares the Inquisitors to those who organized the Shoah, the Gulag, or the genocide of Cambodia, the first appear to be

---

47 *Life and Letters of Thomas Henry Huxley, by his son Leonard Huxley* (London: Macmillan, 1900), t. 1, p. 344.
48 See above, p. ??
49 See the passage from the *Traité sur la tolérance*, cited above, p. 77.

incompetent amateurs, if not choir boys. One therefore needs to revise Rousseau's judgment about the little that one has to fear from atheism.

The question of the social utility of religion has seen a paradoxical reception. On one hand, the social function of religion is generally accepted as a sociological fact. The dream of an atheistic society seems to only preoccupy a few reactionary spirits, more strident the more they feel threatened. On the other hand, the affirmation of such a utility, when employed as an argument, only gives rise to distrust, if not disgust. Since Spinoza and his medieval sources, the distinction between true and false opinions has become commonplace, even banal, and with it the cautionary thought that what is useful is not necessarily true.[50]

In the passage I already cited from the end of the "Profession of faith of the Savoyard Curate," Rousseau distinguishes between the short and the long term. In the short term, fanaticism is certainly dangerous; in the long term, on the contrary, atheism has consequences even more negative.

Here again is an idea of Rousseau that has hardly been accepted. It is only in a rare instance that someone has a clear awareness of the logical consequences of atheism. One of the rare examples is Félix Le Dantec, a French biologist and popular philosopher of the end of the nineteenth century, a bit forgotten today. In a book which appeared in 1907, and which carried the simple title of *Atheism*, Le Dantec explains that life can hold no interest for "the logical atheist"; here would be true wisdom. But that is to go too far. As for what concerns him, Le Dantec is glad that he possesses, alongside the coherent atheism that he professes, a moral conscience which is the result of an enormous quantity of "ancestral errors," and which dictates his conduct in the cases when reason would leave him adrift. In a society of thoroughgoing atheists, he writes, "anesthetic suicide" would be widespread; and because of this, society would probably disappear.[51] More dangerous than suicide attacks would be painless suicides, without attacks.

In the Baconian text I cited above, an ambiguous sentence is found.[52]

50   Baruch Spinoza, *Tractatus theologico-politicus*, chap. XIV, J. van Vloten and J. P. N. Land (ed.) (La Haye: Nijhoff, 1900), t. 2, pp. 109–11; Maimonides, *Guide for the Perplexed*, III, 28.
51   Félix Le Dantec, *L'Athéisme* (Paris: Flammarion, 1907), pp. 101 & 106.
52   See above, p. 71.

As I understand it, atheists would be men who see no further than this life, and who thus are intelligent; they are short-sighted and, paradoxically, precisely because of this, they are prudent. Tocqueville took up this idea, but not without giving it a new meaning, by changing the sign from positive to negative. According to him, the inability to take into consideration the long term is one of the characteristics of democratic man, insofar as he takes his distance from religion. Religion would be a salutary remedy against such an incapacity.[53]

The danger of atheism, if we are to believe Rousseau, can never become actual. But our most actual problem is perhaps precisely that we are only sensible to contemporary questions, to the here-and-now. In this way, Rousseau's question remains open: what are the long-term consequences of atheism? Where does the "indifference to the good" finally lead? Supposing that atheism did show itself beneficial for society, i.e., for the ensemble of men who are living at this moment, has it therefore proved that it can promote life and, before that, produce it?

53 Alexis de Tocqueville, *De la démocratie en Amérique*, II, II, 17, *op. cit.*, p. 663.

5

IS SECULARIZATION MODERN?

The connection between Modernity and a secularization that leads to private as well as collective atheism most often seems to go without saying. One can almost define one by the other. Here, however, as a sort of medievalist, I propose to cast the light of medieval facts and concepts on that proposition. I thereby want to show that to simply associate secularization and Modernity is not entirely legitimate.

My initial theses are the following: 1) the *word* secularization is truly modern; 2) it was with Modernity that the reality that it designates deployed its concrete consequences. Here I only recall facts that are widely known. In contrast, I also wish to maintain that 3) the conditions of possibility for secularization were put in place and brought together during the medieval period. In an image: the modern earthquake that we know had its epicenter in the Middle Ages.

The word and the facts

I will begin by quickly rehearsing the first two points, taking stock of an inventory of things already acquired, although I will make a few comments on the margins.

A remark on the current sense of the word "secular"

The history of the words "secular," "secularism," "secularization," etc. has already been recounted several times, and the bibliography is quite extensive.[1] I therefore will put them in a note, because I only want to add a

---

1   Hermann Lübbe, *Säkularisierung. Geschichte eines ideenpolitischen Begriffs* (Fribourg: Alber, 1965); Hans Blumenberg, *Die Legitimität der Neuzeit* (Frankfurt: Suhrkamp, 1966); Giacomo Marramao, *Cielo e terra. Genealogia della secolariz-*

detail. The use of the word "secular" in opposition to "religious," and taken in the sense of what is called today "secularism," is relatively recent. While reading John Stuart Mill's *On Liberty* (1859) recently, I was surprised to note that, for the philosopher, this use of the term was still a neologism. Mill explained that it would be an error to try to seek in Christian teaching a complete rule by which to guide oneself, a rule that its author had the intention of imposing and sanctioning, but only partially provided. It would be dangerous, he continued, to form one's spirit on an exclusively religious model, while neglecting "secular rules, as one can style them, for lack of a better term."[2] Mill avoids opposing to "religious" something like "irreligion," or to "Christian" something like "non-Christian." He therefore chose a word that already belonged to the Christian vocabulary, which doesn't have meaning except within it, where it designates the lay state of life, and in that sense opposes the "regular" state of the monks. At this fateful date of 1859, which saw the publication of the *On the Origin of Species*, Queen Victoria was on the throne. The intellectual elites of England were in the process of wandering from Christianity. But it still was not respectable to declare oneself an atheist. The precaution in Mill's language is of the same order as what we saw earlier with Thomas Huxley, who ten years later, in 1869, used "agnosticism."

Since then, the term "secular" has become one of those words that expresses the (approving) self-consciousness of enlightened Modernity, satisfied with having left behind everything that it designates in various ways, including "the Middle Ages," in terms sufficient to delegitimize everything that pertains to them. However, as we just saw, the term has a Christian origin and, more exactly, is rooted in canon law, where it designates the one who, while in the bosom of the Church, lives in the "world" (*saeculum, siècle*), unlike the one who is subject to a monastic rule. This semantic evolution has parallels. Thus, the adjective "lay," which has taken on the meaning of "outside the church," originally meant a specific status within the Church,

---

zazione (Rome: Laterza, 1994); Jean-Claude Monod, *La Querelle de la sécularisation. Théologie politique et philosophies de l'histoire de Hegel à Blumenberg* (Paris: Vrin, 2002).

2   John S. Mill, *On Liberty*, 2, in *Utilitarianism, Liberty and Representative Government*, ed. A. D. Linsay (London: Dent, 1968), p. 110.

that of a baptized person who did not have a clerical function. The consideration of linguistic facts of this sort leads to the question of their content. One can ask if the valorization of the people, even its quasi-divinization (*vox populi, vox Dei*), is tenable in the long run if the biblical foundation of the dignity of each human being, and Bergson's thesis concerning the evangelical origin of democracy (a thesis to which I will return), are not, quite simply, true.[3]

In any case, and as a conclusion to this first part, I maintain the following: the process of secularization was first of all semantic; *the words by which secularization is designated are themselves secularized words.*

A skeleton in the European closet

The word "secularization" was, historically speaking, first employed in Europe to designate a very concrete phenomenon, one that pertains directly to Modernity: the confiscation of the goods of the Church effected by temporal sovereigns.

These facts are often quickly passed by in order to focus on the metaphorical use made of them. However, it seems to me illuminating to pause a moment on the events designated by the first meaning of the term, and their intellectual consequences. This, moreover, is what Hans Blumenberg does, albeit rapidly, following Hermann Lübbe, in order to highlight the pejorative cast of "illegitimacy" that affected the term "secularization" from its origin, when a term of religious origin was taken and deployed as a metaphor in a profane context.[4]

As for the original *facts*, one finds the first examples in Germany at the time of the Lutheran Reformation, or the England of Henry VIII, when the goods of dissolved religious orders fell into the hands, here of Germany princes, there, those of the king of England. After a few sporadic cases, for example, the Austria of Joseph II, the apogee of the movement was found in the French Revolution. The goods of the Catholic church were "placed at the

---

3   Henri Bergson, *Les Deux Sources de la morale et de la religion* (Paris: Alcan, 1932), chap. IV, p. 300.
4   Hans Blumenberg, *Die Legitimität der Neuzeit* (Frankfurt: Suhrkamp, 1988), pp. 27–28.

disposition of the Nation" on the second of November, 1789, and their administration taken away from the clergy on the seventeenth of March, 1790. Along with the goods of the emigrés, they became "national goods," whose sale allowed for the issuing of banknotes which were to fund the public debt.

It was later, however, that the *word* acquired European-wide notoriety, in the Germany of the beginning of the nineteenth century, with the secularizations of 1803, now given that name.[5] The operation was of such a perfect Machiavellianism that it perfectly illustrated a maxim of the Florentine secretary, to wit: a prince ought not to make gifts except with what belongs to others.[6] After the treaty of Lunéville between France and Austria, signed in 1801, German princes found themselves deprived of their possessions on the left bank of the Rhine and had to be recompensed. The idea of doing so by secularizations was already in the secret agreement of August 5, 1796, between France and Prussia.[7] The predatory State therefore generously authorized its victims to pay themselves with the possessions of those weaker than they. The princes were authorized to appropriate the goods of the Church that were found in their territories.

It perhaps was to be expected that the Church would lose its temporal power, but no one could defend the legitimacy of this sort of operation with *juridical* arguments. The opponents of the secularizations did not fail to underscore this. This is what Edmund Burke had done in the grand rhetorical style that was his, at the very dawn of the French Revolution.[8] It is a matter of theft, pure and simple, because the rights of the owners were uncontestable and reinforced by millennial custom; they were despoiled without any indemnity; in acting this way, one risked putting in doubt the right of property of everyone.[9] The fact that the one that had made itself guilty of

---

5   All the original documents are reproduced in the excellent little anthology of Rudolfine Freiin von Oer (dir.), *Die Säkularisation 1803. Vorbereitung – Diskussion – Durchführung* [abbreviated as *S1803*] (Göttingen: Vandenhoeck & Ruprecht, 1970).

6   Machiavelli, *Il principe*, chap. XVI, in F. Flora and C. Cordie (dir.), *Tutte le opere* (Milan: Mondadori, 1949), t. 1, p. 51.

7   Text in *S1803*, n. 3, p. 14.

8   Edmund Burke, *Reflections on the Revolution in France, op. cit.*, pp. 205–06.

9   Brief of Pius VII to the emperor Francois II, 27th of June, 1801, *S1803*, n. 9, p. 22; I. H. von Wessenberg, *Die Folgen der Säkularisationen*, *S1803*, n. 10, pp. 24–30.

such a denial of justice was the State, which ought to have been the guarantor and guardian of rights, and, according to Locke, above all of property, increased the scandal. The secularizations therefore had to be defended by vague arguments without any real legal justification. One had to seek refuge in a nebulous heaven of ideas and invoke the "historical necessity" of "the construction of the modern State," "Progress," "Enlightenment," and even "the interest of the Church"—properly understood, of course. Hence, what has been called an ambivalent, even a schizophrenic, attitude toward these facts.[10]

Things did not get any better with the French law of July 3, 1905, since it not only unilaterally abandoned an international treaty, the Concordat of 1801 between Bonaparte and the Papacy, but it also abrogated the arrangements destined to compensate for the losses the Church had suffered during the Revolution. "Not content with seizing centuries-old pious gifts and legacies made by the faithful, the State now confiscated everything the Church had legally acquired since the Concordat."[11]

If one invokes depth psychology, it cannot be ruled out that these denials of justice have remained on the European conscience. Or rather, its subconscious, since their camouflage seems to have had undeniable success. Nor is it to be excluded that the necessity of cobbling together a justification for the unjustifiable is one of the sources from which popular philosophies of history draw their credibility and continue to feed a certain progressive sensibility. It is a long-noted psychological fact that it costs us much more to forgive the evil we ourselves have done, than that which was done to us. And among the ways that allow us to free ourselves from the guilt that we feel toward our victims, the easiest is to continue to accuse them, in keeping with one of the processes of collective scapegoating that René Girard has brought to our attention. The hatred of many of our contemporaries for the Church is perhaps not only the consequence of the injustices, real or purported, committed by her or in her name, but also those committed against her.

10   R. von Oer, in the introduction to *S1803*, p. 8.
11   Michael Burleigh, *Earthly Powers. The Clash of Religion and Politics in Europe from the French Revolution to the Great War* (London: HarperCollins, 2005), p. 362.

In other words, it could be the case that the intellectual movement of "secularization," in the sense of the promotion of a culture that is more and more "secular," is a long-term consequence of very concrete facts that originally bore this name. The trajectory taken by the word we are discussing, and its semantic extension from an event in the revolutionary period to a tendency pertaining to contemporary culture, would therefore be anything but fortuitous, but, on the contrary, the necessary unfolding of an historical logic.

Three steps toward the "world"

Now, in order to consider secularization as an idea, which is the central theme of this exposition, I will take a brief remark by Heidegger as my guiding thread. For him, the idea of secularization is incapable of explaining anything, because it presupposes what must be demonstrated. Indeed, the idea postulates a sort of translation from one domain to another. The arrival-domain must therefore already exist. There must be a *saeculum*, a "world," to which one transfers what belonged to another domain.[12]

Here I would like to reconstruct a few of the steps taken in the direction of the "world," three stages which link together in a chronological order. First of all, primitive Christianity, then the Constantinian turn, then the medieval conflict between the clergy and the Empire.

From the Greek kosmos to the Christian saeculum

The "saeculum" is, first of all, one of those names for what one can also call the "world." The establishment of the world as "saeculum" is an event that revolutionized cosmology, and this revolution derives from a history that I recounted elsewhere, inspired on this point by Karl Löwith.[13] The "saeculum" is what remains of the pagan "world" after the Christian revolution,

---

12 Martin Heidegger, *Nietzsche, op. cit.*, t. 2, pp. 146 & 321; these passages are studied in Jean-Claude Monod, *La Querelle de la sécularisation, op. cit.*, pp. 9–15.

13 See Karl Löwith, "Mensch und Menschenwelt" [1960], *Mensch und Menschenwelt. Beiträge zur Anthropologie*, In K. Stichweh (dir.), *Sämtliche Schriften* (Stuttgart: Metzler, 1981), t. 1, pp. 295–328, and see my *The Wisdom of the World, op. cit.*

itself begun in Judaism. The Greco-Roman world believed it lived in an eternal *kosmos* of endless cycles; Christianity, the heir of the ambient apocalypticism, saw itself as situated in an essentially provisional "saeculum," destined to pass, according to St. Paul's phrase concerning the "figure of this world" (I *Corinthians* VII, 30).

The word *saeculum* is interesting in this regard, that it designates the world—which one could think refers above all to the spatial, with a word that customarily designates time, since in Latin it originally signified "generation." Among Christian authors it translated the Greek *aiôn*, although not without suffering, by way of the Septuagint translation, the contamination of the Hebrew term *'ôlâm*.[14]

There is a profound anthropological truth in this connection between the succession of generations and "the world" as designating a span of one hundred years. A hundred years represents approximately the maximum of a man's living memory, the farthest radiance of the halo of memories that we carry with us. The oldest stories that I heard from my grandparents and that I will retain all my life, or, conversely, the images that my grandchildren will retain of me, added to the average age of an individual's life, together make a hundred years.[15]

One therefore can suggest, in a wordplay that is perhaps quite profound, a connection between a "secular" (*séculier*), someone who lives in the world, and "age-old" (*séculaire*), what lives for a century or several. These are notions that we French speakers take great care to distinguish, but which other languages express by the same word, as the English do with the word *secular*, the Italians with *secolare*, and the Spanish with *secular*. "Secularism" therefore would be understood by way of analogy with "millenarianism." The latter is understood as working for a thousand years; "secularism" in contrast acts as if nothing existed beyond the horizon of a hundred years. An honest examination of our "secularized" societies and their chances of having a future could give some plausibility to this unexpected symmetry: will their own principles, followed with consistency, allow them to live longer than a century?

14 See C. S. Lewis, *Studies in Words* (Cambridge: Cambridge University Press, 1967), pp. 225–26.
15 See Chapter 11 below.

The "rule" against the "world"

As for concrete history, Christianity has this peculiarity, that it was super-added to a preexisting political instance, the Roman Empire.[16] This is what distinguishes it, for example, from Islam, which established its own empire at the time of the Arab conquests of the seventh century. The Roman Empire had nothing "secular" about it. On the contrary it was based on the religious, i.e., the cult of the emperor. But neither he nor it were Christian, since they persecuted the followers of the new faith, precisely because they refused to observe the worship that was intended to concretize the obedience of subjects. As is well known, Christianity ended by absorbing the Roman world. But, and especially in the Latin portion of the Empire, it had this particularity that, if I can put it this way, it spewed it out after having chewed on it. What we call the Middle Ages is the history of this separation.

This began early enough, from the Emperor Constantine who, after having ended the persecution of Christians in 313, attempted to assure himself of control of the Church—whose head he would have willingly assumed—in exchange for the support given to it by the Roman state. Before him, there was hardly any risk of confusion between the Church and State, because the latter persecuted the former. After Constantine, the temptation became strong, and many succumbed to it. The Church reacted by creating around herself a sort of invisible membrane, made of rules of law that made her, in principle, an autonomous entity. Nothing would have been possible, however, without the existence of a social force around which resistance crystalized. This was the monastic movement, which developed at the time among a small elite, as an attempt, perhaps self-consciously, to reconstitute, once the Empire had converted, the precarious mode of life of the martyrs. The network of European monasteries thus furnished the shock troops of the papacy in its struggle against the "secular" power of the emperors of the Holy Roman Empire, then against the kings of France and England.

In other words, what was born with monasticism was a mode of life that defined itself against what was until then normal and unique, what was called "secular." This new and paradoxical mode of life conformed to a

---

16 See my *La Loi de Dieu. Histoire philosophique d'une alliance* (Paris: Gallimard, 2005), pp. 158–60.

"rule" (*regula*) which did not come from this "world." As a consequence, it later took the name of "regular." Behind this etymological history, it is important to see the historical stakes that were involved. The birth of the monastic way of life, which came to be formulated by the three vows of poverty, chastity, and obedience, had indirect consequences on familial, social, and political life. To establish a family, to seek material prosperity, to seek power, all these behaviors ceased to "go without saying" and now appeared as the result of deliberate choices. The object of this choice was "the world." By that, the monastic rule introduced something of a "secularization" for everything that was not regulated by it.

The secularizing Church and the sacral State

After the initial persecution and the Constantinian turn, a third moment occurred in the eleventh century.[17] The reform promoted by Pope Gregory VII, who claimed the monopoly on the nomination of bishops, unleashed the Investiture Controversy opposing popes and emperors. This reform has been understood as a revolution, a "papal revolution," which would have been the first in an uninterrupted series of revolutions that mark European history. The idea is due to Eugen Rosenstock-Huessy.[18] He is now known for having engaged in a correspondence with the philosopher Franz Rosenzweig, but his work possesses intrinsic merit. Following in his steps, his disciple the American legal scholar Harold J. Berman described the way in which the initially juridical revolution spread to all the domains of the medieval world, modifying them profoundly.[19]

This conflict took place with roles reversed. It was not at all the case that the Empire defended secularity, and the Church sacrality, as one would expect. The exact opposite happened. In response to the claims of the papacy, the Empire claimed a certain sacrality, and took the name "holy" and added it to the adjectives "Roman" and "Germanic," thus adopting one of the traditional notes

---

17 *Ibid.*, pp. 166–67.

18 Eugen Rosenstock-Huessy, *Die europäischen Revolutionen und der Charakter der Nationen* [1931] (Moers: Brendow, 1987).

19 Harold J. Berman, *Law and Revolution. The Formation of the Western Legal Tradition* (Cambridge, MA: Harvard University Press, 1983).

of the Church itself. In the *Credo*, "holy" figures among the notes or defining traits of the Church, which is "one, holy, catholic, and apostolic." Quite remarkably, the first to raise the claim of being the sovereign of the "Holy" Empire, Frederick Barbarossa (d. 1190), placed himself on legal grounds. He argued that the Roman Empire is "holy" because a pagan, the Roman jurist Ulpian, in the second century had called the *law* of the State a holy law.[20]

Before speaking of the relations between the papacy and the Empire as a conflict implicating Church and State, it is important to recognize that the existence of these last two institutions is not self-evident, either in general or in the medieval period. And we must not seek the State where we are tempted to seek it. In fact, the Church of the Gregorian reform is the first institution in history that understood itself as, and wanted to be, a State, an administration governing itself according to its own rules: "In the modern sense, the true medieval State, if these words do not constitute a paradox, is the Church."[21] "If one can use the concept of State in the Middle Ages," writes Walter Ullmann, "it can only apply to the pope himself. He alone was superior, he alone, in modern vocabulary, was sovereign, because he held himself above the society of the faithful, his subjects, and he was not a member of the Church."[22] The idea of sovereignty came about to think the power of the pope, before provoking, as a response, its extension to that of kings.[23]

There are even more surprises. The secularizing instance in the Middle Ages was nothing other than the Church, since it was the Church which

20 See Ernst Kantorowicz, *The King's Two Bodies. A Study in Medieval Political Theology* (Princeton: Princeton University Press, 1957), pp. 197, 207; Gaines Post, *Studies in Medieval Legal Thought. Public Law and the State, 1100–1322* (Princeton: Princeton University Press, 1964), p. 535.

21 John N. Figgis, *Political Thought from Gerson to Grotius: 1414–1625. Seven Studies* (New York: Harper & Bros., 1907), p. 19; see Harold J. Berman, *Law and Revolution, op. cit.*, p. 276; Paolo Prodi, *Una storia della giustizia. Dal pluralismo dei fori al moderno dualismo tra coscienza e diritto* (Bologne: Il Mulino, 2000), pp. 111–12. The idea is already found in Nietzsche, fragment 7 [242], Spring-Summer 1883, *KSA*, t. 10, p. 318, cited in Didier Franck, *Nietzsche et l'ombre de Dieu* (Paris: PUF, 1998),p. 240.

22 Walter Ullmann, *Principles of Government and Politics in the Middle Ages* (London/Methuen/New York: Barnes & Noble, 1974), p. 87.

23 See what is implied in the parallel suggested by Jean Bodin, *De la République*, I, 8, p. 132.

forced the State to constitute itself as an autonomous institution, parallel to it. It assigned the State its sole task, which is the good functioning of the temporal city, summed up in the word "Justice." Listen to Jeannine Quillet, who is a specialist in the history of medieval political philosophy: "As paradoxical as it may sound, one can say [...] that it was the action of the popes that in the eleventh century tended to 'laicize' political power, by withdrawing from it every initiative in spiritual matters."[24] And to cite this time Pierre Legendre: "The institutional concept of secularized society is an effect of Christianity in its rivalry with the Empire."[25]

In another text than the one I alluded to above, but which addresses the same problem, Heidegger invokes as the sole cause of the "dediviniza-tion" of the world a retreat of the sacred or the gods.[26] In this way, there would be "secularization," if one persists in using the term, only because the sacred would have already begun to withdraw, a retreat that the sacred itself would have initiated. I have nothing particular to say about this thesis, at least in the sense that Heidegger gives it, because one would have to have a fairly adequate understanding of the idea of the sacred that Heidegger assumes, an understanding I am not sure I possess. As for the concrete unfolding of historical events, however, the example of the way in which the Church under the leadership of monks and the papacy separated itself from the lay mode of life and the temporal power of princes shows that a thesis of this sort possesses a certain plausibility.

Secularism

I have already one or two times employed the term "secularism," a word and an idea that I now need to look at more closely.

---

24 Jeannine Quillet, *Les Clefs du pouvoir au Moyen Âge* (Paris: Flammarion, 1972), p. 44.
25 Pierre Legendre, *Le Désir politique de Dieu. Études sur les montages de l'État et du droit* (Paris: Fayard, 1988), p. 262 (and see p. 257); see also Ernst Kantoro-wicz, *The King's Two Bodies, op. cit.*, pp. 320–21; Harold J. Berman, *Law and Revolution, op. cit.*, p. 115; and Marcel Gauchet, *Le Désenchantement du monde, op. cit.*, p. 118.
26 Martin Heidegger, "Die Zeit des Weltbildes," in *Holzwege* (Frankfurt: Klos-termann, 1950), p. 70, and see above, p. 90.

The word

The Latin word *saeculum* has shown itself to be particularly fecund, and it gave birth to other words as well, three of which I need to briefly define. "Secularity" is a purely descriptive notion, which names a situation in which man, whether an individual or a society, renounces any reference to something beyond the here-below of our material world accessible to the senses. "Secularization" in turn designates, beyond the particular events that history reports, a theory of history in general, a movement that has a spontaneous tendency to take its distance vis-à-vis an initial sacred and to install itself in the profane. Secularity therefore would not only be a factual condition, but the goal of the movement of history. With "secularism" we take yet another step. The suffix suggests a valorization, a stance in favor of the movement toward secularity, which is welcomed with great satisfaction, to the point that some wish to hasten its arrival.

Here, etymology gives us an indication that is both amusing and important. The term "secularism" has entered all the European languages, and has found more or less adequate equivalents in others, such as *'almānīya* in Arabic. It seems though that it was used for the first time in English (*secularism*) at the beginning of the 1850s by George Jacob Holyoake (1817–1906), one of whose main works, published in 1870, was entitled *The Principles of Secularism*.[27] In 1859, as we saw earlier, John Stuart Mill still saw it as a neologism.

As for the substance, the debate for which the term was created turns out to be based on an error. Proponents of secularism imagined that religion is the origin of moral precepts, and that all one had to do was show that those can be grasped without a particular revelation of God. However, this is exactly what Christianity maintained, explicitly since the *Letter to the Romans* (II, 14–15) and implicitly since Jesus himself.[28] The partisans of secularism can be excused, however, because many Christians of the time believed they were defending religion by showing that it is indispensable for the moral education of man.

In the first place, to speak of "secularism" allowed one to avoid the term "atheism," which was still felt to be inflammatory and discrediting in Victorian

---

27   See *Oxford English Dictionary*, 1a.
28   For the issue in its entirety, see *The Law of God, op. cit.*

England. The term "agnosticism" appeared in the same intellectual atmosphere. In Great Britain today, a third term is used in this sense: *humanism*. All that said, it is interesting to ask why one employed precisely this term, "secularism," what is its precise nuance of meaning? Words have their own logic.

French has two different adjectives: on one hand, "secular" (*séculier*), which designates whoever rejects any and all transcendence; on the other, "century-old" (*séculaire*), meaning whatever lasts a hundred years. As for its origin, as we have seen the word is Christian, based on the opposition between regular and secular clergy. But the length designated by the word *saeculum*, that is, precisely a century, one hundred years, is not without importance. A century is the halo of possible experience which surrounds the life of an individual. But what is the case of the groups that are formed when individuals come together in society?

Man and citizen

In the context of modern political philosophy, the central problem is to assure the peaceful coexistence of a group of this sort by finding the rules that allow each to maximize his advantages, but without harming others. This coexistence, however, by definition presupposes that the group already *exists*. Now, individual existence is transitory, limited, and lasts, as we have seen, a hundred years at the outside. Men are individuals of a specific biological species, and the human species, like the other living species, maintains itself by replacing the individuals who disappear with new individuals, engendered by them. The species continues by "surfing" on the lives of individuals.

From this, a tension comes to light between the idea of the individual as a member of the species and that of the citizen as a member of society. This tension does not date from yesterday, because it was already explored by Rousseau.[29] And the young Marx took it up in a different vein, reflecting upon the strange doubling found in the title of the key document of the French Revolution, the "Declaration of the rights of man *and* of citizen" of 1789. His critique bears upon the opposition between the egoistic individual and society. But the two, individuals as well as society, have a common root.

---

29 J-J. Rousseau, *Émile*, I, in B. Gagnebin and M. Raymond (ed.), *Oeuvres complètes, op. cit.*, t. 4, pp. 248–50.

Marx calls man as a generic reality (*Gattungswesen*) by the name of society (*Gesellschaft*).[30]

Man is no longer the adequate support of democracy. As a biological species, he is not capable of realizing the ideal conditions that a perfect democracy requires. This ideal support of democracy, this ideal citizen would be, rather, an angel. But since we are men, what is necessary for humanity to continue to exist, and therefore (since we are not pure spirits) for humans to continue to have children? One can invoke many things, of different orders: economic and social conditions, legislative measures, the psychological climate of a society, etc.

The philosopher in turn must ask what is necessary for those responsible in these areas to have the will to influence these conditions so that humanity can desire to continue to exist. Now, this will supposes two things, a way of looking and a choice. On one hand, it supposes that men think further than a century, i.e., beyond what an individual can experience. And on the other, it supposes a choice. To characterize it, I can think of no better term than "metaphysical." This choice consists in saying that it is *good* that men continue on the earth. I said very precisely intrinsically "good"; I did not say *fun* for the present generation (which I do not doubt). Now, this judgment, who can make it? Certainly not man himself. One recalls Sartre's sarcastic remark on this subject: "One cannot admit that a man can make a judgment on man."[31] The only one who can is he who declared on the last day of creation that all that he had made was not only "good" (*tōv*), but "very good" (*tōv me'od*) (*Genesis* I, 31).

Lacking this, the irony of language realizes the prediction contained in the etymology. The secularist is he whose immanent logic would oblige him (if he were consistent with his principles) to act as if humanity must not last longer than a century. Even more: the secularist is he whose behavior (if it was carried out in a coherent and generalized way) would make it that humanity would only last a century.[32]

---

30   Karl Marx, *Zur Judenfrage*, 1, *in Karl Marx-Friedrich Engels, Werke* (Berlin: Dietz, 1964), t. 1, pp. 363–70.

31   See Jean-Paul Sartre, *L'existentialisme est un humanisme* (Paris: Nagel, 1946), pp. 91–92.

32   Interestingly, the inventor of the word "secularism," Holyoake, was known as a proponent of birth-control by contraception.

6
DEMOCRACY AND THEOCRACY

Our democracies are often thought to be pursuing a process of secularization. But on the way, they encounter various enemies. On the first rank of those who reject it, and whom they must therefore (counter)-attack, is what is characterized as "theocracy." Based upon their etymologies, one can translate the battle between democracy and theocracy as being between "the power/authority of the people" and "the power/authority of God."

I am going to try to nuance this opposition, by showing that the true problem is the nature of Law, because the two conceptions of Law that are opposed in the contrast rest on a common foundation, which is the idea of a divine Law.[1] In this way, our democracies prove to be themselves a kind of theocracy, but with this difference: that the divinity behind the Law is not conceived in the same way in each case. These different conceptions were forged in the Middle Ages, but today they take on striking relevance.

The original meaning of "theocracy"

In everyday language, despite what lexicographers might say, the term "theocracy" has taken on a clearly pejorative sense. To call a regime "theocratic" is to utter an insult. Today, one typically defines as a "theocracy" a political regime in which power is held by a kind of sacerdotal caste, recruited on the basis of the orthodoxy of its members vis-à-vis some religious belief. In the Iran after Khomeini, for example, while it characterized itself as a "government of the jurist" (*wilaya-e faqih*), it was called a theocracy because the Shiite clerics (mullahs) held power, either directly or indirectly, by means of "the Revolutionary Council" which verifies the conformity of

---

1   Here I take up some ideas of my book *The Law of God, op. cit.*

each law proposed by the government with Islam, and determines the orthodoxy of every candidate to high office. A theocracy of this sort hardly has any proponents in the West.

However, originally the word "theocracy" was far from having a pejorative sense. On the contrary, when it was first coined it was a term of praise. It was coined in the first century of our era by the Jewish historian Flavius Josephus. Born Joseph b. Matityahu, the historian had fought against the Romans and, captured by them, he changed camps and was adopted by the family of the emperor Vespasian. In addition to historical writings on the war in which he had taken part, and on Jewish history in general, he wrote a defense of Judaism in response to the polemical work of an Egyptian named Apion. In this apology, Josephus praised the legislation of Moses by arguing that, alone among the nations, the Jewish people who respect this Law did not live under one of the types of political regime that had been defined by the Greek philosophers, but directly under the commandments of God. Consequently, the city founded by Moses was neither a monarchy nor a democracy, but what Josephus called a *theokratia*, the power/authority of God.[2] The sole sovereign of Israel was God, more precisely, God's Law.

Such is the meaning of "theocracy" that would be accepted by the Islamic regimes that exist today, as well as that regime dreamed of by those who wish to give institutional force to *sharia*. Islamic authors in contrast, especially Sunnis, only have disdain for the regimes in which a caste of priests is in power.

Western theocracy: the idea of divine Law

Even though we have the habit of looking down on "theocracies" past or present, our systems of legislation are, or were (I will return to this point), in a certain sense equally theocratic. They are, or were, in the final analysis founded on conceptions that are of theological origin.

The idea of a divine Law is not absent from our own Western tradition; on the contrary, it is emphatically present in its two sources, the Greek and the biblical, in "Athens" as well as "Jerusalem," not only the Old Testament,

2   See Flavius Josephus, *Contre Apion*, II, 16, # 165, T. Reinach (ed.) (Paris: Les Belles Lettres, 1930), p. 86.

but also Sophocles, Plato, and Cicero. Now, in any case, this idea did not become absent until a relatively recent date. The last important author to have mentioned a divine Law among the different types of law was the English jurist John Austin, a disciple of the philosopher Jeremy Bentham, in his lectures on jurisprudence in 1832.[3] Thus, what is exceptional in the intellectual history of the West is the last two centuries, during the course of which the idea of a divine Law has left our field of vision.

However, even when this idea was present in a great part of our tradition, it developed according to different lines than the way in which Islam understood what a divine Law (*sharia*) is or should be. I therefore need to briefly contrast the idea of divine Law in the West and in Islam. I will take as my guiding thread the work of St. Thomas Aquinas, on one hand, because of his immense influence, sometimes in unexpected places, such as Martin Luther King, Jr.,[4] but above all because the medieval development of the Western idea of divine Law seems to me, as to many others, to have been synthesized and achieved its culmination in him.

In the treatise on laws in his *Summa theologiae*, Thomas distinguishes four sorts of law: eternal, natural, divine, or human.[5] The eternal Law is nothing other than the law by which God himself lives and to which he in some way is subject, a law which is charity. The divine Law is the legislative content of the Old and New Testaments, for example, the Ten Commandments and the Sermon on the Mount. The fourth species of law, human law, designates the attempts of humanity to apply to different peoples in various circumstances the natural law of reason which reflects the eternal Law of God.

I need to spend some more time on what Thomas means by the third sort of law, the "natural law." In fact, he does not understand by it what the phrase has come to mean in Modern Times, i.e., the fiction of a pre-political state of things in which human beings would have been governed solely by their desire for preservation. The ideas of nature that underlie classical political philosophy and its modern version are diametrically opposed. Leibniz saw it well, when

---

3   John Austin, *The Province of Jurisprudence Determined*, H. L. A. Hart (ed.) (Indianapolis: Hackett, 1998).

4   Martin Luther King, Jr., Letter from the Birmingham Jail, 16 April, 1963.

5   Thomas Aquinas, *Summa theologiae*, Prima Secundae, qq. 90–97.

he observed against Hobbes: "According to Aristotle, one calls 'natural' what is the most suitable to the perfection of the nature of the thing; but M. Hobbes calls the natural state what has the least of human art[iface], perhaps not taking into consideration that human nature in its perfection carries art with it."[6]

For Thomas Aquinas, the natural law is the law that emanates, not from Nature in general, but from the nature of man. Now, this nature does not mean the animal or (purported) purely biological dimension of human beings. It is rather expressed by the classical definition of man as the "rational animal." In this definition, what best expresses the humanity of man is not his animal aspect, which he shares with certain other living beings, but what Thomas calls *ratio*, the word that customarily translates the Greek *logos*.

As a consequence, the natural law has two aspects: for everything that is animal in man and in the other living beings, it signifies the same thing as for Hobbes or even for Epicurus, to wit: the concern for self-preservation.[7] On this point the natural law has a meaning that comes close to the modern version of this expression.

But a second aspect comes to light in the case of man as such, for whom the natural law is situated in *ratio*, i.e., in reason and in liberty. The natural law for man is therefore the rational law. Now, Thomas Aquinas defines the natural law as "a participation of the eternal Law in the rational creature." In that way, since it reflects the eternal Law, the natural law, as such, is divine.[8] It is no less divine than the writings of the Old and the New Testaments, whose legislative agenda aims to recall the natural law to the humanity that it ought not to have forgotten.

Western theocracy: the idea of conscience

To be sure, today we no longer base our efforts to enact just laws on the idea of a divine Law, revealed or even natural. We prefer to speak of the

---

6   Gottfried W. Leibniz, *Essais de Théodicée*, II, # 220, in P. Janet (ed.), *Oeuvres philosophiques* (Paris: Alcan, 1900), t. 2, p. 234.

7   See Thomas Aquinas, *Commentary on the Nicomachean Ethics*, V, lect. 12, # 1019, R. Spiazzi (ed.) (Turin: Marietti, 1964), 280a. The same distinction is present among earlier jurists.

8   See Thomas Aquinas, *Summa theologiae*, Prima Secundae, q. 91, a. 2, body; ad 1; a. 4, the beginning.

moral conscience of man. That is the result of a long and tortuous history, which has already been recounted and I have no need to do so.[9]

I do have to recall here that the idea of conscience was for a long time conceived as the trace in man of something divine. In a famous passage, Rousseau has his Savoyard Curate exclaim: "Conscience, divine instinct, immortal and heavenly voice!"[10] But the idea of a connection between the conscience and the divine wasn't new and, in particular, had nothing to do with the Enlightenment, a period during which Rousseau, as is well known, was rather a marginal than a representative figure. The idea is found in Antiquity as well as the Middle Ages, among pagan philosophers as well as the Fathers of the Church or scholastic thinkers.

The first to have seen in the conscience something divine was probably the Stoic philosopher Seneca, who wrote: "God (or a god) is near to thee, with thee, in thee. A sacred spirit has its seat in us. He is the observer and the guardian of our good deeds and our misdeeds."[11] The initial words strangely echo a famous passage of the Pentateuch, according to which the Law is "quite close to thee, in thy mouth and in thy heart" (*Deuteronomy* XXX, 14).

The passage from paganism to Christianity did not visibly affect the idea. On the contrary, Paul reprised the Stoic idea of conscience (*suneidèsis*), which performed the same function for the pagans as the Law of Moses did for the Jews (*Romans* II, 15). Since the Law of Moses came from God, by analogy one is authorized to infer that the conscience has the same origin. Augustine explicitly identified the voice of the conscience with the voice of God. "There is no soul, no matter how corrupt, as long as it can reason, in the conscience of which God does not speak. For who wrote the natural law in the heart of men, if not God?"[12]

The idea of the divine that underlies these different declarations concerning the conscience and its origin in a "divine" principle is not one and

9   See Paolo Prodi, *Una storia della giustizia, op. cit.*

10   J.-J. Rousseau, *Émile*, IV, in B. Gagnebin and M. Raymond (ed.), *Oeuvres complètes, op. cit.*, 1969, t. 4, p. 600.

11   Seneca, *Ad Lucilium epistolae*, 41, 1–2, L. D. Reynolds (ed.) (Oxford: Oxford University Press, 1965), t. 1, p. 108.

12   St. Augustine, *De Sermone Domini in monte*, II, ix, 32; PL, 34, 1283 [c]; see *Sermo* XII, iv, 4, *PL*, 38, 102.

the same. The God of Seneca is the Stoic Zeus, who does not radically separate himself from the world that emanates from him. We possess the divine spark of conscience because, literally speaking, our soul constitutes a spark of the primitive creative fire which is identical to God. This is a long way from the God of Paul, Augustine, and Thomas Aquinas, the God of the Bible, who addresses himself not only to human conscience by a silent interior voice, but also enters into the course of history, first of all with Israel and the first Covenant, and finally in the life of Jesus. This biblical God is he who, when the law of nature and/or reason has been stifled or forgotten, recalls it to the conscience by giving Moses the ten commandments.

Democracy and its theocratic foundations

Whether the underlying idea be Law or conscience, both have theological foundations. Therefore, our democratic ideals of a rule of law or of a moral conscience supposed to function as the final authority in the spirit of each human being, be he citizen, judge, or something else, these ideals have a theological origin.

Certain aspects of the medieval origins of democracy can be, and in fact have been, recognized by history. For example, historians recall that our modern election procedures were first elaborated in monasteries and religious orders. Monks elected their superiors, especially the mendicant orders like the Dominicans and the Franciscans, according to majority vote. What was the ultimate foundation of this confidence in a vote? It becomes comprehensible if we recall that the principle of moral choice in man, i.e., conscience, was for a long time considered as a participation in the divine.

In a Western regime, law comes from the will of the people. The people is composed of free human beings whom one believes know what to do because they listen to the voice of their conscience. In the final analysis, law is founded on the moral conscience of man. Behind the principle of "one man, one vote" is the old proverb *vox populi, vox Dei*, a formula found for the first time in the writings of Alcuin of York, an English monk whom Charlemagne, in the first years of the ninth century, had invited to his court and charged with organizing the system of education.[13]

13   Alcuin of York, *Epistolae*, 166, 9, PL, 101, 438.

To make the voice of the people the voice of God was more than a simple *façon de parler*. Thus, in the fifteenth century, the Cardinal and philosopher Nicolas of Cusa defended the preference given to Councils (rather than the Pope) when it came to embodying the principle of infallibility in the Church. He maintained that the mark of the divine character of a decision was the fact that the people agreed on it:

> All legitimate authority comes from agreement on a choice and from free submission. There is a divine seed in the people in virtue of their common birth and from natural right, equal in all men, in such a way that all authority, which comes from God as man himself does, is recognized as divine when it comes from the common consent of subjects.[14]

The Islamic idea of divine Law

After having seen the Western conception of law and its ultimate foundation in human conscience, let us now examine the Islamic conception of a divine Law.

According to Sunni Islam, to establish the law, "to legislate," signifies that one attributes to actions a value (*hukm*) that is at once juridical and moral. The jurists maintain that in principle every human action, without exception, allows itself to be placed in one of these five categories: strictly obligatory; praiseworthy but not obligatory; permitted; blameworthy but not forbidden; strictly forbidden.

Now, the sole power that can attribute a value to human actions is God. As a consequence, the sole legislator (*hākim*) who can exist is God. This is how the jurist al-Ghazali expressed himself at the end of the eleventh century in his treatise on the principles of Islamic law (of which he merely expressed the common view).[15] There certainly are some cases, not many though, where God explicitly issues decisions of a juridical order in the Quran itself, for example in connection with marriage, inheritance, or

---

14 Nicolas of Cusa, *De concordantia catholica*, III, 4, # 331, ed. G. Kallen, in *Opera Omnia* (Hamburg: Meiner, 1963–1968), t. 4, p. 348.

15 See, for example: al-Ghazali, *Al-Mustasfa min 'ilm al-usûl*, I. M. Ramadân (ed.) (Beyrouth: Dār al-Arqām, s. d.), t. 1, p. 222 *sq*.

criminal law. However, in the immense majority of cases, the juridical dispositions have to be deduced, either from the Holy Book, or from the corpus of Traditions about Mohammed (Hadith), or a combination of the two, to which are added other sources of law, whose mixture differs according to the four juridical schools (sometimes called "rites") commonly accepted by believers. The system of rules that in the final analysis is based on these divine and human sources is the Islamic Law, the *sharia*.

Here one must distinguish, and take into account an argument that is often made. There does not exist, and there has never existed, a single unified *sharia*. What exists is a plurality of juridical systems, which propose different interpretations of the sources, Quranic and other, interpretations which are all of human origin.[16] On the other hand, one idea is present always and throughout Islam, according to which God exercises a legislative activity and is the sole being who has the right to do so. Beyond the plurality of *sharias*, there is what we can call the *šar'*, the fact that God imposes a positive law on his creatures, demanding obedience as the condition for salvation.[17] And on any hypothesis, and even for certain authors called "modernists," without the revealed will of God human conscience never suffices to adequately distinguish between good and evil.[18]

The argument of *sharia*'s advocates is not lacking in compelling force. The principle according to which "one does not obey the creature at the cost of disobedience towards the Creator" (*lā tāqata li-mahlūq bi-ma'siyati l'Hāliq*) rejoins St. Peter's formulation before the Sanhedrin: "It is better to obey God than men." (*Acts* V, 29.) But in Christendom, in the seventeenth century Hobbes assured a new foundation for modern political philosophy, taking as his target the very declaration of St. Peter than I just cited (which, however, he cites rarely).[19] According to Hobbes, as long as

16   See, for example: Mathias Rohe, *Das islamische Recht. Geschichte und Gegenwart* (Munich: Beck, 2009), pp. 9–16.
17   See Wilfred Cantwell Smith, *The Concept of Shari'a among some Mutakallimun*, in G. Makdisi (ed.), *Arabic and Islamic Studies in Honor of H. A. R. Gibb* (Cambridge, MA: 1965), pp. 581–602.
18   See, for example: M. 'Abduh, *Risâla al-Tawhîd* [1897] (Beyrouth: Dār lhyā al-'Ulūm, s.d., 1986), pp. 85, 95.
19   Hobbes, *Leviathan*, III, chap. xxxix, M. Oakeshott (ed.) (Oxford: Blackwell, 1960), p. 306; chap. xlii, p. 378.

we can claim that an authority superior to the secular State exists, for example, the Church, so long as we can fear sanctions worse than death (to wit: hell), political life lacks solid foundations. Hobbes therefore sought to show that there is no other way of obeying God than to obey the temporal authority under which we live, arguing that we're never sure that our private inspiration comes from God, and that the Bible can always be interpreted in different ways.

The same procedure would be very difficult in Islam. If God has spoken in person, more precisely, if he dictated a Book to Mohammed, his envoy, if, moreover, he chose and "purified" (*mustafā*) the said envoy in such a way that his entire life had the value of a "beautiful example" (*Quran* XXXIII, 21), why should we still have confidence in our own powers? This is even more implausible as everyone knows that the capacities of human reason are limited.

As a consequence, one can more clearly see the point on which the West and Islam are opposed. They agree on the ultimate origin of legislation, since both are founded in the final analysis upon the divine. In contrast, though, they are opposed over the way in which the law is divine. The ways in which the two civilizations conceive the law and the role that God plays vis-à-vis it are, and always have been, a thousand miles apart. In the final analysis, all this depends on the way in which the two religions conceive of God's Word. In the two biblical religions, God speaks in history, through the voice of conscience, and, according to Christians, in the life of Jesus as the Word Incarnate (*John* 1, 1-14); in Islam, God speaks in the written word of the Book.

I would emphasize the fact that these representations of the Word of God, and hence of the divine Law, were different from the beginning. The West and Islam have never been in agreement on these fundamental points, not even in the Middle Ages, which was perhaps the period when they were most profoundly in disagreement. One could even venture a paradox and say that certain aspects of the ideas of modern politics are in greater harmony with Islamic ideas than they are with the theories of the medieval West. Think, for example, of the way that Rousseau approves of Mohammed because, being at once Prophet and head of State, he did not practice the Christian distinction between the spiritual and the temporal, which had proved disastrous for the unity of our societies.[20] Consequently, we need to say good-bye to the complacent but widely held view according to which Islam would be nothing more than something "medieval" which hasn't (yet) been able to negotiate the turn that the West took in the modern period.

Democracy, a secondary problem

We now can return to the conflict that I mentioned at the very beginning. The political regime that confronts theocracy, is it really democracy? And before that, is the real problem to establish democracy? The lack of democracy is a fact in all the Islamic countries, in any case before "the Arab spring," and in many countries that have nothing Islamic about them. Moreover, we all must admit that what we call "our democracies" are far from being ideal regimes; but Churchill's witticism—that democracy is the worst of all regimes except for all the others—despite being hackneyed, retains all its validity.

However, it seems to me that the question of democracy as a political regime is, in the final analysis, secondary. If one considers it through ancient and medieval eyes, more exactly, through the eyes of Plato and Aristotle, democracy is nothing more than one regime among six possible regimes. It is the rule of the entire "people" (*dēmos*), not that of a small group, called "aristocracy," or that of a single individual, "monarchy". In keeping with the ancient way of looking at things, each of these regimes has a moral qualification: "democracy" is the tolerable version of the government by the people, while its corruption, the domination of the plebs or mob, is called "ochlocracy." In the same way, "aristocracy," which is supposed to be the regime of the most virtuous, can degenerate into "oligarchy," the rule of the few (most often, the rule of the wealthy, i.e., "plutocracy"); and "monarchy," which can be the best regime, can degenerate into "tyranny," the worst of the six.[21]

Democracy, as well as the five other regimes, is the province of political science. Now, political science is itself a part of practical philosophy,

---

20   J-J. Rousseau, *Du contrat social*, IV, 8, in B. Gagnebin and M. Raymond (ed.), *Oeuvres complètes, op. cit.*, t. 3, p. 462 *sq.*
21   See, for example: Aristotle, *Politics*, III, 7.

conceived as the art of governing, which the thinkers of the Middle Ages divided into three parts.[22] Such government can be that of an individual, what we call "ethics." It can be the government of the "household" (*oikos*), and was called by the Ancients "economy," an art that concerns three fundamental relations: husband and wife, parent and child; master and slave.[23] Finally, the government can be the government of the city (*polis*), and this is what we still call "political science."

In all these cases, practical philosophy has as its objective an answer to the question of good government: what ought I to do in order to govern appropriately in these three areas? Ethics tells me how I ought to govern myself; economics tells me, in modernized terms, how I ought to treat my spouse, how I ought to raise my children, how I ought to conduct myself toward the people for whom I am responsible in my business. Political science tells me how I ought to conduct myself as a citizen or a magistrate.

To summarize: democracy is one regime among several, within a domain, that of politics, which is itself part of a greater whole, that of practical philosophy.

The Islamic claim

Now, the Islamic claim does not bear uniquely on political questions, not even particularly on them. It extends to the entirety of the field of what I would call "normativity," to all the rules of behavior—ethical, familial, legal, all the domains in which Islam aims to indicate the right path to take.

Islam as such, Islam as an idea, has nothing to reproach the idea of democracy, insofar as democracy is a defined system of government, distinct from aristocracy and monarchy. To be sure, primitive Islam, such as Islamic historiography constantly recounts and extols as the model of an ideal past, was an absolute monarchy, where Mohammed ruled alone. Or rather: where

22 See, for example: al-Kindi, in E. Rosenthal, "From Arabic Books and Manuscripts, VI, Istanbul Materials for al-Kindî and as-Sharakhsî," *Journal of the American Oriental Society*, 76, 1956, col. 27b and n. 6; Maimonides, *Traité de Logique*, chap. xxiv; Thomas Aquinas, *Commentaire de l'Éthique à Nicomaque*, *op. cit.*, 1, 1, 6, 4a; Nasir ud-Dîn Tusî, *The Nasirean Ethics*, G. M. Wickens (ed.) (London: Allen and Unwin,1964), Preamble, pp. 25, 28.

23 Aristotle, *Politics*, I, 3, 1253b6–7.

God ruled alone through him. This is what the caliphs who succeeded him wanted to do as well. And the Islamic world today consists principally in monarchical regimes, whatever might be the name they give themselves. One can hope that the "Arab spring" will change something, without being too much enthralled to illusions.

On the other hand, many Muslim thinkers, and not only those who call themselves "modernists" or "reformers," rightly observe that the Quran contains no clear indication of the type of regime that has God's favor; it limits itself to requiring that one obey "the Prophet and those who command" (IV, 59). A few underline the fact that certain caliphs were elected by a committee (*šurā*), and that it even happened to Mohammed himself to ask counsel of others, facts from which they infer (not without some boldness) a preference in Islam for representative democracy of a parliamentary sort.[24]

Moreover, the same authors love to strongly emphasize certain features of the Islamic vision of the world that one can characterize as egalitarian, and take them as a point of departure to develop the democratic idea. We can forgive certain anachronisms in their arguments; we can regret that some people regularly oppose Islamic egalitarianism to caricatures of Christianity, for example, concerning the meaning of monastic life and the role of the clergy in the Church. Be that as it may, such democratic features are found in Islam: each human being is responsible before God without the mediation of any leader or priest. Nothing prevents one from taking these as touchstones for a political regime of a popular cast. But still, in each case one must ask, what type of people are we talking about?

What people? Four types of democracy

I have tried to show that to a certain extent we live, or at least we have lived, under a theocracy. Perhaps therefore it would be helpful to look a bit closer at democracy, and ask ourselves to what extent the use of this term is justified. Each has in his memory the definition given by Lincoln in the

---

24 See, for example: Henri Laoust, *Le Califat dans la doctrine de Rashid Rida. Traduction annotée d'al-Hilâfa aw al-Imâma al'uzma (Le Califat ou l'Imâma suprême)* (Beyrouth: s. n., 1938), p. 126.

Gettysburg Address: "government of the people, by the people, and for the people." But what, precisely, does one mean by "people"? Here I would like to provide a typology and distinguish four different models. In order to do so, I will base myself upon four words, three Greek and one Arabic.

Modern "democracies" are described that way on the basis of words of Greek origin. However, it can very well be the case that the identity of the word hides a gulf between ancient and modern times. Those that we today call "democracies" are not exactly democracies in the Greek sense of "the power/authority of the *dēmos*." Some differences are obvious, such as the one that separates direct from indirect or representative democracy. But I see something deeper, which concerns the very nature of the people by whom and for whom power is said to be exercised. In ancient Greece, the *dēmos* of democracy was hardly anything more than a club of adult males, freeborn, sometimes owners of slaves, in any case enjoying the rights of citizenship in a given city.[25] In our modern experience, the best equivalent to such a democracy would be the typically modern phenomenon of a private club, whose members select themselves.

In his first book, René Girard reflected on snobbery and the "private club" (or "country club") as expressing the essence of democratic society. In our societies, which are no longer stratified in "orders" or "estates," social differentiation reconstitutes itself on purely negative criteria. The private club does not derive its interest from the fact that it allows one to encounter interesting people, but because it guarantees that one will not encounter any "slobs."[26] A society without nobility (*s[ine]nob[ilitate]*) must be snobbish. On a greater scale, one can fear that a humanity that conceives the meaning of its own history as an ascent toward "democratization" might change itself into a private club whose definition would be summed up in the ability to blackball anyone it wanted.

Alongside the people as *dēmos*, one can see the people as *ethnos*, as a "nation" in the Latin sense of *natio*, the litter of an animal, that of the Roman wolf, for example. In this way the people is the community of those who live on, and from, a common soil, who share a language that is called

25 See, for example: Aristotle, *Politics*, IV, 4, 1290b1.
26 René Girard, *Mensonge romantique et vérité romanesque* (Paris: Plon, 1961), pp. 223–24.

"maternal," and who feel themselves the heirs of the same history. It is clear that the "nation" is often the more or less artificial result of a construction wrought by a State that has crystalized around a region and a particular dynasty (the Île-de-France, Piedmont, Castile, Prussia), speaking a particular dialect that is imposed by compulsory schooling. The regime founded on a people so conceived (or imagined) can bear the name of *ethnocracy*. The temptation of such a democracy is nationalism, even racism.

What is the subject of modern democracies? It could be the case that these are not conscious of what they share in their inner being. Perhaps they do not even want to recognize that on which they are based. I would echo an insight of Bergson to which I already alluded, according to which democracy has an "evangelical essence."[27] It seems to me that the true subject of modern democracies is the people that is constituted by divine election, which gives each person access to the True and the Good. Otherwise, how to answer the aristocratic objection, which asks why one gives the vote to a Nobel Prize winner and the village idiot?

The vocabulary of the Greek language has a word to designate this way of conceiving the people, a word chosen by the authors of the Greek translation of the Bible, the Septuagint. In order to render the Hebrew word *'am*, and probably to avoid using the term *dēmos*, which had too obvious political connotations, these translators used a term from the language of epics, *laos*, which at their time was rather archaic or provincial. The Greek adjective *laikos* ("belonging to the *laos*") gave the Latin term *laicus*, still living in our Romance languages and in French, in the English word *lay*, in the German *Laie* (which also means "profane, incompetent, amateur"). If I allowed myself to coin an inelegant technical term, I would say that our modern "democracies" are, in the final analysis, and ideally, *laocracies*. And in actual practice, our concrete regimes constitute a mixed regime, with differing mixtures of this ideal laocracy and ethnocracies.

What one expects from an Islamic people is expressed by the concept of *umma*, the "nation [of Islam]" which encompasses and transcends the particular "ethnicities" (*ša'b*). The people thus envisaged is constituted by the call of God (*da'wa*) and by the response to that call, which consists in

27 Henri Bergson, *Les Deux Sources de la morale et de la religion, op. cit.*, p. 300. See above, p. 87.

assuming the yoke of the law (*šarī'a*), to apply and to have it applied by co-ercive measures or appropriate initiatives. The maternal metaphor which is found in the etymology of the term (*umma* from *umm*, "mother") echoes the Islamic idea according to which every man is born Muslim and thus rightfully belongs to the *umma*, in such a way that explicit adherence only ratifies a situation considered to be quasi-"natural". Once again, if I can risk coming up with yet another neologism, perhaps even less felicitous than the previous, I would say that an Islamic democracy, assuming that such could exist, would be an *ummacracy*.

In a regime of this sort, each of the individual citizens would be gov-erned in the last analysis, not by his conscience, but by the positive law of God, drawn from the Holy Book and the deeds and actions of the Prophet, and formulated by the doctors of the Law. As for the technical procedures for selecting representatives and office-holders by vote, the regime would not be distinct from a Western "ethno-laocracy." But its content would be very different. Thus the parliament of such a regime would *a priori* forbid itself from taking legislative actions contrary to the version of *sharia* in place in the country. One has an approximation of this sort in the regime in contemporary Iran.

The secularization of conscience

Our democracies today continue to emphatically defend the idea according to which human conscience constitutes the final authority, to which alone one appeals in the final analysis. But they have severed the thread which connected conscience to divinity, in such a way that the authority of con-science is no longer held to be divine. As the result of a long process, the sovereignty of conscience has thus lost the last vestige of theocracy. To sum-marize it, I will only mention a few extreme cases, since many thinkers have defended more nuanced conceptions. If I wanted to present a complete ac-count, I would have to fill out many aspects.

It has been noted that in Rousseau's exclamation that I cited above, the divine that qualifies the instinct that is conscience is no longer a substantive, but rather a somewhat vague adjective.[28] Forty years later, the German

---

28   See above, n. 10, p. 103.

philosopher Fichte spoke with a good deal of emphasis of "the voice of conscience within me which tells me what I should do in each situation of my life."[29] But this voice is no longer directly the voice of God. What speaks through our conscience is, to be sure, a "sublime will" which "in itself is a law." But Fichte takes care not to name God as the origin of the conscience. With him we find ourselves before the new perspective inaugurated by Kant's revolution in ethics. The moral Law is no longer a cashing out of the Good which is an aspect of God. The existence of the latter is but one of the principles that we must postulate in order for duty to be in harmony with the Good (the other postulates being freedom and the immortality of the soul).[30]

In the tradition of continental philosophy, the last important thinker who provided a theory of moral conscience (*Gewissen*) was Heidegger. Now, the interpretation that he gives of it systematically avoids, and even excludes, every reference to realities that would exist in a way other than the human *Dasein*, whether it be God or a law. By means of the voice of conscience, *Dasein* does not have to hear any message that would come to it from outside itself; there is not even need for it to be reminded that there is something like the Good, like "values," or whatever name one would like to give them. Conscience only recalls *Dasein* back to himself from his dispersion in inauthentic existence.[31]

We today have taken yet another step in the same direction. Presently, no one hesitates to invoke his conscience (usually in a grave tone). But when it is a matter of coming up with a theory about it, people most often are inclined to demystify it, as being "nothing other than" the result of natural selection, of social pressure, of nursery memories, . . . whatever. When one persists in referring to it in ordinary life, it means whatever the individual decides, or rather believes he decides, according to his fancy. That this caprice is rationalized by this-or-that ideology makes no difference.

---

29   Johann G. Fichte, *Die Bestimmung des Menschen* [1800], III, 4, in F. Medicus (ed.), *Ausgewählte Werke* (Darmstadt: Wissenschaftliche Buchgesellschaft, 1962), t. 3, p. 394.

30   E. Kant, *Kritik der praktischen Vernunft, op. cit.*

31   Martin Heidegger, *Sein und Zeit* [1927] (Tübingen: Niemeyer, 1963), # 54, p. 269; # 57, p. 275, 278; # 59, p. 291.

Is a radically non-theocratic regime possible?

Our current regimes in the western world cannot be called laocratic, except in a very broad sense, having undergone the process commonly called "secularization". This concept raises as many questions as it resolves, but I will accept it for the moment.[32] However, this "secularized" state of our democracies is a problem. Over the long term, can a human community continue to understand itself as a *laos* composed of persons capable of liberty and truth, without at least implicit theological underpinnings? This leads me to end with a disagreeable question: Is a radically non-theocratic regime possible over the long term?

If one takes the word "theocracy" in its customary meaning, that of "government by men of religion," which has been so much descried, the experience of centuries has demonstrated that a non-theocratic regime is possible. One can even doubt that there has ever existed something like a theocratic regime, even in Islam. People often imagine that this religion does not make a strict distinction between the political and the religious. That can be true at the level of principles. But if one looks at history, one sees that the identity between religious and political powers, supposing that it was more than a retrospective dream, did not last longer than the decade when Mohammed personally governed his subjects at Medina. Even for a philosopher living in the tenth century under Islamic domination such as Alfarabi, the existence of regimes like this belonged to the distant past. If we are to believe the testimony of later authors, Farabi would have mentioned a regime that approached this type of government, and would have called it by the name of "the regime of the imam" (*imāmiyya*), and he would have said that it had existed in ancient Persia, that is to say, before Islam.[33] An Islamic theocracy, therefore, in the sense of a government by men of religion, is a dream for the future (to be sure, a dream of men of religion), rather than a past reality.

32　See the previous chapter, "Is secularization modern?".
33　See Al-Farabi, cited in Ibn Bâjja, *Tadbîr al-Mutawahhid*, 1, in M. Fakhry (ed.) *Opera metaphysica* [Arabic] (Beyrouth: s. n., 1991 (2nd ed.)), p. 43; Averroes, *Commentaire de la République de Platon*, II, xvii, 5, E. Rosenthal (ed.) (Cambridge: Cambridge University Press, 1969), p. 79, and *Commentaire moyen à la Rhétorique d'Aristote*]1, 8], M. Aouad (ed.) (Paris: Vrin, 2002), p. 69.

The question becomes more complicated if we allow "theocracy" the meaning of a regime in which one considers the norms as reposing on a divine foundation, whether a Law in the Islamic mode, or conscience in a Western one.

Since modern political thought, the final source of political legitimacy is the tacit contract between citizens. To be sure, certain contemporary authors hazard a further step. This type of contract could be the ultimate source of every norm, including moral rules; and it must remain within the borders of humanity. It thus serves to exclude any instance that could claim an extra-human origin.

Now, this radical exclusion of every supra-human instance has a very weighty consequence. On the basis of a social contract, we probably could construct a system of norms that allowed human beings to live in peace with one another. For that, they would only have to follow their self-interest, that is to say, the interests of men who are actually alive. Hence the relevance of the comparison made ever since Hobbes (who probably invented it) of players seated around a table and agreeing on the rules of the game.[34] This, of course, presupposes an earlier agreement: no one can put in doubt the right of those who are already there to take part in the game.

But on the other hand, a contract of this sort, precisely because it includes no external reference, cannot decide the question of whether this existence on earth of the species *homo sapiens* is a good or a bad thing. For that, one needs a transcendent point of reference.[35]

---

34 Hobbes, *Leviathan*, II, 30, *op. cit.*, p. 227; see also Adam Smith, *A Theory of Moral Sentiments*, VI, ii, 2, 17, D. D. Raphael and A. L. Macfie (ed.) (Oxford: Oxford University Press, 1976), p. 234.

35 See my *The Anchors in the Heavens* (St. Augustine Press, 2019), trans. by Brian Lapsa.

7

REACTION TO PROGRESS

Modernity understands all the changes it promotes as representing an advance towards something better than everything that preceded. The idea of progress is a theme, however, that seems to have disappeared from our sight, perhaps because it has become the air we breathe. Ancient man believed in historical cycles which alternate between advance and decline, or, even worse, they imagined a decline from some golden age. We moderns believe that things go from better to better. This is even true during times of crisis which cause us anxiety, our very surprise and indignation revealing our belief in progress: we think that the situation *ought to be* getting better. As a consequence, we try to identify those factors that prevent the ascent to the radiant summits and, once they're unmasked, we turn on them with unvarnished animosity.

It is therefore worthwhile to render this intangible atmosphere visible again, and to reflect on progress, as well as its enemies, those who are bent on slowing it down, or even reversing it.

"Progress is all the rage!"[1]

Progress has been served with all sorts of sauces. In comic books, for example. Thus, the character General Tapioca, in a radio transmission in which he announced that, despite his own ambitions, he was abdicating power in favor of his eternal rival, General Alcazar, entrusting him with the task of leading San Theodoros "on the path of economic, social and cultural progress."[2]

---

1   I borrow this phrase from Philippe Meyer, who used it as the leitmotif of his morning columns on France Culture.
2   Hergé, *Tintin et les Picaros* (Tournai: Casterman, 1976), p. 56.

We are equally familiar with the Leninist use of the term, especially in periods when the strategy of the Comintern was invested in the Popular Front, intended to rally all the "progressive" groups around the Communist Party. One also recalls the more recent contribution of certain pundits, the marvelous phrase "progressive Islamists," to designate one of the camps that fought in the Lebanese civil war.

The public mind of Western societies has made adherence to progress the criterion of the Good, and being suspected of rejecting or opposing it the greatest culpability. The appearance of the adjective "progressive," which has a positive connotation in European languages, testifies to this. It is attested in English as early as 1848, and since then has entered several other languages. The adjective had great success in the European lefts, where it was constantly threatened by adversaries with various names ("conservatives," "reactionaries," "integrists," and "fundamentalists"), but always defeated.

Too often, though, one forgets the Hitlerian version of the idea of progress. The elimination of the Jews planned by the national-socialist State had as its goal, according to an explicit passage in *Mein Kampf*, to eliminate an obstacle to progress conceived not as social, but as racial. Hitler's German is quite ungainly, but I need to translate a few passages that are not very well known: "The man who misunderstands the laws of race and who disdains them deprives himself of the happiness for which he seems destined. He prevents the victorious march of the better race and thus, by this very fact, the preliminary condition of all human *progress*." In contrast, "the Aryan provides the foundation stones and plans for all human *progress*." When he degenerates by mixing with inferior races, "in the same way that the real and intellectual conqueror loses himself in the blood of subject [peoples], it's also the fuel for the torch of the *progress* of civilization (*Kulturfortschritt*) which is lost." As for the Jew, "it is no thanks to him that any *progress* of humanity has occurred, but despite him."[3] This verbal and mental mush at least has the merit of showing that the idea of progress, and the progress of civilization, can also be put at the service of crime.

---

3   Adolf Hitler, *Mein Kampf* [1925], I, 11 (Munich: Zentralverlag der NSDAP, 1942 (665th ed.)), pp. 317, 318, 320 & 322. Also see p. 323.

Progress has a history

The idea of progress is not new, since one encounters it in Antiquity.[4] Among the Stoics, it is present at the level of the individual, when they nuanced the rigor of their all-or-nothing pair, wise/fool, with the notion of moral advance (*prokopē*).[5] One also finds it at the collective level, during periods of ruptures and advances in the sciences, e.g., in Aristotle.[6] However, it is accompanied as a counterweight by the idea of cycles, separated by periodic catastrophes. Thus floods, earthquakes, or cosmic fireballs allow only rustic mountain people to survive, and humanity has to begin again from zero, or just about.

The heir of the Old Testament, Christianity introduced into Western consciousness the representation of a non-cyclical history, one that is linear, stretched between an origin and a fulfillment. However, it was only with Modernity that the idea of progress was rooted in European consciousness. It was installed first of all in the wake of incontestable facts such as the Great Discoveries, made possible by certain decisive inventions. The list of these intellectual conquests, such as the compass, the printing press, and even gunpowder, is constantly found on the pens of writers of this period, starting with Francis Bacon.

In the eighteenth century, the century of Enlightenment, the idea of progress appeared in its full clarity, from now on shorn of the ideas that till then had qualified it. Here too, it was a very real fact, a spectacular victory of science, Newtonian astrophysics, which gave it its plausibility.

From the fact of the growth of knowledge and technologies, the Enlightenment shifted to the idea of an improvement of the human race in terms of morality and civilization. A vision of history animated by a quasi-spontaneous movement toward the better was put in place from the

---

4   I recommend the classical works, beginning with John B. Bury, *The Idea of Progress: an Inquiry into its Origin and Growth* (New York: Macmillan, 1932); now one can add Frédéric Rouvillois, *L'Invention du progrès. 1680–1730* (Paris: Éditions du CNRS, 2010).

5   See the dossier in Hans von Arnim (ed.), *Stoicorum Veterum Fragmenta* [1903] (Stuttgart: Teubner, 1979), t. 3, pp. 140–45.

6   Aristotle, *Protrepticus*, fragment 8 Ross.

middle of the eighteenth century by Turgot (1750) and then Condorcet (1794).[7]

May I be permitted a remark on "history" and its two meanings. Only the fixing of a point of departure can allow one to measure the progress made vis-à-vis it. The awareness of progress entails that one fixes the past, now become "history." The movement of events (in German, *Geschichte*) is a real élan toward the future, while historiographical knowledge (*Historie*) becomes in contrast the inventory of the relics and survivals, sometimes exotic and touching, but always irrevocably superseded.

Rousseau's protest in his *First Discourse*, which shows that progress in the arts and sciences, far from rendering men better, contributes to their corruption, is the exact contemporary of Turgot's hymn to progress.[8] Since then, the two sensibilities coexist and form a complex fabric. Optimism remains the base line, while pessimism, held in abeyance the majority of the time, resurfaces on the occasion of the different crises that the West continues to experience.

Belief or fact?

The question is then posed whether progress is something that one observes or something in which one believes. At the beginning of the nineteenth century, and until the parting of the waters that I will name, progress became the object of a belief, of a sort of religion. Thus the positivism of Auguste Comte made of progress the "truly fundamental *dogma* of human wisdom, be it practical or theoretical."[9]

---

7   Anne Robert Jacques Turgot, "Tableau philosophique des progrès successifs de l'esprit humain. Discours prononcé en latin dans les écoles de Sorbonne, pour la clôture des Sorboniques, par M. l'abbé Turgot, prieur de la maison, le 11 décembre 1750," in G. Schelle (ed.), *Oeuvres de Turgot et documents le concernant* (Paris: Alcan, 1913), t. 1, pp. 214–35; Nicolas de Condorcet, *Esquisse d'un tableau historique des progrès de l'esprit humain*, A. Pons (ed.) (Paris: GF-Flammarion, 1988).

8   J-J. Rousseau, *Discours sur les sciences et les arts*, in B. Gagnebin and M. Raymond (ed.), *Oeuvres complètes, op. cit.*, pp. 1–30.

9   Auguste Comte, *Discours sur l'esprit positif*, 2, in J. Grange (ed.) *Philosophie des Sciences* (Paris: Gallimard, "Tel," 1996), p. 180. (Italics mine.)

A capital stage was reached in the middle of the nineteenth century with Darwin. Progress is then deemed to be an observable fact, because the theory of evolution provides a scientific basis. "The attraction exercised by Darwinism pertains to the fact that it provided a myth that already existed with the scientific guarantees that it required."[10] Progress is no longer simply a fact of human history, it prolongs a universal tendency of nature. For the biologist and popularizer Ernst Haeckel, who did much to popularize Darwinism in Germany, the progress assured by the struggle for existence governs plants and animals, but also languages or peoples: "this progress is a natural law," he maintains. It therefore constitutes an irresistible movement that neither tyrants nor priests can halt.[11] Marx admired Darwin and would have dedicated *Capital* to him. But, even at the beginning of his thought, fifteen years before the *Origin of Species*, he already considered the passage to communism as the result of a natural movement.[12]

By rooting progress in the spontaneous evolution of nature, one entered into an ambiguous dialectic. On one hand, one gained in surety: there is no longer any need to hope, at most it is enough to await, even if it would be better to assist evolution to give birth to what it is pregnant with by pushing it in the right direction, or removing all the obstacles on its path. But on the other hand, the results can hardly be attributed to man's credit, pulled along as he is by a current of which he is not the master and which surpasses him. This is so true that one can ask if the river that comes from well above will not one day leave him on the bank, like an empty husk.

We are there. The man in the street—and all of us are in some part of ourselves—as well as the sophists who peddle him ready-made thoughts, still believe in progress; but those who reflect are more circumspect. During

10 C. S. Lewis, "The World's Last Night," in W. Hooper (ed.), *Fern-Seed and Elephants and Other Essays on Christianity* (Glasgow: Collins, 1975), p. 74.
11 Ernst Haeckel, "Über die Entwicklungslehre Darwins" [1863], in H. Schmidt-Jena (ed.), *Gemeinverständliche Werke* (Leipzig: Kröner, Berlin: Henschel, 1924), t. 5, pp. 3–32, citation p. 28; and see already Herbert Spencer, *Social Statics, or The Conditions Essential to Happiness Specified, and the First of them Developed*, I, ii, 4 (London: Chapman, 1851), p. 65.
12 Karl Marx, *Deutsche Ideologie*, I, in S. Landshut (ed.), *Die Frühschriften*, 7th ed. revised by O. Heins and R. Sperl (Stuttgart: Kröner, 2004), p. 430b.

the centuries of colonization progress had its shadows, to say the least. In this regard one should read the short story that Joseph Conrad located in the Congo, then still the personal property of the king of Belgium, entitled "An outpost of progress."[13]

In the twentieth century, horrors of the same intensity, or worse, had Europe itself for their stage, and gave increased credibility to the contrary mood of the reflective elites.

A challenge for Christians

The notion of progress merits some interest by historians, philosophers, and sociologists. Its reality stimulates that of scholars, jurists, and artists. But why should it attract the attention of Christians? Perhaps because Christianity entertains an ambiguous attitude toward progress, which is worthwhile to clarify.

On one hand, from the time of its appearance Christianity was perceived as a novelty. It was even attacked as such, "the new" being by that very fact considered suspect, even illegitimate. For example, this is the case with Celsus, who, in the third century in his polemic against Christianity, repeated that it only dated from "yesterday" (*khthes*).[14] The adage "Entirely new, entirely beautiful" in contrast exhibits a typically modern attitude. Now, as I recalled earlier, the conception of history as linear and not cyclical comes from the Bible. The currency of this perspective is a collection of concepts which eventually become "unhinged" because uprooted from their native soil (Chesterton), but constitute the current slogans of Modernity. At least three, and perhaps a fourth, of the most fundamental are found in the New Testament: the autonomy (*nomos* [...] *heautô*) of the one who can distinguish Good from Evil on his own (*Romans* II, 14); the emancipation of a humanity that has arrived at the age of an adult and can henceforth do without tutors (*Galatians* III, 25; IV, 2-3); forgetting what one leaves behind and the striving toward what lies ahead (*epektasis*) (*Philippians* III, 13). And

---

13   Joseph Conrad, "An outpost of progress," in *Tales of Unrest* [1898] (London: Penguin, 1977), pp. 83–110.

14   In Origen, *Contre Celse*, I, 26 and II, 4, M. Borret (ed.) (Paris: Cerf, 1967), pp. 146 & 288; VI, 10, *ibid.*, 1969, p. 204; VIII, 12, *ibid.*, 1969, p. 198.

even the idea of an edifice that grows toward its fullness (*Ephesians* II, 21; *Colossians* II, 19).

On the other hand, Christianity has been attacked ever since Modernity for opposite reasons, as an agent of stasis, of slowing progress, even going back. The theme became an obligatory trope of Enlightenment discourse. In the Middle Ages, the "Catholic Church [...] prevented new inventions from developing," as M. Jean-Luc Mélenchon recently maintained in a radio interview, a veritable compendium of ignorance concerning everything that historians have taught us.[15] One can even note a somewhat recent return of the thought in the wake of the ecological movement. Not only would Christianity be responsible for the delay in the development of the sciences and technology, but it also would be responsible for the exact opposite, the excessive developments of the two, by handing the earth over to the disordered appetites of man, whom the Bible would consider as its master. The thesis originally appeared in an article (itself quite nuanced) by the American historian of medieval science, Lynn B. White Jr.[16] However, against this, it has been demonstrated that the text of *Genesis* (1, 26) which seems to legitimate the exploitation of nature was never interpreted in this sense by either Jews or Christians before the advent of the modern project, and that that project is more the cause than the consequence of the meaning erroneously ascribed to the biblical verses.[17] Nonetheless, White's nuanced argument has been taken up with much less nuance by any number of media pundits.

In this way Christianity performs the feat, here with progress as in other ways, of being false in every respect. It is guilty of everything, but also its contrary.

---

15   Répliques (with Denis Tillinac), France Culture, 7 May 2011. On the decisive role of Benedictine monks in technical innovation, see, among others, the very accessible synthesis of Jean Gimpel, *La Révolution industrielle du Moyen Âge* (Paris: Seuil, 1975).

16   Lynn B. White Jr. [1957], "The Historical Roots of our Ecological Crisis," reprinted in *Machina ex deo. Essays in the Dynamism of Western Culture* (Cambridge, MA: The MIT Press, 1968), pp. 75–94.

17   See Jeremy Cohen, *"Be Fertile and Increase, Fill the Earth and Master It." The Ancient and Medieval Career of a Biblical Text* (Ithaca/London: Cornell University Press, 1989).

All the light on obscurantism

The contrary of progressivism is obscurantism, and no obscurantism acknowledges that that is what it is. "Obscurantist!" is an insult, and an insult is hard to transform into a concept. To determine its exact meaning is neither easy nor particularly gratifying. This is even the case when one goes from the language of reckless drivers to that of the media, where a certain number of purported concepts are hardly more than empty insults. To analyze an insult reveals little about the object of the insult. In contrast, it reveals a good deal about the one who utters it. It reveals what he is, those he does not like, and above all, what exactly he does not like in them. He who utters an insult shows that he doesn't expect a response, because he has nothing to learn from his adversary. An insult rarely opens one of those "dialogues" of which our time is so fond, but which it practices so infrequently.

This is the case with the terms commonly used to name what we fear today. In religion, one speaks of "integrism" and "fundamentalism," thus transposing terms that were originally Catholic, then Protestant. In politics, one invokes the danger of "reaction." And finally, in culture, one warns about the "obscurantism" of which I am speaking here. These terms have a common feature. Those on whom one hangs one of these terms find themselves excluded from the discussion and are not allowed to speak: with "people like that" one doesn't talk.

The Enlightenment project

Without any difficulty, however, one discerns behind the word "obscurantism" an opposite image of light, that is, the rhetoric of Enlightenment with a capital E. In the eighteenth century, this historical movement had recourse to the image of light in order to designate itself (to be sure, with complacency) in the various European languages: *Lumières*, *Aufklärung*, *illuminismo*, *ilustración*, *verlichting*, etc. The metaphor is therefore rather old. Clarity is to dispel shadows and darkness, and definitively so; the sun of Reason is to rise and never set.

Darkness makes one blind and one never recognizes that one lives in the shadows, therefore one has no desire to leave them. It is necessary therefore, in order to become conscious of this, to begin by naming them. Different names were mobilized: "prejudices" in general and, in matter of religion, "superstition" or "fanaticism." In principle, for those who created these tags, they were to only have a passive role, one that would end rather quickly with the demise of what they named. What was there to say, therefore, about the adversaries, the active opponents, of those who championed enlightenment? About those who resisted the spread of knowledge? Who remained attached to "prejudices"? Now a word was needed not for the darkness in general, but for active shadows which defended themselves, which even counter-attacked.

For centuries, philosophers practiced a certain elitism and refused to communicate their most profound thoughts to ordinary human beings. Not in order to jealously guard them, but so as not to risk troubling the vulgar in the opinions upon which society depended.[18] Radical Enlightenment broke with this ancient tradition and supposed that it was always good to say the entire truth to everyone. The Christian mission came from a duty to announce the Gospel to all the nations (*Matthew* XXVIII, 19). Once secularized, it became the duty of popularizing knowledge, and in particular the science and philosophy that took it for their model; the task of propagating faith became propaganda. As early as 1753, Diderot came up with the slogan: "Let's hasten to make philosophy popular!"[19]

How to describe the adversaries of Enlightenment? Condorcet invented the figure of "the priest," not only the man of religion, but in general the one who possesses some knowledge that he jealously retains for himself.[20] It may even be the case that this egoist wants to deceive the people in order to assure his domination and that of his ally, the "tyrant." One can find this dark figure everywhere, even in the Prehistory of comic books, as the crazy sorcerer in *Rahan*.[21]

---

18 See Leo Strauss, *Persecution and the Art of Writing* (Glencoe: The Free Press, 1953), p. 34.

19 Denis Diderot, *De l'interprétation de la nature*, XL, in P. Vernière (ed.), *Oeuvres philosophiques* (Paris: Garnier, 1964), p. 216.

20 Nicolas de Condorcet, *Esquisse d'un tableau historique des progrès de l'esprit humain, op. cit.*, pp. 94–95.

21 Roger Lécureux and André Chéret, *Rahan, fils des âges farouches*, comic strip that appeared for the first time in 1969 in *Pif-Gadget*, published for children by the French Communist Party.

These wicked men represent what was called "obscurantism."

The origin of a word

The word perhaps owes its origin to a collection of parodic letters entitled *The Letters of obscure men* (*Epistolae obscurorum virorum*) which appeared in 1515 in Haguenau. Their anonymous author wanted to echo ironically the *Letters of illustrious men* published a year before by the humanist Jean Reuchlin, by pretending to attack him with ridiculous arguments. The adjective "obscure" therefore does not have a direct relationship to the theme, an attack by humanists on the scholastics. However, since Christian scholars debated whether one should burn the writings of Jews, including the Talmud, the image of the battle of light with darkness easily passed from the title to the contents.

Different terms to designate the adherents of obscurantism appeared throughout Europe from the end of the eighteenth century. In German, one began to speak of *Finsterlinge* ("people of the darkness") and in English of *obscurants* and *obscurantism*. The use of these words became general at the time of the Restorations, which were presented as backslidings.

In German the Bavarian philosopher Franz von Baader, a Catholic, used it in an official discourse given on the occasion of the opening of the University of Munich in 1826. He argued for a mutual enrichment of religion and scholarship, which would allow one to avoid the Scylla of nihilism and the Charybdis of obscurantism.[22] In a private letter from the same year he further specified his thought by naming Prussian nihilism and Austrian obscurantism.[23] It is interesting to note that he employed as the antonym of obscurantism the word "nihilism," a term also of recent vintage, but which surprises in this context.

In French, Balzac used it in 1837 to speak of one of his characters, the strongly reactionary Marquis d'Esgrignon: "He only read the *Quotidienne*

---

22 Franz von Baader, "Über die Freiheit der Intelligenz. Eine akademische Rede bei Eröffnung der Ludwig-Maximilians-Universität in München," in F. Hoffman (ed.), *Sämtliche Werke* (Leipzig: Bethmann, 1851), t. 1, n. X, pp. 133–50, citation p. 149.

23 Franz von Baader, "Lettre au Comte Armansperg," 28 November 1826, in E. Susini (ed.), *Lettres inédites de Franz von Baader* (Paris, Vrin, 1942), t. 1, p. 394.

and the *Gazette de France*, two journals that the constitutional papers accused of obscurantism, and a thousand monarchical and religious monstrosities, but which the Marquis himself found to be full of heresies and revolutionary ideas."[24]

To enlighten rather than set afire and burn

Why do we today, even after two hundred years, continue to be fearful of the word "obscurantism"? In asking the question, I am not claiming that we are only threatened by words; far be it from me to deny that there is danger in the world. I do not deny that our democratic societies have enemies, nor that a portion of their hatred has good reasons. In fact, I would validate the courage of acknowledging one's fear, and even more, that of naming one's enemy. But I do ask, why do we use precisely *that* word? Wouldn't it be enough to simply describe what is occurring, and to say that others are killing, kidnapping, oppressing, raping, and mutilating? Why add that these are manifestations of "obscurantism"?

Would it be to avoid the pain and trouble of reexamining the basic assumption of Enlightenment, that the progress of knowledge always entails that of civilization? Or, to use a phrase attributed to Victor Hugo, the thought that "to open a school is to close a prison"?[25] Isn't it necessary to suspect the suspicion that the proponents of Enlightenment cast upon their adversaries, and ask if they might not have something enlightening to say to us?

Roger Shattuck, the American historian of the French culture of the nineteenth century, posed the following simple question apropos to the atomic bomb, pornography, and Sade: "Is it always good to know everything?"[26] Among other audacities, he had the bravado to attack one of the favorite totems of the Parisian intelligentsia, the Marquis de Sade, by deconstructing the genealogy of the infatuation of which he was, and is, the object. When his book was translated into French, the Parisian intellectual guard-dogs duly howled. It was their right. But was it intelligent?

24 Honoré de Balzac, *Le Cabinet des antiques*, chap. II.
25 See all the details in *groupugo. div. jussieu. fr/groupugo/doc/10-12-18ᵗʰrchadi. doc.*
26 Roger Shattuck, *Forbidden Knowledge. From Prometheus to Pornography* (New York: Saint Martin's Press, 1996).

One would be better advised to face the problem, and to cease considering the Enlightenment as something unquestionable. The examination should be conducted on three fronts. On one, on "the Enlightenment" as adequately characterizing an entire century, the eighteenth, which is not lacking in its own dark spots; on another, on the full results of the historical movement of much greater amplitude which claimed "to enlighten" peoples, sometimes against their will; and finally, on the very legitimacy of the enterprise.

The image of illumination, chosen by the Enlightenment itself to express the way it understands itself, harbors an ironic implication and counterpoint. Torches can start fires as well as cast light. This is what a little fable published in the *Berlinische Monatsschrift* in 1784 represents. An ape puts the torch to a forest of cedars and congratulates itself for illuminating the country.[27] The Spaniard Donoso Cortés, having returned from a youthful enthusiasm for liberalism to an attitude today considered to be frankly reactionary, used the same image in the nineteenth century.

> We have all seen pass before our eyes these centuries of prodigious unbelief and very high culture, which in the wake of time left behind them a trail which was less luminous than fiery, and which blazed in history with a phosphorescent light. Fix your eyes on them, look at them any number of times, and you will see that their éclat is a flame, and that they only give light because they burn. Each could say that their ability to illumine comes from the sudden explosion of materials which in themselves are obscure, but inflammable, much more than from the pure regions whence comes that peaceful light which was gently spread on the vaults of heaven by the masterful brush of a sovereign painter.[28]

27 Cited in Peter Pütz, *Die deutsche Aufklärung* (Darmstadt: Wissenschaftliche Buchgesellschaft, 1978), pp. 31–32.
28 Juan Donoso Cortés, *Ensayo sobre el catolicismo, el liberalismo y el socialismo* [1851], I, 1, in J. Juretschke (ed.), Obras (Madrid: BAC, 1946), t. 2, p. 349.

The Italian scholar and lyric poet Leopardi draws a wise maxim from some reflections illustrated by a similar, but calmer, image, which we would do well to adopt: "Reason is a light. Nature wishes to be illumined by reason, not torched by it."[29]

29 Giacomo Leopardi, *Zibaldone di pensieri*, 21–22 [not dated, between 1817 and 1818] (Rome: Newton Compton, 2007), p. 20b.

III
CULTURE

8
ARE THERE REALLY TWO CULTURES?

Modernity prides itself on leading us from an uncouth barbarism, which it supposes preceded it, to culture. We therefore need to reflect upon this notion. I will do so first of all in reference to the little book of Charles P. Snow, *The Two Cultures and the Scientific Revolution*. Published in 1959, the work was reprinted four years later, in other words, a little more than fifty years ago. In it the author, a physicist by training but a university administrator by career, addressed the growing division between two forms of education, which one could call literary and scientific. According to him, people with literary formation and those of scientific training were less and less able to understand each other.

Snow's book stirred many reactions, which can be grouped into polemical and friendly. On the polemical side, the question is revived from time to time when someone interprets a particular controversy as the resurgence of the literary/scientific opposition. This was the case with the debate that was begun in 1996 by the American physicist Alan Sokal. He had sent an article whose content was deliberately absurd, but composed of "postmodern" and "deconstructivist" jargon, to a journal of literary criticism that published it without raising an eyebrow.[1] On the irenic side, people have tried to construct all sorts of bridges between the two cultures. For example, some have tried to show that the gulf that separates them can be surmounted by a third culture, the human and social sciences.[2]

---

1   Alan Sokal, "Transgressing the Boundaries: Toward a Transformative Hermeneutics of Quantum Gravity," *Social Text*, 46–47, 1996, pp. 217–52.
2   Wolf Lepenies, *Die drei Kulturen. Soziologie zwischen Literatur und Wissenschaft* (Munich: Hanser, 1985).

Two human types?

In truth, there is a clear disproportion between people of so-called scientific formation and those of literary or humanistic formation. The first group often possesses relevant knowledge and information about the second's domain, which the second generally do not possess about the first. In reality, scientific sorts, especially the most brilliant in their own fields, are often good connoisseurs of literature and painting, even good musicians in their own right. In this way the scientist who is a musician and lover of fine literature has both cultures, while the literary person only has one. In this case, though, the problem would be resolved by the personal union of the two cultures among a scientific elite, for whom one would perhaps dare to reactivate an old word, one that has become a bit pretentious, of "savants."

In contrast, among those of literary formation the grossest ignorance in the areas of the exact sciences is more the rule than the exception. With this type, even a tincture of the exact sciences is rare. It is therefore often noticed and noted, while the scientific human type qualified in arts and letters, if he elicits admiration or envy, hardly stirs any surprise. This leads us to deepen the observation of the fact (*quaestio facti*) in the direction of the question of right (*quaestio juris*). Ordinarily, it is acknowledged that a scientist cannot completely ignore everything else, while a literary type can allow himself a shameful ignorance in matters of natural science. I will return to this.

In any case, the remarks just made presuppose two things. On one hand, that it is the same meaning of "culture" when it is the sciences of nature and when it is a matter of literature or art. On the other, they suppose that what one means by "culture" in the two cases is some sort of knowledge, even information. However, this seems quite wrong to me. I will therefore argue for a rather restrictive definition of culture. In doing so, I am conscious that I am going against a long-term tendency; I therefore need to briefly retrace its history.

The inflation of the meaning of "culture"

Over the past several decades we can observe an inflation of the meaning of the word "culture," an inflation that seems to me to be due principally to the transgression of two semantic borders. On one hand, the word crossed the border situated on a vertical axis between elite and popular culture. It is no longer reserved to the interests and conduct of a social and intellectual elite. It also designates popular culture, including its most mundane aspects, its most regional or local ones, even the most deviant. It includes life styles, cuisine, folklore. Finally, it's used in the sense of the customs in place in a given milieu, for example, "corporate culture." On the other hand, the word "culture" has stepped beyond the frontier situated on the horizontal axis. It passes to the plural, and one speaks of cultures in the sense of civilizations. One hardly speaks any longer of civilization in the singular, civilization *tout court*, which would be ours. But one also speaks less and less of civilizations in the plural, which was still being done thirty years ago. Samuel Huntington's best seller, which spoke of "a clash of civilizations" not too long ago, raised the concerted outcry of the virtuous.[3] Even if the title used the plural, the book contributed to the discredit of the term "civilization." The word "culture" therefore presents itself as a suitable substitute.

The word "culture" has also come to occupy the position of being the supreme explanatory principle of the human. The opposition between nature and culture has become a primary datum, and it is taught, for those who haven't picked it up in their upbringing, at the beginning of the required philosophy curriculum. Moreover, this opposition is drawn in culture's favor, to the point that in certain contexts the word "nature" has become a dirty word. To claim that certain characteristics of the human pertain to nature is perceived as crudely offensive. This contemporary sensibility is itself the result of a tendency of very long date, whose roots one can find at the beginning of Modern Times, with Descartes and Hobbes, then Locke and Vico.

In order to examine this new enlargement of meaning, I will concentrate for the moment on the French idea of "general culture," although it is not solely a French idea. By this is understood what one *should* know, what one does not have the right not to know, in other words, something like a canon. This knowledge is at once a minimum and something common, to

---

3   Samuel Huntington, *The Clash of Civilizations and the Remaking of World Order* (New York: Simon & Schuster, 1996).

be shared by all, beyond the various specialties. Here too the roots of the idea plunge deep into the past. For example, they recall the idea of "the generalist gentleman" capable of interesting himself in everything, but without ever putting on the blinders of a specialty, found in seventeenth century France. Every Frenchman who has read Pascal in high school knows this expression.

In addition, in the French system there is an academic subject that bears this name. The examination competition for certain prestigious schools, especially the business schools, includes a test of what is called "general culture and the human sciences." I myself taught this discipline for a year in two preparatory classes. The test consists in an essay on a relevant subject. The trick consisted in treating the subject while using the greatest amount of references possible to the works studied in the course, brilliantly interpreted, to be sure, but also, preferably, other such works which the student was deemed to have read on his own, following his or her own tastes. In view of this test, an entire arsenal of pedagogical tools was constructed. At the start of each year, manuals were sold which had been compiled hastily during the summer that followed the publication of the program. There is even a *Dictionnaire de culture générale*, which appeared a few years ago from the University Presses of France.[4]

In the United States, the idea of a canon is sometimes realized in programs where the years of college are devoted to the study of the "Great Books" of Western or world culture. Lists are drawn up of these works, often with the fixed number of one hundred. Great Books Programs exist in several prestigious universities and at lesser known schools, including St. John's of Annapolis and Santa Fe. Just about everywhere, core curricula work on the same principle. Thus, the notion of "general culture" or a "canon" far exceeds the French hexagon.

The meaning of "culture"

If I now ask myself what culture is, it is clear that it is a form of knowledge, but not of just any sort. The possession of facts and information, as extensive and exact as it might be, is not enough. To know by heart the phone

---

4   Frédéric Laupies (dir.), *Dictionnaire de culture générale* (Paris: PUF, 2000).

book is not culture. Facts and information are not called "culture" except to the extent that they constitute a "code" which allows one to be recognized as belonging to a distinct entity—which it is easy to designate by the same word, "culture." In this case, it is tempting to claim that the idea of culture is ideological in nature, that it serves as a password to a particular social status. This temptation has not been resisted.

Still, despite this, it is by starting from this suspect notion that I will develop my own concept of culture. General culture nourishes conversation. And not merely that which goes on in fancy salons, but—here one will excuse the medievalist – in the most general sense of the *conversatio civilis* about which the scholastics spoke, i.e., the human conversation, the social use of *logos* in the city which is the specific difference of man. According to Thomas Aquinas, it is this culture that the Averroist doctrine of the unity of the intellect threatens, because if all the thinkable has already been thought, if I merely have to draw from an existing reservoir of concepts, I no longer have to take upon myself the effort of thinking and communication.[5] In passing, I would note the way that the virtual encyclopedias on the internet resemble a sort of agent intellect with which one simply has to connect in order to know, in this case learning coincides with booting up one's computer . . . .

Culture is what permits orientation in the world. Orientation is not simply a marker, because if a marker allows us to know where we *are*, orientation allows us to decide where we *ought to go*. Culture bears on everything for which there is a *good* way of proceeding. With culture, one introduces the notion of value. Value is not exclusively moral, but also, among other sorts, aesthetic. A useful criterion for it can be that of personal engagement. What I merely know does not make any real difference in my life. To be sure, knowledge helps me make decisions to the extent that it helps me better understand the consequences of my acts. But it is not knowledge that is going to tell me what to decide. If the doctor instructs me on the dangers of tobacco, that is not going to cause me to stop smoking. It's still the case that I may decide to prefer the intensity of a risky life to bourgeois security. An entire way of life is in play. What belongs to culture

---

5   Thomas Aquinas, *De unitate intellectus contra Averroistas*, IV, 240, in R. Spiazzi (ed.), *Opuscula philosophica* (Turin: Marietti, 1954), p. 83a.

obliges me to modify my conduct. To be cultivated is to not allow oneself just any thing, whether it be in connection with the most sublime morality, passing through the aesthetic domain, and ending with etiquette, even one's personal hygiene.

Culture and knowledge

If one applies this criterion, a radical consequence follows. The domain of what is knowledge and only knowledge, in particular science, does not pertain to culture. Therefore, there is no scientific culture. In truth, science describes facts and seeks their laws. But in the objects it studies it does not find any trace of value, which is why it abstains from every value-judgment. This was brought to light no later than the end of the eighteenth century by Hume and Kant, when they made a strict distinction between what is and what ought to be.

On the other hand, is there a literary culture? That is, isn't there *only* literary culture? No, not even here, at least to the extent that one understands by this a form of knowledge. To know poems by heart or to remember historical dates is no more a form of culture than to know the laws of physics. I will put side-by-side two examples given by Snow. To have read a play by Shakespeare and to know the second principle of thermodynamics, i.e., concerning entropy, are two specimens of knowledge, two kinds of information. But neither pertains to culture.

The distinction between the cultural and what is not cultural thus does not neatly cover the division between the scientific and the literary. Everything that only pertains to historical information is outside culture. Literary history, for example, is pure information. In contrast, stylistic analysis, if it is applied, if it teaches me to make a good use of language, pertains to culture. The history of art is not culture; to know how to paint, even to know how to appreciate a painting, is culture.

My definition of culture is therefore extremely narrow. It does, however, compensate for its narrowness by being broader on another plane. The customs of daily life, the forms of manners, cuisine, for me they are also part of culture. If one wants to, one can speak of high and low culture, elite culture and popular culture, but a difference of degree is not a difference of nature. At the limit (and if you'll permit me a smile), what's called "physical culture" does merit its name to the extent that it teaches the correct use of the body and eventually enhances its beauty and grace. "Not knowing how to read or to swim" was a phrase in ancient Greece to describe someone entirely without culture.[6]

Return to the problem

I can now return to a question left open earlier. Why do scientific types experience more of a need for information of a general literary sort, than vice versa? Let's break it into two parts. On one hand, why do they experience the need for general knowledge? On the other, why is this privilege granted to what is literary or artistic?

The first can be explained by reference to the new situation introduced by Modern Times and the "scientific revolution" referred to by C. P. Snow. The amount of knowledge that has to be acquired, makes "universal men" as found in the Renaissance or German classicism, Leonardo da Vinci or Goethe, impossible. A consequence of this situation is that the need for general knowledge is pretty much the same for all. The specialist in one branch of hard science probably does not know much more about the other hard sciences, perhaps even sub-sections of the same discipline, than a totally unscientific literary person. He has the same need as the latter of repairing to popularizations.

But popularization is not necessary for the non-hard forms of knowledge, which in principle express themselves in everyday language, and are therefore accessible to the questions of non-specialists. With respect to the hard sciences, the non-knower knows that he does not know. But everyone believes he understands the soft sciences. The temptation is great, in particular for philosophy, to ape the hard sciences, either by the use of some symbolic formalism or by expressing oneself in a technical way when it is not necessary, and thus to shelter oneself from requests for meaning, often quite naïve but always heartfelt, that come from the man in the street.[7]

---

6   See, for example: Plato, *Laws*, III, 689d.
7   See my "Histoire de la philosophie et liberté," in *Introduction au monde grec. Études d'histoire de la philosophie* (Chatou: La Transparence, 2005), pp. 9–32, especially pp. 13–15.

Because these disciplines do not have need of popularization, attempts in this direction end in nothing good. Thus, we have no example of popularized philosophy. What pretends to be so today is nothing but vulgar philosophy.

Sciences and humanity/ies

The second problem is tied to the emergence of a new type of knowing, the mathematical knowledge of nature as pioneered by Galileo. It had as a result that knowledge no longer provides a moral model. Before the parting of the water represented by Galileo, nature was the model, or the metaphor, or at least the guarantor, of the moral endeavors of man.[8] This was not only true at the political level, where the hierarchical social order mirrored the cosmic order, but also at the level of the individual's efforts at ethical conduct. To be sure, nature did not at all constitute a source of morality. But it showed that since the good was real, it *a fortiori* was possible.

The presence of nature, which premodern man experienced as a *kosmos*, played a role analogous to that of the postulates of practical reason in Kant.[9] These, i.e., human freedom, the existence of a just God, and the immortality of the soul, did not serve to ground the moral law, which sufficed to itself and obliged one to follow it on its own authority. The postulates, though, served to guarantee the possibility of the Good, that is to say, the accord between what the Law required and the order of the real world.

The major difference between the premodern vision of the world and Kant's morality is that the realization of the Good is, for Kant, postulated. It remains in the domain of faith and hope. For ancient and medieval man, in contrast, it is already given in the cosmic harmony, where one only needs to grasp it.

Premodern knowledge was part of what was called "the humanities," the *litterae humaniores*. Its structure included disciplines whose task was to humanize, to make man more human. These subjects pertained to the "literary" domain, but not more than the "scientific" domain. Those who possessed the "hardest" sciences of the period affirmed that the study of them

8   See my *The Wisdom of the World, op. cit.*
9   E. Kant, *Kritik der praktischen Vernunft*, I, ii, 2, iv–vi.

could make one virtuous. Ptolemy wrote in the preface to his *Almagest* that nothing was more suited to make us good men than astronomy, a consequence of contemplating the regularity, good order, harmony, and the modesty of the celestial spheres. And Averroes expressly wrote that the study of physics can teach us the virtue of justice, because nature itself possessed this virtue.[10]

After the scientific revolution connected with Modern Times, nature appeared as totally devoid of meaning and values. Knowledge of nature, in itself, gives us no indication of what we ought to do. In this sense, and in this sense alone, it is not "interesting."[11] This is true for the knowledge of nature, but also for all erudition, be it historical, literary, or even philosophical. The practice of the laboratory or the archives can at most habituate us to a certain ethic. The virtues of courage, above all intellectual courage or probity, humility before the facts, generosity in the exchange of results, are required for research, which favors them in return. But this is the case with all research.

Thus, there are not two cultures. There is only one. But it is quite small, and it is neither literary nor scientific. Quite simply, it does not belong to the order of knowledge. We moderns find ourselves before forms of knowledge that can no longer humanize us. Before this problem, we—whether we are literary or scientific, specialists in what we call either hard or soft knowledge—are all camped under the same banner.

---

10 Ptolemy, *Syntaxis Mathematica*, J. L. Heiberg (ed.) (Leipzig: Teubner, 1907), t. 1, p. 7, 7–14; Averroes, *Grand Commentaire à la Physique d'Aristote*, Preface, Juntes, p. 2C, cited in my *The Wisdom of the World, op. cit.*, pp. 150 and 141, respectively.

11 See my "La physique est-elle intéressante? Quelques réponses de l'Antiquité tardive et du Moyen Âge," in *Au moyen du Moyen Âge, op. cit.*

9

DOES CULTURE SUPPORT
THE IDEA OF TRUTH?

The culture whose definition I just sketched, at least provisionally, constitutes the pride of modern man. It is what he displays against the backdrop, sometimes complacently darkened, of the preceding periods of history. For a long time it seemed obvious that the decisive advantage of this culture over its opponents was that of the truth over the kingdom of falsehood, compounded of error, illusions, and lies. To cultivate oneself, for the individual as well as the collective, was not simply to compile a collection of opinions. The great works of literature, of painting, of music, and, of course, philosophy, were not toys with which one amused oneself, they contained truth.

Truth without pertinence, but dangerous

The current tendency, however, among those who read is to put in scare quotes the truth claims of what they read. The very word *truth* has almost become a vulgar term, which one surrounds, like a cordon sanitaire, with quotation marks. One will speak of the truth *of* someone, or a group, or a civilization, in the sense of "what that person or group holds as true"—in more direct language, their opinions.

May I be permitted to begin with a well-known passage from C. S. Lewis. An experienced devil, Screwtape, writes to his apprentice. The human for whom he is the guardian devil could avoid a quibble of conscience by reading the argument an ancient author made against it. However, the lead devil writes:

> [I]n the intellectual climate which we have at last succeeded in producing throughout Western Europe, you needn't bother

about that. Only the learned read old books and we have now so dealt with the learned that they are of all men the least likely to acquire wisdom by doing so. We have done this by inculcating the Historical Point of View. The Historical Point of View, put briefly, means that when a learned man is presented with any statement in an ancient author, the one question he never asks is whether it is *true*. He asks who influenced the ancient writer, and how far the statement is consistent with what he said in other books, and what phase in the writer's development, or in the general history of thought, it illustrates, and how it affected later writers, and how often it has been misunderstood (especially by the learned man's own colleagues) and what the general course of criticism on it has been for the last ten years, and what is the "present state of the question."[1]

This is very well done, and we ought to enjoy it. However, let's not make our task too easy. It is not enough just to "thunder against" (Flaubert) the attitude that is described. For this attitude does not just repose on an aestheticism that toys with opinions and is delighted at their chatoyant variety. It also comes from a moral concern.

Claims of truth would engender intolerance, it is believed. In particular, monotheism would be dangerous, not so much because of the number of gods that it allows, i.e., only one, but precisely because it introduces into religion the idea of truth. A sole god would be the "true" god, the others being false, that is, "idols." It was the Egyptologist and theorist of culture Jan Assmann who introduced this idea into the learned world.[2]

To the claim to possess the truth—which is actually unknowable—Richard Rorty prefers what he calls "democracy." Across the centuries, his position resembles that of Epicurus, who put "friendship" (*philia*) above all else. Granted that it is theoretically possible, and thus that peace of soul is assured, one can propose any number of explanations of astronomical or

---

1   C. S. Lewis, *The Screwtape Letters*, n. 27 (New York: Macmillan, 1948), pp. 139–40. My italics.

2   See, above all, Jan Assmann, *Die Mosaische Unterscheidung oder Der Preis des Monotheismus* (Munich: Hanser, 2003).

meteorological phenomena as long as they undermine the fear of an intervention in the human domain by powers that transcend it.

Today, one can observe a tendency to not even discuss the truth of a fact or a theory, but to criticize an opinion that one doesn't share by simply repeating it, but under some aspect that makes it look ridiculous; this suffices to discredit it. This tactic reaches its peak (or nadir) among media types today, but in substance it is a rather old stratagem. It was invented by the publicists of the "Enlightenment," and theorized by a genuine philosopher, Lessing, who spoke of "defeating by mocking" (*herauslachen*) one's opponents. Leo Strauss rightly saw in this an acknowledgment of one's inability to argue on the merits and to defeat with reasoning the other's arguments.[3] To echo Valery: "Put the laughers on your side—and the ship will capsize."[4]

Things are even more serious. The nineteenth century played with the idea that truth would not only be useless to culture, but harmful, offering the following argument. Things have no intrinsic meaning; however, we need meaning; we therefore have to construct it. All meaning is fictive and has to be. Culture is a fiction that allows us to live in a world that, in and of itself, is devoid of meaning. Culture is therefore artificial, and it has to be. In our day, Cornelius Castoriadis has developed the theme with great force. But the idea of the fictive character of culture appeared much earlier, under the title of "illusion."

The Enlightenment had already noted, to cite the words of d'Alembert in 1757, that "we hardly ever gain any new knowledge but thereby disabuse ourselves of some pleasant illusion, and our increasing in knowledge is almost always at the price of our pleasures."[5] It was in a similar spirit that Burke regretted that the empire of light and reason destroyed the "agreeable illusions" which make the charm of society.[6]

3   Leo Strauss, *Philosophie und Gesetz. Beiträge zum Verständnis Maimunis und seiner Vorläufer* [1935], in H. Meier (ed.), *Gesammelte Schriften* (Stuttgart: Metzler, 1997), t. 2, p. 18.

4   Paul Valéry, *Mauvaises pensées et autres*, in J. Hytier (ed.), *Oeuvres* (Paris : Gallimard, "Bibliothèque de la Pléide," 1960), t. 2, p. 827.

5   D'Alembert, *Réflexions sur l'usage et sur l'abus de la philosophie dans les matières de goût*, in *Oeuvres* (Paris : Belin/Bossange, 1822), t. 4, p. 333.

6   E. Burke, *Reflections on the Revolution in France, op. cit.*, p. 67.

Transposed into a much more radical key, this idea constituted the common basis of European sensibility from the time of late Romanticism. In Italy, it was already the case with Leopardi in 1818. For this classicist and poet, reason destroyed the illusions without which man cannot live. As a consequence, it leads to its proper contrary, barbarism. The logical result of a total destruction of illusions would be suicide.[7]

At the other end of Europe, in Russia, his contemporary Pushkin said he preferred the heroic legend to the banal image of Napoleon that remained in his contemporaries' memories, and in general, the "deception that elevates us" to the vulgar reality.[8]

The available-for-use truth: technoscience

This rejection of truth for the sake of culture would not be feasible if a second phenomenon did not compensate for the rejection, and make it possible in the first place. It is also contemporaneous with the first, which is not an accident. I have in mind the mathematical science of nature which began with Galileo (d. 1642) and its technological applications; the latter began with the industrial revolution at the end of the eighteenth century, attaining full stature in the nineteenth.

Technology based upon science, or technoscience, is a kind of factory which furnishes us with truth that is tailored to our needs. Or, if one would like another image, it is a mint that prints all the money we would like. Our expenditures initially covered, we can allow ourselves to play at doubting the truth.

For many of our contemporaries, truth reduces to what "Science" (supposing that such exists) says. This sort of truth has many advantages; the first is obvious, even spectacularly so, and the second is more discreet, because it is the flip-side of a disadvantage.

On one hand, science has practical applications in technology. It deploys itself in very effective techniques, and contents itself with "what

7 Giacomo Leopardi, *Zibaldone di pensieri, op. cit.*, 21–22 [no date, between 1817 and 1818], p. 20b, then 216 (18-20 August 1820], p. 83b.
8 Alexander Pushkin, *šepoŭ* [29 September 1830], vv. 63–64, in *Sotchinenija* (Paris: YMCA Press, 1991), p. 362b.

works." To say that the laws that it formulates in mathematical language are "true" would be a useless redundancy. On the other hand, science, like all "hard" knowledge as such, even literary or artistic, is, strictly speaking, lacking in interest (as I defined it earlier).[9]

Science is distant from culture, and even has nothing to do with it. As such, it is neutral. It leaves open the question of the legitimacy of using the techniques it makes possible. The computer, the cell phone, and the jet plane were all used by the kamikazes of September 11. When it comes to the question of legitimacy, science kicks the can down the street.

The official truth: ideology

Can culture as a salutary fiction suffice? Can there be accord among minds without something like the truth? Can one conceive of a common fiction? As long as it is unself-aware, this sort of fiction can suffice. Be that as it may, today one observes an increase of rather piquant formulas tending to dilute the truth, such as "to each, his truth," or "my truth." Similarly, the cult of "tolerance" is at its peak, it has become our last virtue, the one at which no one laughs, or rather: at which it is forbidden to laugh.

However, this is only the self-congratulatory conscience of our societies, not their reality. On this latter plane, the temptation is very strong to put order in the chaos of "truths" by choosing one and imposing it as the official truth. This is more than a temptation, it is the effective reality of all societies, including ours. Some of these official truths are merely insinuated, like advertising; others are quite harsh, like the propaganda of a totalitarian regime. Between the two a rainbow of intermediate forms is deployed, of which political correctness is one of the most visible. An escalation to the extremes is always possible. In the name of what can we oppose such endeavors?

Pascal already saw the phenomenon: "When one doesn't know the truth of a thing, it's good that there be a common error which fixes the mind of men [...] because the principal malady of man is a restless curiosity over

---

9   See my « La physique est-elle intéressante ? », in *Au moyen du Moyen Âge, op. cit.* especially pp. 98-99 and above, p. 141.

things he cannot know, and it isn't so bad for him to be in error, rather than this useless curiosity."[10]

The necessity of ideology comes from this situation, as it fills the void of meaning left by science. This is why ideology adopts the empty form of the latter and apes it. There would be no Leninism without political economy and its critique by Marx; there would be no Nazism without Darwin's theory of evolution. Ideology is deemed to be "true." Lenin said so in 1913: "Marx's doctrine is all-powerful, because it is correct."[11] It also apes religion and utilizes religious affects, extending them to objects that are purportedly accessible to science.

In politics, the truth is less effective than the lie. It has even been observed that a big lie is more effective than a small one. This is what an expert in this domain said, no one less than Hitler himself, apropos to war propaganda, what has been called "brainwashing."[12] Ideology combines the two. In the purest actual realizations that history until now has seen, ideology presents its most shameful lies as the Truth, and publishes them in a journal which bears that title, *Pravda*.

An examination of the very idea of "culture" and its origin will allow us to draw the same dark conclusion. The idea of culture is absent from the Greek source of philosophy, which I need to quickly rehearse. The Greeks practiced a three-fold distinction of realities: nature (*physis*), art or craft (*tekhnē*), and convention (*nomos*), to which a three-fold set of human attitudes corresponded: contemplation (*theōria*), fabrication (*poiēsis*), and action (*praxis*). Each of these human activities is capable of a certain access to the truth; the excellence (*aretē*) of these activities exists to grasp the truth found in each of these three domains. Contemplation welcomes what shows itself "without distortion" (see the use of the adjective *atrekēs*). Fabrication produces what isn't yet, and it must proceed correctly. In all these domains, Aristotle speaks of truth. The dianoetic virtues that he lists, to wit: science (*epistēmē*), art (*tekhnē*), intellect (*nūs*), wisdom (*sophia*), and prudence (*phronēsis*) are the five by which the soul "achieves truth" (*alētheuein*).[13] In cases of fabrication,

---

10   Blaise Pascal, *Pensées*, # 18, *op. cit.*, t. 1, pp. 29–30.
11   Lenin, *Les Trois Sources et les trois parties constitutives du marxisme* [1913], Introduction.
12   Adolf Hitler, *Mein Kampf*, I, 10, *op. cit.*, p. 252.
13   Aristotle, *Nicomachean Ethics*, VI, 3, 1139b15.

art is a true *logos* (*logos alēthēs*) which accompanies the habit (*hexis*) of production.[14] In cases of action (*praxis*), prudence is a true practical habit (*hexis alēthēs*).[15] Aristotle in fact does not hesitate to speak of the "practical truth" (*alētheia praktikē*).[16] But in all of that, there is no appearance of "culture."

Our modern concept of culture represents a fusion of the two last notions of each of these triads of Greek philosophy. The domain of being of culture brings together art and convention; the activity exercised by culture combines fabrication and action.

"Culture," in its opposition to nature, is an invention of the eighteenth century, and found its most powerful expression in Kant.

> Inasmuch as he is the sole terrestrial being who possesses understanding, and with it a power of fixing his goals voluntarily, he [man] is truly the rightful lord of nature; and when one considers the latter as a teleological system, he, as far as its purpose, is the final end of nature. However, he is so only under one condition, to wit: that he understands it and has the will to give it and himself a final destination that can suffice unto itself, thus be the final end, but a goal that one has no need of seeking in nature [...] Only culture therefore can be the final goal that one is justified in posing for nature with respect to the human race . . . .[17]

This culture is not that of technical ability, which develops the capacity of means to attain their end, but does not suffice to orient the will towards a good end. Nor is it that of mere discipline, which liberates us vis-à-vis the instincts, but cannot orient the will any more than the first form. Man does not receive the privilege of being the final end of creation except to the extent that he is "considered as noumenal [...] [as] the subject of morality [...] [as] being moral."[18]

---

14   *Ibid.*, 4, 1140a10, 21.
15   *Ibid.*, 5, 1140b5, 21.
16   *Ibid.*, 2, 1139a26–7, 30, b12.
17   E. Kant, *Kritik der Urteilskraft, op. cit.*, # 83, p. 300 [391], 2.
18   *Ibid.*, # 84, p. 304 [398], 305 [399] and note p. 306 [399].

For Kant, the synthesis still took place under the banner of action, as it is regulated by morality. For us, it takes place under that of production, not so much material production, but the production of representations. Culture no longer is understood as work to arrive at the true, but as the production of the requisite common opinions so that life remains possible. In this way, the idea of culture enters by its own logic into the sphere of ideology.

Truth as a need

We are spoiled children, we who can allow ourselves to play with the idea of truth because we are not forced to lie. The Lie was consubstantial with totalitarian regimes, those happily past, or those that are still surviving in reality (and in the minds of those nostalgic for that past).

> The organized Lie practiced by totalitarian States is not, as is sometimes claimed, a provisional expedient of the same nature as ruse is in war. It is essential to totalitarianism, something that would continue even if the concentration camps and secret police ceased to be necessary. [...] Totalitarianism in fact demands that the past be constantly modified, and at length it demands that one ceases to believe in even the existence of an objective truth.[19]

This Lie is a torture. Listen to the witness of Alexander Solzhenitsyn. In his *Letter to the Leaders of the Soviet Union*, published in 1974, the writer devoted a special chapter, the sixth, to ideology, where he wrote: "This universal, obligatory Lie, one that is compulsory, has become the most tormenting aspect of the existence of the people of our country, worst than all the material adversities, worse than civil non-freedom."[20] Let me underscore this: When Orwell and Solzhenitsyn evoke the contrary of the truth, they do not speak of error, but of the Lie.

19 George Orwell, "The Prevention of Literature," in S. Orwell (ed.), *The Collected Essays, Journalism and Letters*, t. 4: *In Front of Your Nose*, 1945–1950 (London: Penguin, 1970), pp. 81–95, citation pp. 85–86.
20 Alexandre Soljenitsyne, *Lettre aux dirigeants de l'Union soviétique, op. cit.*

What Solzhenitsyn suffered and witnessed to in its particularly virulent form, but also its obvious and so to speak frank form, and thus easier to discern, is still present under softer forms, but also more subtle and thus more difficult to confront. To be sure, the means of diffusion of "official doctrines" are less concentrated in our European societies than they were with the Soviet News Agency, TASS. And the techniques of coercion here are very far from those of the KGB or the Red Army. Nonetheless, today we still have authorized opinion, obligatory opinions, and other interdictions.

Truth, however, is a vital necessity, and our civilization is increasingly aware that the very existence of man on this earth needs to be justified. Nietzsche aids us to see this, perhaps despite himself. In an unpublished fragment when he was writing Zarathustra, one reads: "We are conducting an experiment (*Versuch*) with the truth! Perhaps humanity is going to disappear! Let's go! (*wohlan*)."[21]

For some people, truth is nothing but the result of a consensus. Now, quite obviously, a consensus of this sort must be produced by men who live at the same time. In that way, the truth that they decide has to be imposed on future generations. To be sure, those generations will also have the ability to seek a new consensus which will make new decisions about the nature of the truth. But they will have to do so by basing themselves on the "truth" of the previous generation, which will be present in them and will mark them, whether they are aware of it or not. Thus, this absolute democracy must necessarily degenerate into a dictatorship of the present over the future, in other words, the absence of democracy. There must be something like objective truth, independent of our will, that one can transmit from generation to generation, if the future generations are not to be abandoned to the caprice of their ancestors without any defense.[22]

Two types of truth

I now need to ask, what a culture of the truth would be? It would be culture *tout court*. Culture not only supports the idea of truth, but demands it. But what truth?

21 Friedrich Nietzsche, fragment 25 [305], Spring 1884, *KSA*, t. 11, p. 88.
22 For a striking illustration of this point, see C. S. Lewis, *The Abolition of Man*, *op. cit.*, chap. iii.

With St. Augustine I will distinguish two faces of the truth. In his *Confessions*, Augustine posed a very interesting question, to wit: If the happy life consists in rejoicing in the truth, why is it written in the New Testament that men "hate the truth"? Wouldn't it be more normal that they love it, because it undeniably is a good? Augustine answers by making a distinction between two sorts of truth: "*Amant eam lucentem, oderunt eam redarguentem.*"[23] Truth can be *lucens*, shining and illuminating, in which case we love it; but it can also be *redarguens*, convicting, in which case we flee it, even wish that it did not exist – which means: we hate it.

The first truth is like a light that illumines the objects that we wish to see. We wish to see them in order to be able to act on them, use them, consume them. Augustine expresses the second sort of truth with a word that is very hard to render, a verb composed of a prefix and a root. The root, *arg-* , suggests the idea of brilliance, as in *argentum*, silver, the metal that shines. The prefix *re(d)-* indicates a repetition or return to oneself, a reverberation. The French translators of the Bibliothèque Augustinienne render the Latin word by "to accuse." This seems to me to be an excellent choice, on the condition that one understands the word not only in the sense of "to reproach," but also "to cause to stand out," in the sense when one says that the light, being more lively, accuses the shadows.

Truth is the light that we shine on the things we desire to know, and which assures us control. But it is also what turns back upon us and indicates to us what we ought and ought not to do, what we ought to be and are not; it even is what brings to light all the dirty little secrets that we would prefer to leave in the shadow; it is what speaks frankly, even brutally, to us. Thus, while we love the first sort of truth, we flee the second. Now, if we truly loved the truth, we should also want it to shed its light on us.

This distinction allows us to do justice to the contemporary distrust exhibited to the idea of truth, seeing what is valuable in it and, on the contrary, what is unacceptable. The *lucens*-truth can be taken as an idol, even more dangerous because it is noble. Pascal already recalled this: "One makes

---

23   St. Augustine, *Confessiones,* X, xxiii, 34, *BA*, t. 14, pp. 202–04. Heidegger saw the importance of the passage for his analysis of human existence, see *Augustinus und der Neuplatonismus*, summer course (1921), C. Strube (ed.), *Gesamtausgabe*, vol. 60 (Frankfurt: 1995), pp. 199–201.

an idol of the truth itself, because truth without charity is not God, it is his image and an idol one must neither love nor adore, although one must love or adore its contrary, which is the lie, even less"[24]

Therefore one must ask those of our contemporaries who are so severe toward the idea of truth, what is the real reason for their attitude? Perhaps one must turn the suspicion back on the suspecter. What motivates our animosity against the truth? Is it the fear of seeing it degenerate into an oppressive fanaticism? Or would it be the fear of seeing it direct its demands toward me? To say "to each, his truth," to reject a truth that would be the same for all, isn't that to say: above all, not a truth that could say the truth about me?

Culture as veritas redarguens

Augustine's analysis is very illuminating, permitting one to characterize knowledge and culture in a few words. I therefore would propose the following double definition: *knowledge is the sum of all the* lucentes *truths; culture is the ensemble of all the* redarguentes *truths.*

In order to continue, I will return to the passage from C. S. Lewis that I cited near the beginning, because it suffices to read the devil's argument against the grain to draw profound wisdom. The passage continues:

> [S]ince we cannot deceive the whole human race all the time, it is most important thus to cut every generation off from all others; for where learning makes a free commerce between the ages there is always the danger that the characteristic errors of one may be corrected by the characteristic truths of another. But thanks be to Our Father and the Historical Point of View, great scholars are now as little *nourished* by the past as the most ignorant mechanic who holds that "history is bunk."[25]

24 Blaise Pascal, *Pensées, op. cit.*, Br. 582, t. 3, p. 26.
25 C. S. Lewis, *Screwtape Letters*, n. 27, op. cit., p. 140. (My italics.) The allusion at the end is to a statement of the industrialist Henry Ford: "History is more or less bunk. It's tradition. We don't want tradition. We want to live in the present, and the only history that is worth a tinker's damn is the history that we make today" (interview with Charles N. Wheeler, *Chicago Tribune*, 25 May 1916).

But the very diversity of cultures invites me to seek what might be true, and to contest my own limits. Culture isn't a museum in which various opinions are merely displayed, but it allows opinions to correct each other. We therefore ought "to consider the ancient writer as a possible source of understanding, and expect that he might say something that could eventually modify our thought or our conduct."

One can generalize and apply Horace's formulation to everything that pertains to culture: "under another name, it is your story that is recounted." Or the "You are that man!" that the prophet Nathan said to king David after having stirred him to indignation against the wicked man he had just talked about in a parable.[26] In culture, it is always "of me" that the text or object speaks. The message of the Beautiful is always the one that Rilke drew from his contemplation of a Greek statue: "You ought to change your life."[27]

The ocean of truth

Modern conscience is ill at ease before this sort of truth, because it imagines it, wrongly, as an ensemble of ready-made objects. As a consequence, it places the search for truth higher than its possession. One recalls Lessing's parable. If God were to present us with the truth in one of his hands and the endless search for it in the other, and asked us to choose, we should prefer the latter.[28] The choice however is not so simple. In fact, how would we know, if we prefer the search to the truth, that the object of our search is truly the truth, and not, let's say, the Donjuanian excitation of discovery? Still, one must comprehend the aspiration expressed here, and far from dismissing it, do justice to it as much as possible.

Now, the Christian tradition has for a very long time contained an idea that would be worthwhile to reconsider, because it could prove to be more

---

26 Horace, *Sermones*, I, 1, vv. 69–70: "mutato nomine de te fabula narratur"; see also II Samuel, XII, 7.

27 Rainer Maria Rilke, "Archäischer Torso Apollos" (Spring 1908), *Du musst dein Leben ändern*.

28 G. E. Lessing, *Eine Duplik*, 1, end, in *Werke* (Darmstadt: Wissenschaftliche Buchgesellschaft, 1996), t. 8, p. 33.

acceptable to modern thinking. According to this way of seeing, truth is not something that one possesses, but something *in which* one is, a space more than a thing, a theme found in, although left implicit by, some of the Greek Church Fathers. They loved to speak of the "infinite ocean" (*apeiron pelagos*) of the Divinity.[29] This expression entered the Latin West by means of the commentaries on the work of Pseudo-Dionysius the Areopagite by John Scotus Eriugena in the ninth century or Hugh of St. Victor in the twelfth.[30] In a shocking but very revealing way, their use of the expression was diametrically opposed to that made much later by John Locke, who recommended modesty in metaphysical matters, and wrote that we must avoid "loosening the reins of our thoughts and letting them enter the vast Ocean of Being."[31]

By means of this image God is conceived, not as an object, but rather as a field, as a space that is freely left open. One cannot attain God, one can even less "take him in," but, if I can speak this way, one can ride or surf on him. St. Augustine formulates it this way: "He [God] is hidden, so that we can seek him in order to find him; but he is infinite, so that having discovered him, we can continue to seek him."[32]

Culture correctly taught can therefore derive from that truth in charity that Pascal implicitly opposed to the idolatrous cult of the true.[33] In this case, the truth is no longer what one possesses in order to vaunt oneself vis-à-vis one's neighbor, much less to dominate him. By making me come to know myself, it makes me understand that there is nothing that I have not received and do not owe to another. Saint Augustine said this too: "One

---

29 St. Basil, *Contre Eunome*, I, 16, *PG*, 29, 548c; St. Gregory of Nazianzus, *Discours* 38, *PG*, 36, 317; Pseudo-Dionysius the Areopagite, *Hiérarchie céleste*, IX, 3, in M. de Gandillac (ed.), *SC*, n. 58 (Paris: Cerf, 1958), p. 135.

30 John Scotus Eriugena, *Expositiones super Hierarchiam caelestem*, *PL*, 122, 218a; Hugh of St. Victor, *In Hierarchiam caelestem*, *PL*, 175, 1093d–1094a.

31 John Locke, *An Essay Concerning Human Understanding*, I, 1, 7, in J. Yolton (ed.) (London: Dent, 1965), t. 1, p. 8. The use of this metaphor was brought to my attention by John Hittinger.

32 St. Augustine, *Commentaire de l'Évangile de Jean*, 63, 1, in *Corpus Christianorum Series Latina*, t. 36, p. 485: "Ut inveniendum quaeratur, occultus est; ut inventus quaeratur, immensus est."

33 Blaise Pascal, *Pensées, op. cit.*, Br. 582, t. 3, p. 26.

does not enter into the truth except by charity."[34] I will add a preamble of my own invention and say: "One does not enter into culture, except by the truth."

---

34 St. Augustine, *Contra Faustum*, XXXII, 18, PL, 42, 507, in *Corpus Scriptorum Ecclesiasticorum Latinorum*, 25, p. 779: "Non intratur in veritatem nisi per caritatem."

10
HEIRS WITHOUT A TESTAMENT?

The culture of our late modernity, at least in Europe, distances itself from Christianity, and it does so in the name of culture. When Bismarck launched his attack against the German Catholic Church, his endeavor took the name of *Kulturkampf*, a "battle for the culture." More recently, some have gone so far as to want to deny entirely the evidence of the decisive role of Christianity in Western culture. The civilization that emerged from Christianity is now trying to depart from it. But can it neglect the relation with its religious heritage?

I have chosen as the title of my response a formulation that alludes to a saying of René Char, found in a war poem: "Our heritage was preceded by no testament."[1] It acquired some fame when Hannah Arendt chose it as the epigram of a book she published in 1961, *Between Past and Future*.[2] But I have to ask, is the content of a religious message truly something like an inheritance or heritage? This concept, or rather this metaphor, seems suspect to me. So much so that I am tempted to rework the formulation and venture: "Our testament is followed by no heritage." Nonetheless, despite my reservations, I will accept the question.

A world without Christianity

I am not the first to ask what the world would be without Christianity. This was the case with my predecessor in the Romano Guardini Chair in

---

1   René Char, *Feuillets d'Hypnos* [1943–1944], n. 62, in J. Roudaud (ed.), *Oeuvres complètes* (Paris: Gallimard, "Bibliothèque de la Pléiade," 1983), p. 190.

2   Hannah Arendt, *Between Past and Future. Six Exercises in Political Thought* (London: Faber & Faber, 1961).

Munich, Hans Maier, in a little book published in 1999, and which, chock full of facts and thoughts, richly deserves to be translated. It is entitled *A world without Christianity? What would that change?*[3]

Nor would I be the first if I responded that without Christianity, there would be no European culture. To cite but one example, this is the case with the American, become English, poet and man of letters, T. S. Eliot, who in a lecture given just after the war in Germany, in 1946, proposed the trenchant formulation: "I do not believe that the culture of Europe could survive the complete disappearance of the Christian Faith. [...] If Christianity goes, the whole of our culture goes."[4]

Here, I will not ask if this is true. On the contrary, I am going to begin by posing an even more radical question. Supposing that our civilization disappeared, would this truly be a bad thing? Many are the voices today who remind us that our civilization has not only pages of glory, but that it has committed not a few misdeeds. In fact, self-flagellation is almost *de rigueur* in intellectual circles. And the same voices tell us that our civilization is not the only possible one, and, in any case, not the only one that exists. Some add to the observation, comparison and evaluation. They sing the praises of other civilizations, of Islamic tolerance, Buddhist pacifism, the Chinese sense of harmony with nature, and so forth. All this teaches us a good deal about the imaginations of these extollers, and rather little about the historical reality.

Difficulties of a balance sheet for Christianity

A tempting solution would be to come up with a list of the cultural elements of Christian origin present in Western culture, or rather, in world culture. This has been done in different veins. The majority of the time, it has been done in an apologetic mode, for example with Chateaubriand and his *Genius of Christianity*. Sometimes though, and more recently, it has been done in order to charge Christianity with all sorts of catastrophic misdeeds and to

3   Hans Maier, *Welt ohne Christentum—Was wäre anders?* (Fribourg-en-Brisgau: Herder, 1999).
4   T. S. Eliot, Appendix to *Notes towards a definition of culture*, III, in *Christianity and Culture* (San Diego: Harcourt, s. d.), p. 200.

explain how much better the world would be if there hadn't been this noxious accident, this "parenthesis" that, hopefully, is about to end. One finds this sort of accent, for example, in Nietzsche, to name only respectable authors.[5]

The disadvantage of this way of proceeding owes to the consequences it entails, which seem to me to be negative. I will list three.

First, if one speaks of the Christian contribution, one must also mention, if one wants to be honest, the contributions of others, and thus draw up a catalogue of non-Christian influences as well. But then it would be necessary to classify them according to religious criteria (Jewish, pagan), geographic (Mediterranean, Nordic) or ethnic (Celtic, Germanic, Slavic, without forgetting the Finns and the Hungarians). In this way, one would put different things on the same plane and only end in confusion. As proof, I will offer one example. A few years ago, not without anger, I read one of the many texts that explain to us that Muslim Spain, "Al-Andalus," was not only a refined and culturally fecund civilization—which no one denies— but a paradise of peaceful coexistence and mutual tolerance between communities, which is a pure legend. The author of the article also spoke of the "irrigation techniques of *the Muslims*" which would have assured the agricultural wealth of Spain.[6] What was the problem with this claim? It was to attribute a fact of civilization, in this case Mesopotamian rather than Arab, to a religion. If we want to proceed that way, why not speak, therefore, of "the *Christian* horse-collar," "the gun powder of *Confucianists*," or the "numerical place-values of the *Hindus*"? Not to mention the two nuclear physics, "Aryan" and "Jewish," which knew a few years of existence in the Nazi discourse between 1933 and 1945.

Next, one would have to weigh and compare the different elements from the point of view of their relative importance. That would lead to a lot of haggling in order to come up with various percentages. A thousand sensitivities would show up, each human group having the tendency to consider itself as issuing from the marriage of Alexander Popov and the little match-girl, in other terms, as having invented everything and being the victim of all. Hence, mutual accusations *ad infinitum*, each recalling its glorious contributions to world culture and displaying its wounds.

---

5   Friedrich Nietzsche, *Der Antichrist*, # 59, *KSA*, t. 6, pp. 247–49.
6   Agnès Rotivel, *La Croix*, Monday 9 August, 2010.

Finally, one would have to appreciate the positive or negative character of these elements, which would also lead us into endless discussions. I have already recalled the ambivalence of cultural contributions. Here too, a single example will have to suffice. Christianity and, with it, the entire background of the Old Testament, have been blamed, first of all, for having prevented the sciences from progressing (this is the position of radical Enlightenment and their interpretation of the trial of Galileo). Then they were praised for having made them possible, thanks to the desacralization of natural powers. Finally, they have been blamed again for being responsible for the devastation of nature by a technology that the Bible would have delivered to the *libido dominandi* of Adam and his descendants. All this while we wait the next tipping of the scales.

For all these reasons, one will understand that here I will not adopt such a strategy.

"Culture" as a Christian novelty

Here I will defend a thesis that is at once more modest and at the same time a thousand times more bold. I maintain that *it is Christianity that invented culture*. Obviously, I do not mean by that the absurdity that material civilization, science, literature and the arts, and even religion, did not exist before it. Even a provocateur of my type would not risk an enormity of that caliber. On the other hand, I will defend the idea that culture *as such*, a culture that would be culture and nothing but culture, is an invention of Christianity and, more precisely, of St. Paul.

Let's begin with a few words on what culture is.[7] Culture is essentially normative. It encompasses all the domains of human activity in which one can distinguish a good manner of proceeding from a bad. What is considered "good" or "bad" is so for a given culture, and not always for another. For what allows one to distinguish them is precisely the different answers that they give to certain fundamental questions, which themselves are pretty much the same everywhere because they pertain to the nature of man. How to communicate with others? Whom do I have the right to marry? How ought I to educate my children and respect my parents? What

7   See Chapter 8 above.

do I have the right to eat, and how ought I to prepare it? What deserves to be admired, respected, imitated? What are—lifting out of context a fine phrase of the American political scientist Charles E. Merriam—the *credenda*, the *miranda*, and the *agenda*, the things one must believe, that ought to be admired, and that should be done?[8] The field of culture is therefore quite large; it goes from the most sublime to the most humble, from morality to cooking, passing by the rules of manners, refined prose, and law.

In contrast, culture includes *nothing* of what is purely knowledge, mere description of reality. This is true for the sciences of nature, but also for historical knowledge. Mere knowledge, whether it bears upon nature or upon man, of itself has no cultural value. I am not privileging "the literary" over "the scientific" in the "two cultures" of C. P. Snow. I deny this same cultural value to historical, literary, or artistic erudition. Unless it claims to provide models to imitate, e.g., the heroism of great men or the beau style of great writers. In this case it ceases being simply factual and takes on a normative value.

Paul's razor blade

Now I need to proceed to what at first glance will seem to be a detour, and reflect upon the revolution wrought by St. Paul.

The revolution did not consist in rejecting "the yoke of the Law" of Moses. What Paul really rejected was the idea that God formulates rules of conduct. Paul retained the idea of a system of rules, and even their divine origin. However, he placed this idea on a different plane. The norms are not dictated by God by the intermediary of a prophet, they are written in the "heart" of man, which he translates from the Semitic to the Greek as "conscience" (*syneidèsis*) (*Romans* II, 15). If I can apply here an anachronistic opposition, the norms do not pertain to the domain of history but of "nature," understood as created by God. Elsewhere Paul names nature as the principle of action of the pagans who, even though they did not know the Law of Moses, nonetheless conducted themselves "decently" (*Romans* II, 14).

---

8   Charles E. Merriam, *Political Power: Its Composition and Incidence* (New York: McGraw & Hill, 1934), p. 4.

I had to recall what should have been obvious, because the Pauline rev-olution was misunderstood even in Paul's lifetime as a pure and simple claim to exempt oneself from the Law (anomie). It was probably Paul him-self who coined the phrase "everything is permitted" (*panta [moi] exestin*), and he had to explain himself by adding a qualification: "all things are per-mitted to me, but not everything is expedient (*sumpherei*); everything is permitted, but everything is not edifying (*oikodomei*)" (I *Corinthians* X, 23; see VI, 12). Paul's "everything is permitted" therefore does not mean that the line between good and evil is abolished, as was the case in the famous "everything is permitted" that constitutes a veritable leitmotiv in the dis-cussions between the brothers Karamazov.[9] In fact, the line that separates good and evil, between which one must choose, loses none of its gravity, because it is nothing other than that which separates life from death. The verse of *Deuteronomy* which presents the choice between good and evil as a choice between life and death (XXX, 19) has lost none of its pertinence.

Paul's formula really means that this line is not adequately expressed by the opposition between the permitted and the forbidden, especially if one understands them simply as what pleases or displeases God. The true alternative is rather between what leads to life and what leads us to death. To say that God commands or forbids certain actions is a *façon de parler* ap-propriate to children (see *Galatians* III, 24–25). Thus, when we speak to infants who have no idea of electricity and who want to put something in an electrical outlet, we can (and have to) speak directly: "You can't do that!" What we really wanted to say, however, is "that's dangerous." Some behav-iors are permitted because they are intrinsically good, vivifying; others are forbidden because they are intrinsically bad, lethal.

The fundamental idea is that God does not take our place, he doesn't replace our own judgment about the right way to proceed, but he gives us the means of doing it. His instruction enlightens us, and as needed, recalls certain basic rules, but God never *dictates* to us what we must do.

What remains after Paul's use of the razor was the minimal survival kit of humanity. The necessary content of this was already found in the seven

---

9   Dostoyevsky, *Les Frères Karamazov*, I, ii, 6 (Moscow: ACT, 2006), p. 73; II, v, 5, p. 267; IV, xi, 4, p. 589 and 593; 5, p. 605; 8, pp. 625 & 633; 9, p. 651; xii, 6, p. 699.

commandments that, according to the Sages of the Talmud, were given to Noah at the exit from the ark, and in the Ten Commandments given to Moses.[10] One could add that it is nothing other than the eternal Tao without which humanity could not live an authentically human life, perhaps not even live at all.[11]

The filling-in

It is clear that these elementary rules of correction do not provide answers to the multiple questions that human life poses, both in its personal and its social dimensions. That is why the Torah is far from reducing itself to the Decalogue, but contains six hundred and thirteen commands. That is also why, by going into even greater detail, Judaism developed a "path to follow," if one can translate the Hebrew word *halakhah* that way. The insufficiency of the survival kit is already evident in what concerns juridical systems and political organization. It is even more striking if we think about the different ways that human life can flourish in the different domains of high culture, encompassing artistic creation, worship of God, the care and control of the body, the refinement of manners and morals.

On all these points, Paul says almost nothing, if one excludes certain basic principles, for example, the necessity of political authority towards which obedience is a duty (*Romans* XIII, 1). As for the other elements of culture, Paul probably had a tincture of Greek literature and philosophy. He was capable of quoting poets like Aratos, Epimenides and Menander. But his writings do not evince any *interest* in these questions. Nonetheless, the religious revolution that he introduced has among its most lasting consequences a new attitude toward culture, even—as I said earlier—the birth of the very idea of culture.

How so? It starts with the fact that Paul's Christianity lacked definite normative content. And because it was empty, it produced what one could call a gigantic ebb, which was to lay open the entirety of the field of norms.

---

10 Respectively, *Sanhedrin*, 56b, and *Exodus*, XX, 2–14.
11 See C. S. Lewis, *The Abolition of Man or Reflections on Education with Special Reference to the Teaching of English in the Upper Forms of Schools* [1943] (New York: HarperCollins, 2000), p. 18.

It had to fill itself in with a content that it had to borrow from elsewhere. Christianity was forced to absorb what was already available on the market of civilizations. And this is what it did, first with Roman civilization, i.e., the Roman system of law and administration, which included what the Roman world itself had already borrowed from Greek civilization in the scientific, literary and philosophical domains. This borrowing, of course, was complex and even tortuous. The "pagan" culture was not swallowed whole; it was digested, subject to many rendings, even rejected in part. On all this, there is an entire library of books to write, although a large portion is already composed.[12]

For Paul, the surrounding culture was, as he himself said several times, "Greek." Now, I maintain the following: it is only since the Pauline revolution that something like "Greek culture" exists. What already existed beyond any shadow of doubt was Greek *paideia*. This meant a comprehensive style of life. To be sure, this *paideia* included what we today call "culture," for example, literature (Homer) and art, and even physical culture. To use Plato's terminology, it was inseparably gymnastics and "music."[13]

The Hellenism that the Maccabees encountered in Palestine in the second century before Christ did not particularly spread by means of temples. It fact, it seems that the rival gods of the YHWH of Israel were west-Semitic gods, the "Lords" (*ba'alim*) of Canaan, rather than the twelve of Olympus.[14] It spread itself even less via the philosophical schools. The danger was perceived as coming from the gymnasia: the nudity tied to the practice of sports rendered circumcision ludicrous (I *Maccabees* I, 14). But Hellenism was a bloc, and also included what we call "religion," a cult of the gods that for the Greeks was not distinguished from it. This amalgam was not acceptable to the Jews, nor, for that matter, the Christians. One therefore could formulate the following equation: "Greek culture" = *paideia* minus religion.

We therefore cannot grasp the core of the Pauline revolution if we are content to say that it constructed a synthesis between the Greek and the

---

12 See, for example: Werner Jaeger, *Early Christianity and Greek Paideia* (Cambridge, MA: Harvard University Press, 1960).

13 Plato, *Republic*, III, 403c.

14 See Elias J. Bickerman, *Der Gott der Makkabäer. Untersuchungen über Sinn und Ursprung der Makkabäischen Erhebung* (Berlin: Schocken, 1937).

Jewish and allowed the Greek element to enter into the Christian synthesis. More radically, at the same time it allowed the Greek element of culture, once cleansed of its religious dimension, to develop itself as such, that is to say, while still preserving its alterity vis-à-vis the synthesis into which it entered, but without being dissolved in it.

This allows me, if I can say in passing, to point to a connection between my book on *The Law of God* and another on the essence of western culture, *Eccentric Culture*.[15] To express the situation in concepts that I put forth then: the secondarity of Christianity vis-à-vis Judaism made possible the secondarity vis-à-vis Hellenism. Or in other terms, once again employing notions I believe I have justified elsewhere, Greek culture could be *included* and not *digested*.[16]

A culture without Christianity?

I now can turn to my initial question, which I recall: The civilization that has emerged from and wishes to depart from Christianity, can it neglect its relationship with its religious heritage? In other words, if I may be permitted a rather banal image: once the culture has been built that one can rightly qualify as "Christian," if not because of its content, at least because of its origin, can one do away with the religious scaffolding that allowed its construction?

What, therefore, would remain without Christianity?

There would be *science*. Now, it is arguable that the birth of the science of nature was made possible by the Bible, at least in the final analysis, after an entire series of mediations. I myself recalled this view earlier. But it has been quite a long while since science took up its independence from theology, and even from faith. No doubt it can continue on that path indefinitely, as well as the technology it makes possible.

Perhaps we will see the disappearance of the interest in *truth* as such. For one must believe that the truth is good, even beautiful, in order to be able to love it; and that does not go without saying. This belief, as

---

15 See *Eccentric Culture* (South Bend, IN: St. Augustine Press, 2002); *The Law of God* (Chicago: The University of Chicago Press, 2007).

16 See my "Inclusion et digestion. Deux modèles d'appropriation culturelle," in *Au moyen du Moyen Âge, op. cit.*, pp. 187–204.

Nietzsche rightly saw, is the last ray of a fire lit by Plato and by the Christianity which, he also said, is its popularization.[17] A mathematician of great distinction, Laurent Lafforgue, winner of the Fields Medal, recently recalled this.[18]

However, to begin with, one can ask if there really is a need for the idea of truth. Is it not the root of all fanaticisms? Can't one replace it by democracy, or by a "weak thought," as two philosophers, respectively Richard Rorty and the Italian Gianni Vattimo, suggested?[19] And on the other hand, won't the technology that science makes possible continue to be the best guarantee of science's survival, because technology is its best publicity? It allows the constant growth of available commodities and an ever greater comfort.

Without Christianity, there would still be what is needed to organize a viable *society*. Traditional societies based social order on customs rooted in and guaranteed by a cosmic order they were held to imitate. Thanks to several factors, this articulation of the political on the cosmological has disappeared.

As a counterpoint, modern political philosophy since Hobbes has succeeded in constructing the living-together of human beings on immanent bases. It only takes an agreement, a sort of non-aggression pact, with each one abstaining from doing evil to his neighbor in order to receive the same assurance. Modern thought thus arrives at having the social bond depend upon the self-interest rightly understood of each individual, who, above all, seeks his own preservation, then his comfort.

However, this thought seems to me to suffer from a devastating defect. It has nothing to say about the continuance, or interruption, of the human adventure.[20] For it, the existence of man on this earth is neither a good nor

---

17 Friedrich Nietzsche, *Die Fröhliche Wissenschaft*, V, # 344, *KSA*, t. 3, p. 577.
18 Laurent Lafforgue, "Le Christ est la vérité, fondement d'un enseignement catholique," a lecture give at Poissy during the annual convention of the ADDEC, 19 November 2009. Accessible at: http://www.ihes.fr/-lafforgue/textes/ChristVeriteEnseignementCatholique.pdf; see also "La recherche fondamentale a-t-elle un sens?," *Revue catholique internationale Communio*, XXXVIII, 1, n. 225, Janvier-Février 2013, *L'Idée d'Université*, pp. 27–41.
19 See my "Possiamo amare la verità?", op. cit., pp. 48–52.
20 See my *Anchors in the Heavens, op. cit.*

an evil. And in this it is right, because man does not have the right to pronounce on his own legitimacy, as party and judge in the case. In order to say something about the value of man's existence, one must place oneself at a vantage point outside of man, and invoke a creative principle capable of affirming that what he created was "very good" (*Genesis* I, 31).

But would there still be *culture*? It could very well happen that the University continues its trajectory and produces historical, literary, artistic erudition. But culture as I have defined it is a system of norms, which all aim at assuring the continuity of man and the human. It does so at two levels. First of all, at the most humble level of all, that of the substantive, man. By forbidding murder, requiring the respect of one's parents, this allows the survival of man as a species. Then norms promoting what makes man human, in the valorizing sense of the adjective. As I said, these vary according to different cultural eras, as they do not all have the same idea of what ennobles man and makes him truly human.

Religion as it is understood by Christianity does not intervene at the level of culture by proposing specific norms. It contents itself with saying that it is good that the human exists. This "goodness" of the human is not of a moral order, but a metaphysical order. Not the good of "to do," but the good of "being." This metaphysical "goodness" is the condition—the foundation—of the possibility of all other "goodnesses"—moral, aesthetic, social, etc. One must first of all be convinced that it is worth the trouble of pursuing the human adventure in order to seek the most likely means of assuring its perpetuation.

I spoke of religion as understood by Christianity. Christianity does not content itself with affirming the goodness of man in a theoretical way. It goes so far as to bestow confidence upon him in the practical domain, which is even more difficult. It lets man invent, according to the times and places, climates and temperaments, his way of "cashing out" the Decalogue, although ready to alert him when he loses his way. In a word, it lets culture be culture, to be entirely culture, but only culture.

Therefore, we have to ask: Could a culture that would turn its back on Christianity continue to be only a culture? I fear that it would spontaneously seek to reconstitute itself on the basis of religion, whatever that might be. What is called fundamentalism is an attempt of this sort. This is a religion that tells us whether Darwin was right or wrong, what to eat, how to dress. All this while there are other authorities whose competence is other than its own, and which, as in these cases, do their work well as biology, nutrition, and fashion.

That a culture is nothing but a culture is, at bottom, a paradoxical thing. The Christian relationship to culture is, as I have recalled, rather an exception than the rule, even if as members of Western civilization it seems obvious to us. Nothing is more tempting than to seek to legitimate norms by invoking the most sublime source, and to have the most crushing burden, the divine, rest upon man. It is also from this weight that Christianity delivers us. It substitutes holiness for the sacred. It replaces the sacred that demands with the holy that frees.

I therefore would answer the question posed at the beginning in this way. There exists a culture that received the mark of Christianity. It is present in the Western world and, under certain of its features, in the entire world. It is worth being promoted, to the extent that it contains the principles of civilization, e.g., renouncing violence, promoting justice, which it itself has observed more and less well during the course of its history, and which in any event deserve to be better applied and observed.

Must one defend this culture because it is Christian? Christianity, where it is most purely itself, which is to say, as a religion, puts forth arguments that ask to be appreciated as such: its conception of God, of creation, of the relation of the human to the divine. There is one thing that Christianity, following in the wake of the Old Testament, is perhaps the sole institution to be able to provide. And this thing is the ultimate foundation of culture. If culture is the way in which the human arrives at its flourishing, before every attempt to cultivate the human plant, Christianity knows why it is good that it grows on the earth.

IV
TO TEMPORIZE

11

FROM TIME TO TIME

Since Modernity above all designates a certain sort of time, in this case "Modern Times," underneath the different goals that it pursues ("emancipation," "enlightenment," and others), even beneath the direction in which it feels itself as a whole to go (an advance toward "progress"), it is important to grasp the relationship that it has with temporality.

Known time and imagined time

I will begin with a joke that puts two fine fellows talking in the following way: "A: Did you see what they said in the paper? It seems that the sun is going to go out in a billion years! B (trembling with his entire body): What!! A: Yes, the sun's going to go out in a billion years. B: Whew! You scared me. I thought you said, a million."

What does this rather silly joke tell us? The same thing that Descartes had noted: that the imagination, in this different from reason, does not distinguish between a polygon with a thousand sides and one with ten thousand sides.[1] A distance of one billion or of ten billion light years, if they are easily and precisely determined by figures, make no difference to the imagination. This is what led C. S. Lewis to formulate the following paradox: the *kosmos* was experienced by ancient and medieval man as grander than the universe in which we now live, which has expanded beyond measure. Medieval man could compare the Earth, a simple mathematical point, to the last sphere, which was absolutely, not relatively, grand. While for us, the Earth is almost nothing vis-à-vis Pluto's orbit, which in turn is next to

1   Descartes, *Meditationes de prima philosophia*, VI, *AT*, t. 7, p. 72.

nothing relative to the Milky Way, which itself is next to nothing vis-à-vis the entirety of the universe.[2]

Since Freud, people speak of the "wounding of human narcissism," which would be illustrated by the idea that man descends from the animal, i.e., the ape, two formulas which are more journalistic than rigorous.[3] Supposing that this idea is less false in the case of Darwin than that of the end of geocentrism connected to Copernicus—which I do not believe[4]—the real uncertainty of European minds would have occurred a few decades before Darwin. This would be the appearance of periods of time that surpass the imagination. This was done by geology, which explained the formation of the materials that make up the globe by basing itself on eras of unimaginable length. Since then, one speaks in a joking manner of "ice ages" to express waiting forever for someone to show up.

Geology assumed its classical form, and succeeded in making headway with the public, in the work of Charles Lyell, *Principles of Geology*, which appeared between 1830 and 1833. We have written testimonies of the way the hypotheses of geology, hypotheses which became more and more plausible as science progressed, did away with the faith of men of the caliber of Matthew Arnold and John Ruskin. They had difficulty in reconciling the biblical chronology, then taken as a tenet of faith, and the immense periods postulated by geology. Ruskin exclaimed in a letter of 1851, that is, eight years before *The Origin of Species*: "If only the geologists would leave me alone! I would be fine, without these terrible hammers! I hear their pounding at the end of each cadence of the verses of the Bible."[5]

Here, I will only speak of lived time (*temps vécus*), or rather the periods that one can imagine as lived; in brief: livable or at least imaginable times. It is because one can imagine them that these periods have an *interest* for

2   C. S. Lewis, *The Discarded Image. An Introduction to Medieval and Renaissance Literature* (Cambridge: Cambridge University Press, 1964), pp. 98–99.

3   S. Freud, *Eine Schwierigkeit der Psychoanalyse* [1917].

4   "See "Le géocentrisme comme humiliation de l'homme," in *Au moyen du Moyen Âge, op. cit.*, pp. 261–84.

5   John Ruskin, Letter to Henry Acland, 24 May 1851, cited in M. H. Abrams et al. (dir.), *The Norton Anthology of English Literature* (New York: Norton, 1974 (3rd ed.), t. 2, pp. 881–82.

us. They are capable of having some importance when we ask ourselves, what to do? And, how to do it well?

The long duration

Here I would like to examine certain periods of long duration, because they seem to me particularly pertinent, and in both directions, toward the past as well as the future.[6] I will arrange these periods inversely to their length. Then I will try to formulate their possible significance and interest.

In a general way, I would note that our experience situates itself, as it were, at the center of a temporal halo. Or if you prefer, our existence is surrounded by an aureole of past and future time. This is true in a general way, but with this qualification: the diameter of this halo or aureole varies according to the distance our camera travels in its final shot.

The longest duration, I said this earlier, is not always the subject of a living representation, and most often remains an abstraction. The longest period that can have any interest for us in the direction of the past is that of man's existence on earth, understood as a determinate living species. As Max Frisch recalled in a book that appeared in 1979, man appeared in the geological period of the Holocene.[7] In another direction, the future, one can also make long-term conjectures. Certain biologists suppose that each biological species is programmed to produce a determinate quantity of individuals. After this period, it will have exhausted its possibilities. It then must cede to another species.

Duration of such dimensions is hardly helpful for my problem. It does not allow itself to be represented by images. For the imagination, it means as little as the distances that are called—and for good reason—"astronomical." I will limit myself therefore to the periods that appear pertinent to us, and that can be grouped under the notion of "historical duration."

What is the maximal duration of what man makes, and which survives him? Here it is best to make a distinction that Aristotle seems to have been

---

6   I make use in part of the beginning of the work of Jan Assmann, *Das kulturelle Gedächtnis. Schrift, Erinnerung und politische Identität in frühen Hochkulturen* (Munich: Beck, 1977 (2nd ed.), in particular pp. 50–51.

7   Max Frisch, *Der Mensch erscheint im Holozän* (Frankfurt: Suhrkamp, 1979).

the first to make. *Poièsis* is action that produces an object by fabricating it; *praxis* is an action that has no other goal or result other than the accomplishment of the action itself.

A few thousand years is the longest documented duration for a human work in the domain of fabrication. Here one can apply an old distinction, one that Peirce perhaps found in the Stoics, between index and sign.[8] I will briefly recall it. Both indicate the presence of a phenomenon, but the first is involuntary, the second, voluntary. Smoke indicates the presence of fire, but fire has no intention thereby of drawing our attention.

Now, indices are more durable than signs. The works that have been explicitly constructed to last, monuments for example, last less longer than bones or stone tools, which maintain themselves for extremely long periods. The Great Wall of China is an example. And today, the peaks of the Egyptian pyramids look down upon us, forty-two centuries old.

A thousand years represents the longest possible duration for a human action in the domain of *praxis*, of action properly speaking, more precisely, the construction of a political reality. This period in fact touches upon the almost impossible or the hyperbolic. For Chinese poetry, "a tree of a thousand years" is the *adynaton* pure and simple, parallel to the impossible "flower with four colors." I note that when such a period seems to occur, the anniversary is celebrated with an almost religious emotion. This was the case a few years ago for the nations of central Europe such as Poland or Hungary.

A human work does not necessarily mean a work that man alone can realize. To create a work with such an imposing duration, one has need of more than the human. In *Revelations* (XX, 1–6), the millennium is established by God and received by man, who inhabits it. Even Hitler, for his "thousand-year Reich" had need of that somber power he often invoked under the name of "Providence."

In this way, the millennium would be the unit of measure of events that unfold in the human world but which touch upon the superhuman. The unit of measure that is strictly human would therefore be the century (*siècle*). Secularism therefore would be the attempt to create a purely human

8   Charles S. Peirce, *Philosophical Writings*, J. Buchler (ed.) (New York: Dover, 1955), p. 102.

chronology, in this different from the millenarian chronology which implies the superhuman.

The duration of human existence

Let's move, at least for the moment, from the duration that surpasses man to that of man himself. I will first envisage man beyond individual existence, as a generic being. What would be the maximal duration of an enterprise that would understand itself to be merely human? For me, I think just a few centuries. More precisely, perhaps,

four centuries. Let's begin with something quite strange. According to certain demographers, very serious men, only four hundred years remain to humanity to live. In any case, this is what would happen if the birthrates that today are the rule in the most developed countries were to be extended and generalized to the rest of the world.[9]

Four hundred years are perhaps the limit of immediate mutual understanding within a linguistic community. Language changes constantly, and in a way that is subtle and insensible. After four hundred years, the style of writing, vocabulary, and, even more so, pronunciation, will be so modified that the possibility of intercommunication between speakers who, by a miracle, would find themselves in contact is in no way guaranteed.

As a consequence, four hundred years are perhaps the outer limit of a given population's sentiment of identity. In any case, this is what the Bible seems to have assumed. In it, four hundred years represented the length of the stay in Egypt. This number is raised, very precisely, to four hundred and thirty years (*Exodus* XII, 40), a number that is equivalent to four centuries, but with a generation superadded. If the Egyptian captivity had lasted longer, perhaps the Jewish people would have been dissolved among the inhabitants of the Nile valley.

From this one can derive the limit beyond which, except for particular circumstances, an event is transformed into "history." The phenomenon is visible in connection with a very concrete fact, that of affective value. One can ask: What historical person can one make fun of in a particular country? The

9   Jean Bourgeois-Pichat, "Du XXe au XXIe siècle: l'Europe et sa population après l'an 2000," *Population*, 1988, pp. 9–44.

English can gibe Elizabeth I, but not the second. In France, one can caricature Henry IV or Francis I. On the other hand, the French Revolution or Napoleon are still figures of strong emotions, be they admiration or antipathy.

One is on more solid ground when one brings in the perspective of kinship. Objectively speaking, of course, the blood of countless generations of unknown ancestors flows in our veins. Even more, the information encoded in our genes is older than the entire history of our species.

In contrast, though, this is not the case with our awareness of our genealogy, which is rather limited. Language presents us with names for six generations of ancestors and six of descendants. Then, it leaves us wordless. In this way, one hundred and fifty or two hundred years is the ultimate limit, above and below, of kinship identifiable as such. Moreover, what is true in the vertical direction is true in the horizontal. The extreme limit is the sixth degree of consanguinity, cousins beyond the sixth degree do not have a name. Isidore of Seville saw profound meaning in this. Six generations are the limit of kinship, just as the world was created in six days and the total duration of the world will comprehend six eras.[10] Be that as it may, it is a circle of kinship of four hundred years that surrounds the ego.

Three hundred and nine years. The sleep of the famous "seven sleepers" of Ephesus is deemed to have lasted somewhat less than four hundred years. The story of the sleepers is recounted in a Christian legend which found its way into the Quran, where it gave its title to the eighteenth *sura*, called "the cave" after the designation of the sleepers as "men of the cavern" (*ahl al-kahf*).[11] According to the legend, they would have hidden themselves in a cave to escape martyrdom. And they remained there no less than three hundred and nine years. This corresponds to four centuries, minus three generations.

The sign used by the *sura* to indicate that time has greatly elapsed is very interesting. It was the coins with which the sleepers attempted to pay for their purchases once they awoke. Their money was no longer good and merchants refused to accept it. In the poem of Goethe which takes this legend as its subject, *Die Siebenschläfer*, the theme returns yet again. The money that was used has become a treasure, i.e., something that one does

---

10   Isidore of Seville, *Étymologies*, IX, 5–6, citation 6, # 29; see Pierre Legendre, *Le Désir politique de Dieu* (Paris: Fayard, 1988), p. 52.
11   *Quran*, XVIII, 9–26.

not spend but rather hides away.[12] With the de-monetization that is changed to a hoarding, it is political authority that reaches its limits. No sovereign can hope that the currency that bears his image will be accepted three centuries after his disappearance.

After having spoken of the duration of the collectivity, let's now move to that of the individual. And with it, we arrive at the limit of a century.

70 + 30 make **one hundred years**, and represent the maximal duration of a normal human life and of a generation.

The Latin word *saeculum* above all signifies the maximal length of a human life. It is thus that the astronomer Censorinus defines it: "A century (*saeculum*) is the longest span of human life, delimited by birth and death."[13] It was only later that the word took on the meaning that it still has today, to wit: a determinate length, measured in abstract fashion by the number 100, which no doubt was determined by the fact, itself contingent, that we count in the decimal system.

In ancient Rome, a century represented the length that in principle separated two occurrences of what were eponymously called "the Secular Games," such as those that were held in the year 17 B. C. E. and for which Horace, at Augustus's command, composed his *Carmen saeculare*. For the Latin poet, the length of a *saeculum* was not yet the 100 years that we know, but rather 110.[14] The herald charged with announcing these exceptional games solemnly proclaimed that no one who attended had already seen them, nor would see them again. The formula was cited by Suetonius when the games were celebrated under the emperor Claudius. The historian Herodian (170–240 A. D.) wrote: "The men of that day called these 'secular (*aiônios*) games' because they had heard that they were only celebrated once every three generations. Heralds traveled throughout Rome and Italy proclaiming that one would see a spectacle that had never been seen and that one would not see again."[15] However, it seems that this was something of a hyperbole, and people made fun of such an exorbitant claim.

---

12 Goethe, *West-östlicher Diwan*, "Buch des Paradieses," "Siebenschläfer," vv. 60–65.

13 Censorinus, *De die natali*, XVII, 2.

14 Horace, *Carmen saeculare*, v. 21.

15 Suetonius, *Vie des douze Césars, Divus Claudius*, xxi, 2, J. C. Rolfe.

It remains true, however, that the length of a century is not without concrete foundations. In the direction of the past, a century is the limit of the living memory of the individual "I." I can retain a memory of my grandparents and, more rarely, my great grandparents. A century is also the limit of living memory, of what my grandfather told me and what I in my turn can tell my grandchildren.

In the other direction, a century is also the limit of the concrete concerns of the I. I can occupy myself with the future situation of my children, my grandchildren, perhaps even my great grandchildren. But I have a very hard time being personally concerned with the generations that will come after.

If, by a miracle, the previous generations had survived or, conversely, if our far-off posterity was now called to life, these human beings would not mean a lot to us. This unenviable fate is what the Struldbrugs in *Gulliver's Travels* had to suffer, the unfortunate immortals of the land of Luggnagg. Until their thirtieth year, the span of one generation, they behave like normal mortals. Then they begin to suffer from a melancholy that only grows until they attain the age of eighty. At Luggnagg, as elsewhere, this age is the upper limit of the normal hope for life. When they attain that age they are considered legally dead and lose all their goods, which are given to their heirs. Their natural affections do not extend beyond their grandchildren. And at the end of two hundred years, they barely understand their fellow citizens' language.[16]

In the legal domain, one hundred years are also an upper limit, that of the longest length of a contract, what is called *tempus memoratum*.[17] Beyond it, one enters the domain of the "immemorial." The longest possible contract, called "emphyteutic," approaches the limit of a century, but without touching it, because it designates a contract for ninety-nine years. On the other hand, there is a commonplace of French law called a "brocard," which

16 Jonathan Swift, *Gulliver's Travels*, III, 10 (Oxford: Oxford University Press, "World's Classics," 1986), pp. 259–61.

17 Henry de Bracton, *De legibus et consuetudinibus Angliae* [...], fol. 230, G. E. Woodbine (ed.), t. 3, p. 186: "Item docere oportet longum tempus et longum usum qui excedit memoriam hominum. Tale enim tempus sufficit pro jure, non quia jus deficiat sed quia actio deficit vel probatio." The passage is cited in E. Kantorowicz, *The King's Two Bodies*, op. cit., pp. 180–83.

says: "Whoever has plucked the king's goose gives back its feather after a hundred years." More clearly stated: For crimes against the State, there is no statute of limitations.

Human life

When one moves to the reality of an individual life, one arrives at periods that take on importance, either because they coincide with the existence of the ego, or because they occupy a period within the duration of the ego. I do not have to speak of the normal length of human life, the Bible already fixed it at

seventy years, and it adds that eighty years represents an exploit (*gevurah*) (*Psalm* XC, 10). (It is under this same name that Jews today still celebrate the eightieth birthday of their kin and neighbors.) This length of seven times ten corresponds to a certain wisdom, about which we have a large number of witnesses. Dante said that he found himself "midway this way of life" when he was thirty-five.[18] And five centuries later, in 1803, Hölderlin entitled a poem "Half of Life," when he was thirty-three.[19]

The length of seventy years is also significant in our statistics, even if the average length of life in our developed countries easily attains what previously was called an exploit, as eighty no longer surprises us. Not to mention the promises of some doctors, who grant us a maximum of one hundred and twenty years.

Thirty to forty years constitutes a generation. This is a length that is not fixed, but approximate, precisely because it is not determined artificially, but naturally for the most part. One can situate it between two lengths that are themselves artificial. The longer one is the period that separates two jubilees (*yovel*), i.e., forty-nine years (*Leviticus* XXV, 8–16). At the end of this period, debts are remitted.

And on the other hand, there is a period that is a bit briefer:

Thirty years. According to Roman law, this is the period that allows

18 Dante, *Divina Commedia*, "Inferno," I, 1.
19 Friedrich Hölderlin, *Sämtliche Werke*, F. Beissner (ed.) (Stuttgart: Kohlhammer, 1951), t. 2, 1, p. 117.

what is called *usucapio*.[20] Thirty years of peaceful, uncontested possession of a good received in good faith (*bona fide*) on the part of the one who believes himself to be the owner of the said good, suffices for it to be recognized as his legitimate property.

Among these various long periods, generation occupies a place apart. It is among those that are the smallest possible, and thus the shortest of the long periods. But one can also say that it is the longest of the short periods. To credit Marcus Aurelius, it suffices to live forty years to exhaust the possibilities of human experience.[21]

A generation is not the minimal length a human being needs to procreate or give birth to another human being. This would only be about fifteen years, in other words, half a generation.

In the Bible, a generation—this is very important—lasts just forty years. These are the number of years the people had to spend in the desert. The oldest ocular witnesses of the exodus from Egypt have died and been replaced by a generation raised in hardship, in the precarious conditions of nomadic existence. In this way, it became capable of confronting the challenges, both physical and moral, that the conquest of Canaan would require. This at any rate is the rationalizing interpretation of this length given by Maimonides, then, no doubt following him, Ibn Khaldun.[22]

The "specious present"

This length of thirty years has a biological basis. A generation basically represents the span of a woman's sexual maturity from fecundity to menopause. As a result, it is also the maximal distance between two children born of the same mother. But the theoretical possibility exists that a child and

20 *Institutiones* (Digest), XLI, iii, 1, P. Krueger (ed.), col. 703a–708a; *Codex Justiniani*, VII, 39, 4: "De praescriptionibus XXX vel XL annorum," P. Krueger (ed.) (Berlin: Weidmann, 1915), pp. 311a–313a.

21 Marcus Aurelius, *Pensées*, XI, 2, A. S. L. Farquharson (ed.) (Oxford: Clarendon Press, 1968), p. 214.

22 Maimonides, *Guide des égarés*, III, 32, I. Joël (Ed.) (Jerusalem: Junovitch, 1929), pp. 385–86; Ibn Khaldun, *Muqaddima*, II, 18, E. Quatremère (ed.) (Paris: Duprat, 1858), t. 1, p. 256, 2–257, 8.

grandchild of the same mother might be born at the same time, or that a child has an uncle or aunt of his own age.

This length is even more interesting as the entire history of humanity depends upon, or better put: rests on this mobile, extremely fine, point. The length of the past history of the species, several hundred millions of years, or the current number of living individuals, which is several billion, here play no role. Theoretically, it would suffice to put an end to reproduction, for this span and number to disappear definitively, without hope of return.

It was ages ago that someone calculated how much time it would take, if everyone abstained from procreating, for humanity to become extinct. The number was sixty years. The figure is already found in the second part of the *Romance of the Rose*, completed by Jean de Meun toward 1280.[23] Later, in a famous sonnet Shakespeare recommends to his young friend, who perhaps was also his lover, to marry and to have children, for without marriage and procreation humanity would come to an end: "Threescore years would do the world away."[24]

In this way, from the biological point of view humanity rests entirely on the narrow base of a generation.

Psychology knows the concept of the *specious present*, brought to light by William James. Psychologists designate in this way the present, but not as an instant without any dimensions, the *nun* of Aristotle that evaporates as soon as one seeks to grasp it. Rather, it designates a certain duration, for example, the perception of a melody or an action, during which everything still seems reversible and reparable. They have been able to measure such a length. It lasts two or three seconds, which James summarizes this way:

> In short, the practically cognized present is no knife-edge, but a saddle-back, with a certain breadth of its own on which we sit perched, and from which we look in two directions into time. The unit of composition of our perception of time is a *duration*,

---

23 Jean de Meun, *Le Roman de la Rose*, vv. 19583–19598, D. Poirion (ed.) (Paris: GF-Flammarion, 1974), p. 519.
24 W. Shakespeare, Sonnet #11.

with a bow and a stern, as it were—a rearward- and a forward-looking end.[25]

It is interesting to see that James attributes a Janus-face to the specious present. In it, past and present do not merely touch. They overlap.

Now, one could employ James's concept and say that a generation is something like the specious present of humanity, that is, a present which doesn't simply concern the knowledge (*ratio cognoscendi*), but also, quite emphatically, the existence (*ratio essendi*) of humanity.

As a length, generation thus occupies a somewhat awkward place, like a bum between two chairs. On one hand, it is considerably shorter than the life of an individual (seventy/eighty years), and even more so, much less than the chronological aureole or aureoles that surround it, be they one, two, or four centuries. On the other, it is longer than the temporal window within which one can make decisions, and longer still than what is called "contemporaneity," which rubs shoulders with the minimal dimension of the instant.

The individual is immeasurably more ephemeral than the species in all its temporal extension, past and eventual. But, paradoxically, the time during which the individual is real covers a longer period than that during which the species is possible.

Beneath the threshold of a generation

The terms that are shorter than a generation are all in one way or another artificial and juridical. More precisely, each expresses in its own way the highly problematic articulation of the natural and the cultural. Let us therefore consider

ten years. This is the customary period for the prosecution of a murder. A serious crime that was committed ten years ago and which led to the extinction of a life can no longer be punished. The reason usually given is

---

25 William James, *The Principles of Psychology* [1890], chap. XV: "The Perception of Time" (pp. 605–42), "The Sensible Present has Duration" (pp. 608–10), citation on p. 609. The concept was used by Bertrand Russell, *The Analysis of Mind* [1921], Chap. IX (New York: Humanities Press, 1971), p. 174.

that after ten years the memory of witnesses is no longer worthy of credit. The past few decades, certain crimes, starting with crimes against humanity, have been declared to be imprescriptible.

Other periods of prescription are even shorter, such as the famous year and a day at the end of which an object that has been found but not claimed becomes the property of its finder.

In the Bible, **seven years** constitute the period in which the sabbatical year is placed, after a "week of years" (*Leviticus* XXV, 1–7). The land cultivated during six years is to be returned to its natural state by leaving it fallow for a year. It is as if the number "seven" had some secret rapport with the articulation of nature and culture. In a somewhat enigmatic way, Maimonides noted this when he reflected upon the reason for the Sabbath commandment of resting on the seventh day.[26]

The age of seven is ordinarily known as "the age of reason." Whoever has reached this age becomes a reasonable creature, capable of choosing *en connaissance de cause* (or in British English, having arrived at his *years of discretion*) and therefore his actions are at least partly imputable to him. It is at the age of seven that a child is deemed to have appropriated the customs of the group to which he belongs. The young boys who were to become the kings of France experienced this in a brusque and cruel manner. The very day of their seventh birthday, they were abruptly ushered from the permissive universe of childhood, where everything was play, to the pitiless discipline of the dauphin.

The period of seven years has even been taken up in a proverbial phrase, at least in German, the "wretched seventh year" (*das verflixte siebte Jahr*) during which it often happens that an amorous relation dissolves. In English, an analogous formula furnished the title of Billy Wilder's famous 1955 film, *The Seven Year Itch*. In an interesting way, here too this period seems to have some affinity with the tension between nature and culture, in this case represented by the legal institution of marriage and sexual desire.

In the series of what is called "the long term," the meaning given to the phrase by politicians comes in last place. When a politician speaks of the long term, he often just means two or three years. In general, that

---

26 Maimonides, *Guide des égarés*, III, 43.

means, until the next election. In a few special cases, ten years. In democratic countries, the summit of a political career, the most audacious dream of those who have entered that path, is the office of president of the country. In France, until a recent reform, that was seven years and, according to an unwritten rule, two terms of seven years. Today, it has been reduced to two five-year terms. In the United States, at least since Truman, who succeeded Roosevelt and his four terms, the maximum has been fixed at two terms.

To look behind and before

The periods I just enumerated concern the future as well as the past, two dimensions of time that communicate with each other.

The relationship between our attitude toward the past and our attitude toward the future was formulated at least since 1790, by Edmund Burke in his *Reflections on the Revolution in France* (which, however, he only began and never finished). He wrote the following:

> [I]t has been the uniform policy of our constitution to claim and assert our liberties as an entailed inheritance derived to us from our forefathers, and to be transmitted to our posterity— as an estate specially belonging to the people of this kingdom, without any reference whatever to any other more general or prior right. [...] This policy appears to me to be the result of profound reflection, or rather the happy effect of following nature, which is wisdom without reflection, and above it. A spirit of innovation is generally the result of a selfish temper and confined views. People will not look forward to posterity, who never look backward to their ancestors.[27]

Burke wrote the last sentence a bit in passing, in the context of a critique of the politics of France at the beginning of the Revolution, which attempted to proclaim a new constitution, while the English system knew only inherited rights. But all that is consonant with an entire way of looking at human life in the city, which he summed up elsewhere:

27   E. Burke, *Reflections on the Revolution in France, op. cit.*, p. 29.

[O]ne of the first and most leading principles on which the commonwealth and laws are consecrated is, lest the temporary possessors and life-renters in it, unmindful of what they have received from their ancestors or of what is due to their posterity, should act as if they were the entire masters, that they should not think it among their rights to cut off the entail or commit waste on the inheritance by destroying at their pleasure the whole original fabric of their society, hazarding to leave to those who come after them a ruin instead of an habitation—and teaching these successors as little to respect their contrivances as they had themselves respected the institutions of their forefathers. By this unprincipled facility of changing the state as often, and as much as, and as in as many ways as there are floating fancies or fashions, the whole chain and continuity of the commonwealth would be broken. No one generation could link with the another. Men would become little better than the flies of the summer.[28]

Here I would like to ignore the content, tied as it is to circumstances, and look only at the structure. That is, without entering into a discussion of the political reference of the declaration, I would underscore only one point. The neglect of the origin and the rejection of the future, or negligence towards the two dimensions of time, form a closely knit system. The point formulated here is already found, at least in an implicit way, in many other places, in the Bible for example, which contains simultaneously the command to honor one's parents (*Exodus* XX, 12) and the interdiction of sacrificing one's son (*Leviticus* XX, 2–5).

The chronological problem of democratic societies

In the democratic age, the paradox of the generation which I invoked above, to wit: the paradox of a period that floats between two temporalities, that of the individual and that of the species, becomes even more urgent. The democratic form of the regime and the democratic society that it

28 *Ibid.*, p. 83.

determines (and which is to be distinguished from the regime: Athens knew democracy as a regime, but not as a society) attain their peak in Modern Times.

These are notably the period when the human consciousness of time has expanded fantastically, after the abandonment of the narrow biblical chronology. To this is added the phenomenon known since the French historian Élie Halévy under the name of "the acceleration of history." The idea itself appeared earlier, in Kant, or in German historians like Gervinus or American ones like Henry Adams.[29]

However, there is something new in our democratic societies. The longest period during which politics can orient a society is much shorter than even the shortest version of a generation. One can put it this way: the *decision-making* period is much shorter than the *decisive* period. To be sure, history shows that democratic cities can treat questions that concern the long term, and that they succeed better than others.[30] However, the problems that they have to resolve, and that they handle well, concern above all what *present* citizens have *to do*, and less what concerns their perpetuation, that is, what is necessary for the city, and even the human race, to continue to exist. Until now, this perpetuation went without saying, confided as it was to instinct. This is no longer the case.

In pre-democratic societies, the "old regimes," a prince was enthroned who had care of the very long term, and who could take care of it because he had to do so. The king could remain in power longer than a generation. Thus, Louis XIV reigned from 1661 to 1715, that is, fifty-four years. The record is probably held by the Emperor of Austria and King of Hungary, Franz-Joseph, who reigned from 1848 to 1916, thus sixty-eight years. Among other things, the sovereign understood himself to be responsible for the royal family and the dynasty in its entirety. His goal was to at least maintain and, if circumstances permitted, to enlarge the domain he had inherited. That is why the edicts of the kings of France addressed themselves "to all, present and to come." More generally, the nobility had as their first

29 See Reinhart Koselleck, *Vergangene Zukunft. Zur Semantik geschichtlicher Zeit* (Frankfurt: Suhrkamp, 1979), pp. 199–201.

30 See Jean Baechler, "La démocratie et le long terme," *Bulletin de l'Académie des sciences morales et politiques*, 5, March–August 2013, pp. 47–65.

duty to have a descendant, because they knew it had been the first care of their ancestors.

One of the characteristics of our societies is the absence of any authority established and responsible for the very long term. However, the most serious problems are often precisely those that concern the very long term: education, environmental protection, demography. It is therefore important for our democracies, for whom autocracy is, happily, very much in the past, to have an equivalent, a consciously willed equivalent, that can perform the function previous fulfilled by monarchy.

Perhaps I may express my hope in an ironic manner. The "number ones" of many "earthly paradises," *caudillos*, *líderes máximos*, "dear leaders," and other "presidents for life," have recovered this wisdom, and for the "greater good of socialism" and the "greater happiness" of their unanimous and enthusiastic subjects, they have taken care to make their children or brothers their successors.

The disproportionately long duration that Darwin assumed in order to account for the evolution of species is now ended. And it ends . . . today. The past of the human species does not depend upon us. What made us belongs to the past. But what does depend upon us, what we make, is the future, and whether this future will be as long as the past.

Today, people perhaps talk a bit too much about the *dignity* of man. As for me, I would prefer to speak of his *nobility*, and thence to venture a thesis. It could be that the most urgent task of our time is to create a new nobility. Here I take hold of an intuition of Nietzsche, who never missed an opportunity to insist on the importance of the long term. He defined nobility *a contrario*, by characterizing the vulgar: whoever did not look beyond his grandfather.[31] In the past, the nobility constituted a dominating elite. What I hope for, however, is not at all the restoration of such a social stratum. It is rather the establishment in each and every man of an ennobling awareness of temporality.

I therefore would say, not without a smile, that it is the grammatical particle that makes nobility. How so? Someone is noble who is *of* someone, *of* somewhere, *of* some thing. And who, knowing himself to be in this way, also wants something, and someone, to come *from* him.

---

31 Friedrich Nietzsche, *Also sprach Zarathustra*, III, "Von alten und neuen Tafeln," # 11, *KSA*, t. 4, p. 254.

I will end with a final question. If, as everything leads us to believe, the theory of evolution is more than a hypothesis, what interpretation of the discoveries of Darwin and his successors allows us to conceive of the *nobility* of the human in the meaning I just limned, and thus gives us good reasons to continue the human adventure?

12

HOW ONE WRITES HISTORY

Modernity understands itself as a rupture with the past which, nonetheless, led to it. It is the result of a history, of a process whose history it is pleased to recount (thus, a second sense of "history"). It is historical science that gives us knowledge of the past, although not without doing so in a particular manner, marked with the spirit of Modern Times. We therefore need to examine the way in which we, we modern men, write history.

My title above contains several allusions. First of all, to the current ironical expression: "Look how one writes history!," which is employed when one wants to emphasize that a fact has been misinterpreted and, quite possibly, error has been passed on to posterity. Then, to a little satirical treatise in Greek by Lucian of Samosata (second century A.D.), with a similar title: *How one must write history*.[1] Finally, I distinguish myself on more than one point from a well-known book on the same subject, and with the same title.[2]

In this way, I will describe an actual practice of historiography, but will also indicate some of the rules that should be observed.

Knowledge by traces

History has as its object the past, that is, what no longer exists. Now, we can only perceive what is present. Therefore, we must found our knowledge of the past on the knowledge we possess of certain present facts, among which those that indicate a past fact can be called *traces*. The art of the historian consists first of all in identifying certain facts, certain objects, as

1   Lucian of Samosata, *How one must write history*, treatise n. 59.
2   Paul Veyne, *Comment on écrit l'histoire. Essai d'épistémologie* (Paris: Seuil, 1971).

constituting traces. It then consists in interpreting them correctly. The great historian will be he who knows how to make traces speak that no one before him had thought of interrogating, and connecting them.

One can draw a negative consequence from this thesis. Where no trace subsists, there is nothing to do, because there is nothing to interpret. The most perfect forgetting is forgetting the forgetting. We do not yet have forgetting when one remembers that he forgot something.

The subsisting traces must be correctly understood. Thus, the archeologist must explain the meaning of the objects he discovers. To do so, he is obliged to venture hypotheses, a risky venture. What would one say about our own civilization if every written or recorded text disappeared?

This, by the way, is not an abstract possibility. The new computer discs and flash drives allow us to stock and transmit many more elements than ancient materials such as inscription stones or papyrus, parchment or paper, did. But they are only readable on fragile machines that wear out rather soon, while the more primitive materials can sometimes last for centuries.

Recently, some archeologists amused themselves with an exhibition of objects of today, but artificially aged by various procedures. The archeologists who had this idea impishly avoided in their commentaries giving these objects very specific interpretations; but the deliberately fantastical hypotheses that they did provide were all perfectly plausible. For example, the remains of a crucifix were connected to the photo of a cyclist holding up his arms at the finish line, and a garden gnome was understood as a field deity, etc.[3]

An incomplete knowledge

We only know that of which we possess traces. Whatever has totally disappeared, we do not even know that we don't know it. And of what subsists, we are never sure that we have the context which renders it intelligible.

As a consequence, the danger is great to *reduce* the past to what we have traces of, to equate the past with what we can know of the past. This is the case with prehistoric humans. We are tempted to confuse what is

---

3 See, for example: Laurent Flutsch, *Futur antérieur. Trésors archéologiques du XXIiem siècle après J.-C.*, Catalogue de l'exposition Musée romain de Lausanne-Vidy, October 2002–April 2003, Infolio, 2003.

primitive with what is brutish. But what do we know about the intellectual and spiritual life of peoples before writing, of their vision of the world, of their religion?

Example 1. The Australian aborigines, even today, annually celebrate festivals during which clans of the same tribe who ordinarily live apart, come together. Goods are exchanged, marriages concluded, poems are recited. At the completion of the festivities, a summary is painted on the wall of a grotto.[4] In this way, we only have rather impoverished traces of events of great richness. When similar paintings are found on the walls of prehistoric caves, we ought to recognize that they only represent a very small part of what the humans of the time lived and experienced.

Example 2. Plato's dialogues bear subtitles, for example, *Charmides or On moderation* (*sôphrosunè*), *Meno or On virtue* (*aretè*), which reflect the main theme of these works. But these subtitles ought to make the reader laugh out loud: Charmides was the most extreme and sanguinary of the Thirty Tyrants; Meno handed over the Greek army to the Persians and was the very archetype of the traitor: we would call him "Judas." We are lucky enough to know the lives of these men by other means. How many other allusions escape us?

Example 3. In European literature there is a recurrent phrase: *to be or not to be*. One can also find the ironic version, for example in Emmanuel Levinas: "To be or not to be, is that the question?"[5] How would we interpret those words if we had not preserved the works of Shakespeare? Perhaps we would think of Parmenides, lacking a precise indication of the source. Now, please note the paradox: The most well known passages are precisely those that one would be ashamed of giving the exact reference, for fear of appearing to be a pedant.

From events to "causes" that are not always knowable

All history bears upon events. To speak of "historical events" is to state a pleonasm. But events unfold according to different rhythms. There

---

4   Here I recall a lecture by the Italian historian of prehistory, E. Anati.
5   E. Levinas, *Éthique comme philosophie première*, 6, J. Rolland (ed.) (Paris: Rivages poche, 1998), p. 107.

are those that are very rapid, such as the birth of an heir to the throne, or a battle. There are those that are slower, like a war. There are those that are very slow, such as what Fernand Braudel recounts in his masterwork, the displacement of the center of gravity of international commerce from the Mediterranean to the Atlantic in the sixteenth century.[6]

Now, the causes of some events, which are among the most important, are unknown, and perhaps even unknowable.

Example 4. The lowering of the birthrate in eighteenth-century France. Contraception previously was the privilege of a small urban elite, noble and bourgeois. Around 1750, peasants started limiting births by different means. The consequences were vast, and continue to affect us today. At the time of the Revolution, France had a population equal to that of the rest of Europe; today, it represents about a tenth. If it had continued to develop according to the rate of the other European countries, today it would have two or three hundred million inhabitants. In fact, France would have begun to depopulate in the nineteenth century if not for successive waves of immigrants, Italian, Polish, Spanish, Portuguese, then Chinese and Maghrebian. As a consequence of this demographic weakness, France was not able to populate the New World, with the exception of a province in Canada. In contrast, the British Isles were able to do so because their birthrate didn't lower until the middle of the nineteenth century. Today, the international language is that of the most powerful country in the world, the United States of America. To sum up this line of reflection: If today we are obliged to speak English, it is because our ancestors practiced contraception. The phenomenon was noted at the time and raised some alarm. However, when it comes to this massive fact, with its enormous consequences, no one knows its causes. And no one will ever know them, because, even if by a miracle we could go back a few centuries in time, that would be of no help. The people then did not know exactly why they acted the way they did. For, do we ourselves know why *we* act? In fact, do we really know that we are acting?

6   Fernand Braudel, *La Méditerranée à l'époque de Philippe II* (Paris: Colin, 1949), 2 vol.

Spectacular "causes" and real causes

When we recount the past, we have a tendency to prefer ostentatious, spectacular causes to those that are real, but lacking in luster. Our vision of the past is irredeemably marked by the cinema. One could say that we have a Hollywood vision of the past. We privilege the most striking events, even if their explanatory value is modest, even nil.

Example 5. The population of the New World experienced a precipitous decline after its discovery. We do not have precise statistics, but reasonable estimates indicate a demographic catastrophe. In face of this, one imagines collective massacres of unheard-of amplitude, which, however, were technologically impossible. What, then, were the real causes? There were two. The first was physiological. With the conquistadors came microbic and viral strains that the natives did not have. These were organisms for which Europeans had learned over the centuries to produce antibodies. However, isolated during these centuries, the Amerindians no longer produced them. They therefore succumbed to diseases that had become rather innocuous to the Europeans. There are contemporary parallels: when an unknown tribe is discovered, as was the case in New Guinea a few years ago, people hasten to isolate it, so as not to infect it with our diseases.

The second cause of the demographic collapse was psychological. It was the disorientation, the despair before the lost points of reference, which led to a cratering of births. To be sure, there were also Indian revolts that were cruelly repressed. But their effect was limited. Spain and Portugal, it seems, killed many fewer in Latin America than the British in North America or in Australia. The fact therefore is known. However, in a certain way it is deceiving. We don't regret the lack of bloody massacres, at least one hopes not, but we experience a certain regret or even irritation before explanations that are so mundane. Hollywood has played tricks on us by forming, or rather deforming, our vision. One can make a film with lots of colors and sounds involving a battle between conquistadors and Indians. But not with an Indian who is dying of fever on his mat, or even less so, featuring a native who does *not* sleep with his wife.

A history written retrospectively

We ask: "How does *one* write history?" Yes, but *who* exactly is this "one"?

First of all, it is professional historians, those who possess a professional ethic, a deontology, which has been defined since Antiquity, for example by Lucian, whom I already mentioned, but even before him by Tacitus. The historian is the one of strict impartiality, who writes *sine ira et studio*, without partisan anger or zeal.[7]

In any case, history is written by someone in the present, a truism that can take on a negative cast. History is often the way in which a present institution recounts the past so as to understand *itself* as the necessary culmination of that past. What is called "the history of France," and which was taught for a long time in the schools with the aid of images and stereotypes, is a discipline that was cut off from the rest of European and global history. It was to show either how the French nation was formed and had grown great thanks to the ruling dynasty, or, conversely, how it led spontaneously to the establishment of the republican regime.

Example 6. The French Third Republic chose Vercingetorix as its first national hero. Hence the weirdness of academic manuals which speak of "our ancestors, the Gauls," then observe that at a certain moment "Gaul" was called "France," without explaining the change of name. The reason, above all, was that one must not begin the history of France with the Franks, which began with the baptism of Clovis. The history of the nation had to be severed from its baptism. At the time, the Republic fought against the remains of the Old Regime and against the Catholic Church. To choose Vercingetorix, the enemy of the Romans, was to kill two birds with one stone.

"History is written by the victors." This phrase has become proverbial. Hence, the new task of the historian is to scour the historical materials to reconstruct the point of view of the vanquished, a program announced by Walter Benjamin.[8] History can thus take on a subversive value.

In this connection, we could note a paradox. The fact that history is written by the victors can be turned against them. We possess photographic

---

7   Tacitus, *Annals*, I, 1, 3.
8   Walter Benjamin, *Geschichtsphilosophische Thesen*, # 7, in *Schriften* (Frankfurt: Suhrkamp, 1955), p. 498.

evidence of the way that whites treated black slaves in the nineteenth century. The reason for this is two-fold. On one hand, and obviously, they had slaves; but above all, because they had cameras. In contrast, we have no images of ancient or medieval slavery. For this reason, they speak less to our sensibility and excite less scandal.

History as the objectification of the past

This thesis is implicitly contained in the very phrase "to write history," a paradoxical expression because it means to inscribe by writing, and thus to fix, what might fall into oblivion. This was already Herodotus's intent: that noble actions might not be effaced. One writes history for posterity, to leave a "possession for all time" (*ktèma es aieí*), as Thucydides put it.[9]

The enterprise of objectifying the past does not occur automatically. On the contrary, it represents something deeply contrary to nature, even violently artificial, because what we really live in is tradition, not history, and tradition is not objective, but marks us even more. By way of imitation, without willing it, or even being particularly aware of it, we receive the essentials of our lives from it. Above all, we receive language (which is always one or more definite languages) and all that language conveys. But also stylized gests, eating and clothing habits, all that we take for granted.

Why then objectify the past? Once it is objectified, the past can be shared. One can come to an agreement concerning the facts. The intentions of agents can be the object of various hypotheses, their moral appreciation subject to controversy, but the narrative of the facts ought to be common.

If each has his own history, dialogue is impossible. The strongest will impose his narrative. Conversely, the past that has become the object of history loses its virulence. Here, however, we encounter a circle. A common history is not possible unless a desire to have a common future exists; and this desire supposes that the wounds of the past are healed, or at least acknowledged and bandaged.

Example 7. The Franco-German reconciliation of the 1960s, brought about by de Gaulle and Adenauer, made possible the writing of common manuals of history that put the accent on a European perspective. This perspective itself came from an attitude of pardon vis-à-vis the past, a

9 Herodotus, *Histories*, I, 1; Thucydides, *Peloponnesian War*, I, 22, 4.

mutual awareness of common faults, and a refusal to consider the other as alone culpable and oneself as completely innocent. Those who effected this reconciliation were Christians. They aimed to extend God's mercy in a mutual forgiveness of offenses.

History as an enlargement of perspective

This has been known for a long time, and it can even be repeated with Seneca: Thanks to history, we can, in principle, enter into communion with the entire past of humanity.[10]

In some famous verses, Goethe gave us the task of knowing how to find ourselves in *three* thousand years of history, without which we would grope in the darkness: "He who of three thousand years/Does not know how to give an account/Let him remain in the darkness, without experience/And live from day to day."[11]

One, moreover, can note that these three thousand years from Goethe's time are lacking in ambition vis-à-vis the beginning of history, which is conventionally located at the invention of writing, towards 3000 B. C. E. To begin with Homer, who dates from the tenth century of our era, or by the oldest texts of the Bible, which date pretty much from the same time, is to agree to miss out on two thousand years. One would have to go before the two sources, Greek and biblical, Athens and Jerusalem, to the great fluvial civilizations of Egypt and Mesopotamia.

In French, "to enlarge" also means "to liberate," as when one says, "to put a prisoner at large." The word play is significant because history in fact has a liberating function. This is what Wilhelm Dilthey wrote: "History makes us free, in that it elevates us above whatever conditioned our perspective concerning the importance of things that we imbibed during the course of our life [...] To meditate on life makes one profound; to study its history, makes one free."[12]

10 Seneca, *De brevitate vitae*, XIV, 1–2, A. Bourgery (ed.) (Paris: Les Belles Lettres, 1923), p. 68.

11 Goethe, "Und wer franzet oder britet . . . ," in *West-östlicher Diwan*, "Rendsch Nameh—Buch des Unmuts," H.-J. Weitz (ed.) (Frankfurt: Insel, 1988), p. 53.

12 Wilhelm Dilthey, *Der Aufbau der geschichtlichen Welt in den Geisteswissenschaften*, Gesammelt Schriften, vol. VII (Leipzig/Berlin: Teubner, 1927), p. 252.

History raises us above our smallness. In truth, it could very well be the case that men of the past were greater than we. One has to be great oneself in order to understand great men. "To judge great and high things, one needs a soul of that sort, otherwise we attribute to them our vice."[13] Hegel reflected upon the proverb "for his valet, there is no great man." This is true, he admitted; but it is not because a great man is not great, but because the valet is a valet, who only sees the small aspects of things.[14]

To be sure, the historian should not allow himself to believe and accept as gospel truth everything recounted by flatterers. But a history that would deprive us of the capacity to admire would be a very impoverished thing.

To write and to rewrite history

The past doesn't change. What does change and does not cease to change is our knowledge of the past and our understanding of it. One therefore must constantly rewrite history. It is too bad that the adjective "revisionist" has been monopolized by historians who have suspect motives, because I would like to say that history is essentially revisionist. In fact, it makes progress by constantly revising its results.

For a long time history consisted in reading the works of earlier historians. History in the modern sense of the term was born in the seventeenth century with the works of those who were called "antiquarians," who collected ancient documents or objects such as coins. These antiquarians studied the monuments and inscriptions of Antiquity, until the day when they perceived that the information furnished by the objects did not always coincide with the narratives of classical authors. They ended by calling into doubt the veracity of the Ancients, either by bringing to light the motives (propaganda) or the biases that motivated them.

One could therefore say that history began to be written at the moment

---

13 Montaigne, *Essais*, I, 14, P. Villey (ed.) (Paris: Alcan, 1930), t. 1, p. 120; an almost literal quote from Seneca: "magno animo de rebus magnis judicandum est, alioqui videbitur illarum vitium esse quod nostrum est," *Letters to Lucilius*, 71, 24.

14 Hegel, *Phänomenologie des Geistes*, J. Hoffmeister (ed.) (Hamburg: Meiner, 1948), pp. 467–68.

when people grew distrustful of what had already been written. The history being written did not trust the written history.

This work has been well advanced for the history of the West, Antiquity included. It remains to do it for large areas of the history of the Middle East.

Since then, people have not ceased to find new traces, thanks to archeology and the other auxiliary sciences of history such as numismatics, epigraphy, or papyrology. Dendrochronology studies the years of growth of trees and allows one, by means of their width, to know the climate of past centuries. Genetics allows one to reconstruct the migrations of peoples.

One poses new questions to the available traces thanks to the appearance of new disciplines such as the human sciences. Psychoanalysis allows us to better understand the motivations of individuals, even collective representations. Sometimes it allows us to judge them in a more favorable light.

Example 8. The medieval ordeal, what was called the "judgment of God." First of all, one needs to consider this practice as it really was, not as it is imagined. An accused was asked to take hold of an iron bar red from the fire. Today, as I heard recently on the radio, we imagine that if he wasn't burned, he was innocent. This would mean that it could not happen except by a literal miracle. In reality, though, it goes without saying that the accused would always burn his hand. It was covered with ointment, bandaged, and one waited a few weeks. If the wound healed well, that spoke in favor of the accused; if it delayed in healing and became infected, that was a bad sign.[15] At first glance, we only see superstition and savagery. But this impression dissolves if one examines the problem to which it was the solution. The Middle Ages did not know scientific policing, fingerprints, DNA. A forensic examination was impossible. One had to have recourse to witnesses and oaths. Without the ordeal, it would be the most insolent liar who would win. The ordeal worked on the basis of the somatic consequences of the sentiment of guilt. It was to bet that the one who was and knew himself innocent, thus confident in God's justice, would heal quicker. This was a self-fulfilling prophecy of sorts, which had a good chance of being correct.

15   See Peter Brown, "Society and the Supernatural: A Medieval Challenge," *Daedalus*, 104, 1975, pp. 133–51.

For a "de-moralization" of history

With the thesis indicated in the title above, I oppose Schiller's famous play on words: "The history of the world (*Weltgeschichte*) is the judgment of the world (that is to say, the final Judgment) (*Weltgericht*)."[16]

My thesis has a very contemporary context. Europe today suffers from a relationship to its own past that has become diseased and even toxic. Here the past is considered in an entirely negative light. A particularly revealing case is the celebration of the discovery of America which took place in 1992, but which quickly turned to remorse and repentance. Everything took place as if Europeans had adopted the Christian sacrament of penance and had given themselves over to a confession of their sins, but without any hope of absolution.

In this connection, I have the habit of recounting a fable of my own invention (with apologies to La Fontaine). I call it "The elephant and the mouse in the china shop." A very gentle elephant and a very wicked mouse each entered a china store. Who caused the greatest commotion? It was the elephant, of course, not because of its ill will, but because it was huge. The mouse, who as a matter of fact did want to destroy everything in the store, was too small to do so. Europe has done much ill in, and to, the rest of the world; in part, because it did not limit itself to sending saints, but even more so because it had the material means to intervene from outside that other civilizations did not possess.

History recounts facts that merit a moral judgment. The past exists under the same sign as the present and the future: all three are subject to the exigencies of good and evil. But history is not, *in itself*, a universal tribunal. Before judging, and above all before condemning, one must try to understand the actions of historical agents, first of all as responding to problems posed at a specific time. As such, one needs to begin by grasping their internal rationality from what we could call an economic point of view. Were the means that were employed, among those that were available at the time, were they the most apt to obtain the maximum result with the minimum of expense (in money, energy, time, men)? The moral judgment will come after.

16   Schiller, *Resignation* [1786].

Example 9. "Tolerance" is a virtue extolled by all the world. Its historical origin is however more sober. First of all, it was a *modus vivendi* following the failure of the so-called Wars of Religion, which aimed, for Protestants, at taking power, for Catholics, at eliminating the rebels. It was a consequence of another principle, formulated in the Treaties of Westphalia (1648): *cujus regio, ejus religio*. The subjects of a State are deemed to have the religion of the reigning family; if this is not the case, and if they refused to convert, they could emigrate, or (here's the word), be "tolerated." Today this seems to us to be monstrous. But we need to look closer. The principle came after the Thirty Years War, which saw the loss of a *third of the population* of Germanic countries. In other words, it needs to be seen as a solution. The princes had every interest in tolerating minorities for the sake of economic reasons. Moreover, in the regions we are talking about, which formed a mosaic of small States, in the worst case "emigrate" meant moving a few kilometers. This compromise thus constituted a means of limiting disputes and avoiding a new bloodbath.

In the preceding, I believe I have recalled something obvious, that to write history is a task that has its special rules. I also tried to show that to turn to the past can have, even ought to have, positive effects on the present. To be sure, this is on the condition that we show the past the same concern for the rules of justice that each man, here and now, owes to another. Modern Times, though, have a way of looking at the past, in fact are constituted by this way, which detaches them from the past, and which is, precisely, "the historical perspective." To become aware of this particular optic, which is not the only one possible, would be a first step toward a better relationship with the past that made us what we are.

13

THE CONDITIONS OF A FUTURE

Modernity quite obviously had a past. That it should have a future is much less clear, if only because the future in general is not clear. For how to speak about the future, how to make conjectures about its content, that is, about future events about which we know nothing? Here I will simply ask, what are the conditions for having a future? The first, the only indispensable one, is that there are men to live it. But what conditions must be met to satisfy that one?

Implosion?

It has been a while since people have talked about a "demographic explosion." The expression seems to have been first employed in Boston on August 28, 1968, not by a demographer, but by the American sociologist Philip M. Hauser, in the opening address to a sociology conference. He spoke of a *population explosion* as one of four factors in a "revolution" in the "social morphology," meaning by the phrase "the remarkable increase in the birthrate of the world population, especially during the course of the three centuries of the modern era."[1] Since then, the expression has known enormous success, to the point of becoming commonplace, but at the price of a distortion of meaning, since today it means an *exponential* growth in the world population. However, professional demographers have known from the beginning that such an idea is false; more and more even think that it is the contrary of the truth. Today the idea of a demographic explosion is dead and buried, except among certain reactionary sorts who have remained where they were in the sixties.

1 Philip M. Hauser, "The Chaotic Society: Product of the Social Morphological Revolution," *American Sociological Review*, 34, 1969, pp. 1–19, citation on p. 3b.

Today, the dominant model is that of a classical "demographic transition," like the one that took place earlier in the West. With progress in hygiene and in medicine, mortality lowers, and in particular infant mortality drops in a spectacular way, and ends by only touching a tiny sliver of the population. Births drop too, because it is no longer necessary to have many children to assure the replacement of generations. The impression of an explosion in the Third World comes from a process that in Europe unfolded slowly, over a long time, and hence was imperceptible, but elsewhere has occurred suddenly. Doctors and medicines from the West have caused infant mortality to drop abruptly, and the various populations have taken a certain amount of time to adjust their birthrates to needs, by lowering them. But one eventually should arrive at a stabilization of the world population, with a rate of 2.1 infants per woman, ending with an order of greatness of ten billion human beings in total.

This model is the official model of the United Nations. It is the most widely adopted, the most financially supported by international organizations, as well as the media. But it isn't the only possible one, and certain demographers contest it, among them some of the best-known. I will take as my point of departure an article already become classic, published in 1988 by Jean Bourgeois-Pichat, former director of the French *Institut National d'Études Démographiques*. The famous demographer was then at the peak of his career and toward the end of his life (he was to die in 1991). He had nothing to gain or lose. He therefore delivered, in a calm tone and in a very technical journal, a synthesis of his views of the future, even ending with a bit of science fiction. He notes that the rates of European countries seem to have settled in a lasting way *below* those that allow social reproduction. He therefore did not hesitate to speak not of an explosion, but an implosion.[2]

Since then, the idea of a demographic decline is found just about everywhere. Even among men of balanced judgment and little inclined to

2   Jean Bourgeois-Pichat, "Du XXe au XXIe siècle: l'Europe et sa population après l'an 2000," art. cit., pp. 9–44, citation p. 16. The expression is also found in Hauser, *op. cit.*, p. 41. But he understood something completely different: "the cumulative concentration of the world population on a small portion of the earth's surface, the phenomenon of urbanization and metropolitization."

enthusiasms such as Raymond Aron, who in his *Mémoires* published in 1983 wrote: "Europeans are in the process of committing suicide by their drop in birth rates."[3] Some politicians took up the idea. Thus Michel Rocard (†2016), in a speech given at the Congress of families when he was Prime Minister, reprised the phrase: "The majority of western European States [sic! He should have said, "nations"] are in the process of committing suicide by demography, without being aware of it."[4] The former President of the Republic, François Mitterrand, followed his lead. However, it is important to note that the majority of politicians give the same speech at election time, especially when they address family associations, thus preparing public opinion for measures they will never enact.

To be sure, the population of Europe continues to increase, but at a less and less rapid pace. It probably will continue to do so until the thirties, even forties, of the twenty-first century. What will come next is very conjectural, but everything leads one to believe that it will begin to decline. We do not know at what pace. In any case, if one supposes that the figures concerning Germany, the most populated country of Europe (if one excepts Russia, which isn't entirely in Europe) and the most advanced, will be generalized, it is easy to foresee the disappearance of European peoples around 2250. That is the date rather calmly put forth by Jean Bourgeois-Pichat.

The injection of barbarians

Are we going to be "overwhelmed by barbarians" come from outside? That certainly is a fantasy, but it is not entirely implausible. It would not be the first time that a civilization disappeared in this way. The barbarian invasions leading to the fall of the Roman Empire are well-known, they are among the fundamental traumas of Western history, to the extent that, as Tocqueville put it, "we are perhaps too inclined to believe that civilization cannot die otherwise."[5] Now, one of the hypotheses concerning the reasons for

---

3   Raymond Aron, *Mémoires. Cinquante ans de réflexion politique* (Paris: Julliard, 1983), p. 750.
4   Michel Rocard, concluding speech at the Conference of families, 20 January 1989.
5   Alexis de Tocqueville, *De la démocratie en Amérique*, II, 1, 10, op. cit., p. 557.

this fall is the lack of human material, what the Ancients (the historian Polybius for example) already called "oliganthropia." Max Weber took up the idea.[6] What are called the barbarian invasions would have been, among other things, the consequence of the inhilation produced by this demographic void.

However, the current tendency of historians is to minimize the quantitative importance of population transfers. Nor are we obliged to see this process as we too often do, which is to say: from the point of view of the invaded. The ancient world found itself regenerated by what are called "the barbarian invasions." I myself would not call them that. For one reason, because "barbarian" is a biased term that reflects the prejudice of the Greeks and Romans against those who did not speak their languages; and for another, because it seem to me better to speak of barbarian *injections*, an infusion of new blood, a revitalizing transfusion in an anemic organism, an idea that is already found in the eighteenth century with Herder.[7]

One can dream of something analogous for the exhausted West. The barbarians who would be able to invade are not so bad. Everything taken into account, those of Antiquity weren't either. There are examples of Roman peasants going to barbarian lands in order to escape the intolerable pressure of a Roman State that had become despotic.[8] If one draws up the West's ledger, does it have so much about which to pride itself? Would it not have reached its end?

I therefore will restate my question. Are we going to be overwhelmed? Alas, no. Not at all. For the problem is that barbarians are not so abundant on the market. The regions of the world from which one might hope for an influx are themselves afflicted with lower birthrates. Certain zones from

---

6   See Max Weber, "Die sozialen Grundlagen des Untergangs der antiken Kultur" [1896], in M. Sukale (ed.), *Schriften zur Soziologie* (Stuttgart: Reclam, 1995), pp. 49–75; on the problem, see Santo Mazzarino, *The End of the Ancient World. Avatars d'un thème historiographique*, trans. G. Holmes (Paris: Knopf, 1966), chap. III, pp. XXX–XXX.

7   J. G. Herder, *Auch eine Philosophie der Geschichte zur Bildung der Menschheit*, 2. Abschnitt, the beginning, in W. Pross (ed.), *Werke* (Darmstadt: Wissenschaftliche Buchgesellschaft, 1984), t. 1, p. 622.

8   See Henri-Irénée Marrou, *Décadence romaine ou antiquité tardive? III-Ve siècle* (Paris: Seuil, 1977), pp. 140–41.

which not so long ago one feared disturbing rumblings, such as the Brazilian Nordeste, are now destabilizing. In addition, we now see that previously forecast figures were considerably inflated. The most striking example is perhaps Nigeria. One formerly estimated that it was going to have 122 million inhabitants in 2000; the first credible census, that of 1991 (which took place before the civil war) counted 88 million. At most we can hope (or fear, depending upon one's view) that a portion of the population of the Third World will come to populate the north of the planet.

But the real question is to know if depopulation is something that necessarily affects developed countries? Therefore, supposing that the rest of the world becomes developed, it too would become a victim. If the rest of the world is to follow the lead of the West, this immigration would only be a temporary answer. Again according to Bourgeois-Pichat, it is the entire human race that is to disappear, a bit later than Europe, around the year 2400.

At this point I leave the terrain of demographic conjecture. Not without underscoring that, on one hand, I am not in my element here, and, on the other, that even the rapid incursions of an amateur show that it is a rather fraught field. In it, facts and arguments are often overwhelmed by political interests, taboos, even account-settling between individuals or institutions.

I, therefore, am unable to judge the probability of the different scenarios that are proposed. But it is permitted to examine them as hypotheses that can allow certain thought experiments. The atomic bomb give Karl Jaspers the occasion of reflecting upon the possibility of humanity annihilating itself. A nuclear conflagration is improbable, no doubt, but it has become a real possibility since the material means of achieving it exist.[9] Almost twenty years after Hiroshima, the "pill" allowed a limitation of births much less disagreeable than the contraceptive procedures used until then. Henceforth, humanity has the real possibility of a more subtle self-destruction, what one could call a *soft* apocalypse. Perhaps philosophers, without playing prophets, should at least reflect upon such a possibility.

9   Karl Jaspers, *La Bombe atomique et l'avenir de l'humanité* [1958], trans. E. Saget (Paris: Buchet-Chastel, 1962).

The children of Mohammed and those of Maurice

This catastrophic scenario supposes that the rest of the world will follow the West on the path to disappearance. Now, why wouldn't it? The model of a two-child family, or of happy singlehood, has been diffused throughout the planet by television series produced by Western media. And what the West has diffused is not only second-order entertainment, but far better things as well. Among the things come from Europe are the increase in lifespan, lowering of infant mortality, the extension of the period given to the education of the young, greater participation of women in professional activities and public life, in other words, elements difficult to deny that they are benefits. All of them, however, can contribute to a reduction in the number of children per family.

Now, immigration cannot have positive effects if this number declines among the newcomers. In a poster which appeared in November 1997, the association "SOS Racism" invited the French to reflect upon immigration by featuring a figure who symbolized them, and who was given the smartly chosen, very French name, "Maurice." The text went: "If there weren't any children of Mohammed, there would be no pension for Maurice." The subtitle was even clearer: "Starting in 2000, the contribution of the children of immigrants will be all-important to pay for pensions."

Given in response to a maladroit comment by Jean-Pierre Chevène-ment, the goal was to combat the idea of "national preference." With its excellent intentions, the poster nevertheless gave the game away, and cast stark light on a rather sordid economic situation. In a word, immigration is a good deal. It imports producers whose development and education cost nothing to the receiving country. I will not enter into a discussion of the truth or not of the slogan. The validity of the economic argument, which seems at first glance so obvious, has been contested.[10]

The problem is that "Mohammed" is no more stupid than anyone else, and he understands very well what "Maurice" expects from him: to slave away and to raise his children. His children's work will maintain Maurice in his palatial residence. One can understand that Mohammed is hesitant

---

10   See in particular M. Tribalat, *Les Yeux grand fermés. L'immigration en France* (Paris: Denoël, 2010).

to bring children into the world for such a noble task, and that the size of immigrant families tends after one generation to be the same as those of families said to be "indigenous."

Let's return to our European societies, to "Maurice" and his children. How can one blame them for being so little generative? How can one criticize the generations capable of reproducing? Still, our societies do need to encourage them to do so. However, this is not what happens. A belated entry into professional life, one that begins and continues in uncertainty, with the threat of unemployment, and many other economic and psychological factors, including the sentiment of guilt inherited from previous generations—all that does not encourage the formation of families. Especially when the image of the family circulated by certain medias is hardly positive. In such a situation, why aid the young to start a family? This would entail a redistribution of social wealth in their favor. A change of this sort is very unlikely, while the opposite is more likely.

The aging of the population unleashes a multiplier mechanism.[11] The generation that has children is, in general, between twenty and forty years old. Those of less than twenty, minors, don't have a vote in the matter. The retired, say those from sixty to sixty-five years old, have a good portion of the wealth, but their influence is less. The real deciders, those who have the economic, financial, and media power, are between thirty-five or forty and the aforementioned age of retirement. And their power only grows with age. Society is controlled by people who are between fifty and seventy years old. The center of gravity thus moves towards the retired.

As for political power, in our democratic societies it rests on the principle of "one man, one vote," which neglects the age of the voters. Now, the average age of a voter in France is already around fifty. And it regularly grows older.

Therefore, when the distribution of the national wealth is to be decided, it is easy to wager that those who do so, will do so in favor of their own age-group, and the age-group that follows them, which, thanks to nature, is destined to join them. The portion dedicated to young married couples will accordingly be diminished in favor of the retired. Our society will then rest on an alliance of mature adults and seniors against children.

11   Jean Bourgeois-Pichat, *art. cit.*, pp. 13–15.

In face of this, some will feel like responding with moralizing fervor. "What selfishness!" To be candid, I have the same feeling myself, although I would not beat up someone else about it. If there is a generation to blame, it is my own, children of the baby-boomers, who were twenty in 1968, often arrested adolescents, but who are currently at the helm.

Democracy and demography

However, I will abstain from doing so, and I prefer to pose a fundamental question. By what right can one protest? Isn't this system perfectly legitimate? The retired vote, while children cannot. And those who have not come into the world, even less so. How can one do otherwise? This system flows from the logic of actual democracy. One must occupy oneself with those who are here, one must "take care of the present," and, in any case, "in the long run we are all dead."

This is even a direct consequence of the democratic ideal. Democracy takes decisions by an assembly of voters. Now, there is at least one condition that voters must fulfill. They must exist. By what right, therefore, deprive the people who presently exist of anything, in order to have the absent come into being? By what right privilege nothing over being? Here we are in full metaphysical mode. Or at least engaged in reflections over the nature of man.

The nature of man: this is what a famous passage from Kant puts in play, where he explains that the problem of the construction of a State is perfectly solvable even for a group of devils, if only they understand their self-interest correctly.[12] I will allow myself a follow-up point. In a sense, this problem is easier with devils than with men. In orthodox theology, devils are fallen angels, thus spiritual creatures who do not need to reproduce. We humans, however, cannot subsist as a species except by reproducing, that is, by replacing the dead, by bringing individuals into the world who weren't there before.

Our actual democracies are certainly not perfect. But I have no objec-

---

12   E. Kant, *Zum ewigen Frieden*, "1. Zusatz: Von der Garantie des ewigen Friedens," in *Werke*, t. 6, p. 224.

tion to democracy. I am unable to imagine a better regime. Democracy is the best way of allowing living persons to live together. But concerning the persons who do not yet exist, democracy has nothing to say, it has no right to say anything. Democracy therefore has but one defect, which is, left to itself and pushed to the extreme, its logic entails the eventual extinction of humanity.

Among other traits, Tocqueville clearly saw this feature of democracy, that it concentrates exclusively on the present. He also saw the consequence, even if, as was his wont, he merely suggested it. According to him, democracy effaces the future as well as the past: "Not only does democracy cause each man to forget his ancestors, but it also hides his descendants from him."[13] Tocqueville connected this fact to the loss of religious beliefs:

> When once they have accustomed themselves to no longer occupy themselves with what must happen to them after their life, one sees [democratic men] easily fall into that complete and brute-like indifference for the future which is only too consonant with certain instincts of the human race. As soon as they have lost the practice of placing their principal hopes in the long term, they are naturally led to want to realize their least desires immediately, and it seems that from the moment when they despair of living eternally, they are disposed to act as if they only were to exist for a day.[14]

The extinction of the fires

I just said that I do not know any better political regime than democracy, and I believe that. But I also observe that what one means by "democracy" is often more than a political regime. Democracy is overdetermined by the project that is often identified with Modernity, to wit: the claim by man of total autonomy vis-à-vis all transcendence.

Shouldn't we take note of the failure of this project?

---

13   Alexis de Tocqueville, *De la démocratie en Amérique*, II, ii, 2, *op. cit.*, p. 613.
14   *Ibid.*, II, ii, 17, p. 663.

Jean Bourgeois-Pichat makes a striking comparison, which he borrows from astronomy. He considers humanity in its entire trajectory, starting from a few individuals six hundred thousand years ago, and describes the curve of its demographic evolution in this way:

> These curves, completed by the third scenario, [...] the scenario of catastrophe, describe a phenomenon which unfolds a little like that of the life of a star. The latter, after having burned with a modest light during millions, even, billions, of years, sees its brilliance abruptly brighten in gigantic proportions. Astronomers give this the name of supernova. But the phenomenon doesn't last very long. The star rapidly becomes extinct and literally collapses upon itself, without anyone knowing very well what happens in this final phase. For astronomers, the star has disappeared.[15]

This image is powerful. It is also ironically appropriate. In fact, the appearance at the end of the sixteenth century of *novae* (technically: *supernovae*) was one of the events that marked, and were recognized as such, the entrance into new times. The phenomenon obliged people to reconsider the idea, until then uncontested, of an incorruptible celestial matter, distinct from the four terrestrial elements.

Isn't Modernity—*res novae*—therefore one of these stars?

Now, Christians, as such, do not have anything to worry about in this connection. Christ himself said that the gates of hell would not prevail against his Church (*Matthew* XVI, 18). On the other hand, it is the future of the human race that seems seriously compromised. Permit me the worst of scenarios, and let us suppose that humanity were to disappear. Who would be bothered? Christians could draw from the dust an old idea, sketched in the New Testament (*Revelation* VI, 11) and systematized by the Church Fathers, then the medievals.[16]

---

15 Jean Bourgeois-Pichat, *art. cit.*, pp. 29–30.
16 See Henri-Irénée Marrou, *Théologie de l'Histoire* (Paris: Seuil, 1968), pp. 40–41; for the Middle Ages, see, for example, the text by St. Bonaventure cited in my *La Sagesse du monde. Histoire de l'expérience humaine* (Paris: Fayard, 2002 (2nd ed.)), pp. 247–48.

They would say in substance, if not this language: The universe is a factory to produce holiness; it therefore needs to be shut down once it produces the quantity of saints foreseen by the divine plan, since the merits of these saints suffice to assure paradise to those who want it. Who knows, perhaps this number is almost attained . . . .

If Christians, therefore, can sleep soundly, "humanists" on the other hand need to be very anxious. Those for whom the five acts are performed in this life do not have another stage. To cite Diderot: "Posterity is for the philosopher what the other world is for the religious man."[17] But what if there is no posterity? In the response to the letter where this phrase is found, the sculptor Falconet opposes an analogous objection to Diderot. Suppose that some meteor destroys the Earth, where would posterity be then? To which the self-proclaimed "philosopher," as happens often, only responded with declamations.

There is even more to exploit in the image of Bourgeois-Pichat concerning the light of the stars. If non-European peoples are to follow us and adopt our way of life, they too will disappear. The question then is raised whether Enlightenment would not be lethal, rather than light-bearing. We know Paul Valery's phrase, perhaps a bit too often quoted, concerning "civilizations that know themselves to be mortal." Well, one must ask if the adjective "mortal" must not take on a new sense. For Valery it meant "capable of dying." But we also know a "mortal poison" or a "mortal disease." What if Western civilization was mortal in that sense? What if we ought to wish that other civilizations do *not* imitate us? That they remain unenlightened?

In that case, one cannot but approve of those in Europe and elsewhere who refuse what we call "progress," for it is those who have not yet been infected by the virus of Modernity (what I called earlier, "modernitis") who have lots of kids. The demographic weakness of developed countries provides arguments to those who resist modernization. The prospect of a world peopled with Catholics who are followers of Archbishop Lefebvre, Muslims

17 Denis Diderot, Letter to Falconet, Feb 1766, *Le Pour et le Contre ou Lettres sur la postérité*, in E. Hill et al., *Oeuvres complètes* (Paris: Hermann), t. 15, p. 33. The importance of this phrase was pointed out by Carl Becker, *The Heavenly City of the Eighteenth-Century Philosophers* (New Haven: Yale University Press, 1932), pp. 119 & 150.

of the Taliban sort, or ultra-orthodox Jews, is perhaps not exactly the world of which we dream. But is it not the logical outcome of some of our practices?

Metaphysics as infrastructure

What are the psychological wellsprings of these practices? We do not know much about the motivations that invite couples to desire children or to limit the number of births. We don't know, to repeat an earlier striking example, why the French began to limit births around 1750. It is even probable that the reasons were so deep that even the interested parties were not aware of them.

However, there is an author who seems to me to have said something very plausible about the psychological source, not exclusive but ultimate, of reproduction. He is a Tunisian of the fourteenth century, the historian and precursor of so many of the human sciences, Ibn Khaldun, who asked why conquered peoples tend to disappear. And he answered: because of despair. A despairing people ceases to reproduce because, very literally, "hope makes us live." More precisely, Ibn Khaldun wrote:

> It is the strength of hope (*šiddatu l-amal*) and the energy (*našāt*) that it communicates to the animal faculties that allow man to reproduce and to establish himself on the earth (*i'timār*).[18]

Where hope is present, a virtuous circle is put in place. Hope is produced by the idea of a better future, but, conversely, it is hope that creates the future. There is a future because there is hope. You know the proverb: "Where there's life, there's hope." One should turn it around and say: "Where there's hope, there's life."

But why hope? Why continue the human species? The question can seem otiose or academic. No doubt it was for Ibn Khaldun; perhaps also

---

18   Ibn Khaldun, *Muqaddima*, II, 23; I cite the translation of A. Cheddadi (Paris: Gallimard, 2002), p. 409. E. M. Quatremère prints *hiddatu 'l-amal*, "the acuity of hope" (Paris: Duprat, 1858), t. 1, p. 268, 6–7; trans. E. Rosenthal (New York: Pantheon Books, 1958), t. 1, p. 360.

for Tocqueville. It is less and less so for us. In any case, it no longer was for Ernest Renan in the nineteenth century, who devoted a long passage of the first of his *Dialogues philosophiques* to it, where he took up one of Schopenhauer's ideas. Nature deceives individuals by means of sexual pleasure, duping them for the sake of an interest superior to them: procreation. The universe is a crafty tyrant, and among the prejudices demanded by the interest of humanity, nothing is more deceitful than the familial spirit. For Renan, one must see this deceit for what it is and still submit to it.[19] I have to confess that I am not inclined to wager on that last formulation. To consciously accept to be deceived is not very plausible. And even when it would be, would it be the same for the other party, the unborn? In the famous phrase by Pascal, we are already embarked in life; we enjoy, as it were, an already-acquired advantage, although we also suffer its somber, sometimes horrible, aspects. But do we have the right to introduce new beings to life, without being able to ask them their opinion?

We have the right if, and only if, we can affirm that life is intrinsically good, an absolute good, a good for the one who already lives, but also for the one who does not yet exist. That it is a good for the one who already exists, even with all its tragedy, can be affirmed, Nietzsche tells us, granted that one adopts the Dionysian perspective. But this point of view is that of an Olympian god, not that of a human being. What is possible for Kant's fallen angels and Nietzsche's gods is less so for us others, human beings. In any case, assuming that we could attain such a perspective, we still could not impose it on another.

Therefore, can we affirm that life is a good, such that when one "inflicts" it on his neighbor it is justified?[20] In the final analysis, we cannot, without something like a metaphysical hook. Here, one needs to confront a widespread view and maintain, to the contrary, that it is metaphysics that grounds the natural, the physical. We have to disabuse ourselves of an idea

---

19 Ernest Renan, *Dialogues philosophiques* [1876], "1: Certitudes," in H. Psichari (ed.), *Oeuvres complètes* (Paris: Calmann-Levy, 1947), t. 1, pp. 571, 573, 575, 579.

20 I borrow the grandiloquent formulation from Chateaubriand, *Mémoires d'outre-tombe*, I, 1, P. Clarac (ed.) (Paris: Hachette, "Le Livre de Poche," 1973), p. 21.

that has become customary ever since Marxism, the idea that distinguishes the infrastructure from the superstructure and makes the second depend on the first. We need to reverse that. Without transcendence, no life.

Everything transpires as if we could invert Nietzsche's formulations. One no longer has to say that transcendence judges life, that, from the very fact that it compares and measures it against another measure than its own, it condemns it.[21] It is not a matter of asking if one must prefer immanence to transcendence. As if we had the choice! Left to itself, immanence has an internal tendency to self-destruction. Between transcendence and immanence a logic is at work, such that one does not need to choose between them, but the choice of the first is the condition for the continuation of the second.

From on high to below

To formulate this logic in its negative form, I could cite Malraux, according to whom the death of man cannot fail to follow that of God, a formulation that has been often plagiarized since then.[22] However, I prefer to cite Nietzsche again, and a famous passage, although also changing the meaning. It is the last stage of a history that the philosopher recounts, that of the representation of a "true world" launched by Plato with "the ideas" and taken up by Christianity with "heaven," then Kant with "the postulates of practical reason," and, finally, arrived at its exhausted end. I quote:

> [6.] We have abolished the true world. What world remains? The apparent world, perhaps? But no! *At the same time as the true world, we have also abolished the apparent world.*[23]

Once the purported "true world" is abolished, it is also the world of appearances that is. Nietzsche does not mean by that that it too would fall

---

21 See, for example: Friedrich Nietzsche, fragment 7 [6], end of 1886–Spring 1887, *KSA*, t. 12, p. 274.

22 André Malraux, *La Tentation de l'Occident* [1926] (Paris: Hachette, "Le Livre de Poche," 1972, p. 128.

23 Friedrich Nietzsche, *Götzendämmerung*, "Wie die wahre Welt zur Fabel wurde," *KSA*, t. 6, p. 81.

into nothingness, but that it no longer would be measured by an ideal that it could not measure up to, and hence it was returned to its "innocence." Once "there-above" has been suppressed, there is no longer any "here-below," but only reality, *tout court*.

Above, I invoked a poster. Another one will provide me with a final image, or rather a series of posters, much more famous than the one I mentioned earlier. The series dates from the end of August-beginning of September 1981, and came from the photographer Jean-Francois Jonvelle (1943–2002), who had made himself a name in soft pornography. It has remained a classical example of the advertising technique called *teasing*. The series contained three images in which a young female bather progressively revealed her richest treasures every two days. After having unveiled the upper portion, she fixed her gaze on the spectators, to whom she also promised to take off what hid the lower part. The same logic as in Nietzsche governs the relationship between transcendence and immanence: if "I take off the top," it is necessary that "I take off the bottom." Perhaps we live in something like those few days which separate the two fleshly revelations. And the frustration of the desire for the things here-below is perhaps the first consequence of the decline of belief in those above.

The posters were an advertisement for advertisement itself, more precisely for an agency that was called (I can't make this up), L'Avenir (the Future), deemed "to keep its promises." At the awaited date, the young woman in fact kept hers and showed herself without any covering. But she had also rotated her body, thus maintaining, even in the absence of shame, the rules of the profession. Here too one can find a meaning. Perhaps we have to expect that history, once emptied of transcendence, will—let's speak politely—will turn its back on us. And that like the seductive model, it will present not what the painter Courbet called "the origin of the world," but now that other aspect from which only unpleasant digestive products have, or will ever, come.

V
RECONSTRUCTION

14

THE TRANSMISSION
OF THE CLASSICAL HERITAGE

Modernity has not only succeeded what came before it. It also received from what preceded it. To recall its use of the legacy of Antiquity could contribute in turn to what will succeed it.

My title is doubly tautological. First of all, at the level of words. The French word "tradition" at bottom is only the transliteration of the Latin *traditio* which, precisely, signifies nothing other than "transmission." But this tautology is a fortunate one. The word "tradition" has become suspect. Many people, whose brains explode at the second or third syllable of words, do not distinguish "tradition" from "traditionalism," or for that matter "nation" from "nationalism." However, the word loses its reactionary aura and takes on the aspect of a sober description by means of a simple intellectual operation: substituting for transliterated Latin its French translation, which, as I just said, is "transmission."

The second tautology bears upon the concept. There is no heritage without transmission; there is no transmission without a heritage. In order to show this, I need to take a detour through some history.

Bloody ink

"The classical heritage" was and still is the object of a series of almost uninterrupted renaissances. They followed Antiquity and occurred almost as soon as one became aware of a possible, or real, *estrangement* from it.

This millennial process saw many stages. To depict it, one would have to paint a huge fresco in which one would see the appropriation of the *Corpus areopagiticum* in the ninth century, the reading of the *Timaeus* and Ovid at Chartres and elsewhere in France in the twelfth century, the Italian

Renaissances of the thirteenth to the sixteenth century, Racine, the infatuation of the English aristocracy with Rome, then Napoleon's, Weimar classicism, the philological movement lasting until our own day, and, in its wake, its concrete implementation in the middle schools of the Jesuits and Oratorians, the Republican or Imperial *lycée*, the British *public school*, the humanistic Gymnasium in Central Europe, and a thousand other examples.

I would especially emphasize the tragic aspects of this history, because transmission is not a long, tranquil river. It is a history with many colors, and not only that of ink. Concerning ink [*encre*], one says "to be worried sick [*sang d'encre*]." One must also say, "bloody ink" [*encre de sang*] as well. Even the most peaceful scriptorium in the most sheltered monastery, even the desks of the calmest learned men, were animated by the sentiment of a threatening catastrophe that they must ward off, or at least delay. In this history, violence from without and anxiety from within are never far off.

The two were encountered from the beginning, with the emblematic figure of Boethius at the beginning of the sixth century. This Roman patrician in the service of the "barbarian" king Theodoric conceived the titanic project of translating all of Plato and Aristotle's works from Greek to Latin, and then to comment on all of them. Why this project? Until his day, the small cultivated elite of the Republic, then the Empire, hardly had need of translations. Since the age of the Scipios (the second century before Christ), it learned Greek, spoke it, read it. Boethius, however, felt that the immediate relation to Greek, which had been ebbing for centuries, was about to be lost.[1] If one wanted to safeguard the classical heritage it was necessary to get to work translating. But Boethius was lost by his political role. He was suspected of collusion with the empire of Constantinople, which was already preparing the reconquest of the West that it would commence with Justinian. He was executed for treason in 524. The death of Boethius deprived the Latin West of the works of classical Greek philosophy. Europe had to wait until the thirteenth century to have the entirety of Aristotle's treatises, and until the fifteenth century, the dialogues of Plato.

---

1 See Henri-Irénée Marrou, *Histoire de l'éducation dans l'Antiquité* (Pari: Seuil, 1965 (6th ed.), pp. 380–85.

A generation later, toward 555, another Roman patrician, Cassiodorus, founded the monastery school of Vivarium, in Calabria.[2] The connection between work and prayer was traditional among cenobites. But Vivarium was distinct in that the monastery had a library at its center, and the work of the monks consisted above all in recopying manuscripts, correcting them, sometimes translating from the Greek. The goal was to preserve Christian literature, but also medical works. Cassiodorus had a model which he explicitly recognized at the beginning of his *Institutiones*, the school of Nisibis, a monastic school of the Syriac language situated on the border between present-day Turkey and Syria.[3] The work of Cassiodorus is thus one of the rare traces of an initial *translatio studiorum* between the Middle East and Europe. It was a matter of doing in the Latin West what Nisibis did for the Syriac world.

In connection with these two examples, one did not yet speak of "renaissance." The use of the term presupposes death, always threatening, on the point of winning definitively, and needing to be warded off against a variety of barbarisms. The word served as a slogan from the time that we still call "the Renaissance." But it is also found in the writings of modern historians in connection with the famous "Carolingian renaissance," instigated by king Charles the Great, and put in effect by men such as Alcuin of York or, among the successors of Charlemagne, Rhabanus Maurus. This renaissance consisted above all in correcting already available texts.[4] That means that they were corrupt.

Here too, one sees the will to confront an always-threatening danger of loss or distortion.

The political and affective context

This leads us to take into consideration another aspect of the enterprise, its political and affective context.

2   A recent synthesis can be found in Franco Cardini, *Cassiodoro il grande. Roma, I barbari e il monachesimo* (Milan: Jaca Book, 2009), III, 3: "Vita e lavoro a Vivarium," pp. 139–49.

3   See Cassiodorus, *Institutiones*, I, 1, *PL*, 70, 1005.

4   A recent synthesis in Emilio Mitre, *Una primera Europa. Romanos, cristianos y germanos (400–1000)* (Madrid: Encuentro, 2009), pp. 144–56: "El Renacimiento Carolingio, una vía para la cohesión cultural," above all p. 147.

The first, the political, can already be read, although implicitly, in the instructions of the emperor of the West. Its aim is to have correct texts, as Charlemagne explicitly says in his *Admonitio generalis* of 789. The significance of this directive is considerable, since it goes to the very highest level, that is to say, to the relation with God. To have correct texts allows one *to pray correctly*.[5] Philological exactitude has a goal: to assure the salvation of souls. This policy thus wants to show that the strong man of Western Europe, who shortly will proclaim himself emperor, concerns himself with the eternal salvation of his subjects, for which he considers himself equally responsible. Indirectly, to be sure, philology has as a goal the legitimation of political authority. This is neither the first nor the last example, far from us to deny it, of a simultaneous religious and political recuperation of classical studies. The effort to transmit the legacy of the past is suspended, sometimes torn between, the noblest concerns and the most sordid calculations.

In a general way, and not only with Charlemagne, the *translatio studiorum* took place in the wake of military conquests. The famous verse of Horace, "Captive Greece led captive its captor," indicates that Greece first lost its independence in the most concrete way on the battlefield when it was defeated by Rome. In the seventh century it was the conquest of the Middle East by the Arabs that made possible, two centuries later, the passage into Arabic of available Greek learning. The conquest of Toledo by the Castilians (1085) allowed for the translation into Latin of a part of what was available in Arabic, either what had been translated or was directly composed in that language. The taking of Constantinople by the Turks (1453) accelerated the departure to Italy of Byzantine scholars who fled the new conquerors, bringing with them their manuscripts.

All these events weren't strolls in the park. Elsewhere, I already cited a rather amusing and very ironic example, that of the Arabic holdings of the Escorial library. This is not at all a legacy of Muslim Spain, as one might think. This fund of books fell, literally, on the shores of Spain when a ship containing an Arabic library shipwrecked.[6]

---

5   Charlemagne, *Admonitio generalis*, # 72, in A. Boret (ed.), *Monumenta Germaniae Hisorica*, "Leges, II: Capitularia regum francorum," t. 1 (Hanover: Hahn, 1883), p. 60.

6   See my *Au moyen du Moyen Âge, op. cit.*, p. 244.

As for the affective tonality that governs the ensemble of this movement, it is only rarely, perhaps never, the sentiment of a peaceful and legitimate possession of a good that one cannot lose, and that is merited. On the contrary, it is animated by the poignant sentiment of fragility, of strangeness, of illegitimacy. It is a matter of holding fast to what can slip into oblivion. Or to recover what has been forgotten.

The ancient world is perceived as a lost origin towards which only nostalgia—home-coming—can build a fragile bridge. This affective coloration is refracted in different hues among a number of poets and writers. In Italy with Petrarch, in England with Gibbon, in Germany with Schiller and Hölderlin.

To decide in favor of transmission

To fend off this danger of loss requires constant work.

As a result, it seems to me that the word "heritage" needs to be used with a thousand precautions, because it introduces the idea of a will on the part of the testator as well as the legatee. However, in cultural transmission, everything happens on the part of the legatee. There is no heritage without appropriation. Goethe said it in an often-cited phrase, perhaps become hackneyed, but profoundly true nonetheless: "What you inherited from your ancestors,/Acquire it, in order to possess it."[7] One can say of tradition what Renan said of the nation: it is "a daily plebiscite."[8]

But what happens when the result of the vote is negative? It is death without recall. It is possible to understand this by the example of what we have received of the ancient heritage, which is very partial and incomplete. And this, precisely because it too depended upon the interest it was able to elicit. What seemed interesting was conserved, what had ceased to be so went down, all hands on deck.

Towards their own heritage, the Ancients were in a situation that resembles ours in one respect, while being different in another. It was

---

7   Goethe, *Faust* I, vv. 682–83: "Was Du ererbt von Deinen Vätern hast,/Erwirb es, um es zu besitzen."
8   Ernest Renan, "Qu'est-ce qu'une nation?" [1882], III, in H. Psichari (ed.), *Oeuvres complètes, op. cit.*, t. 1, p. 904.

different in that the printing press did not exist. As a result, written works were much harder to reproduce and the number of available copies was restricted. It resembles ours, though, to the extent that here too an active decision to transmit was required, which nothing could replace.

It can happen that an entire world therefore rests on a very small point, and we owe the survival of some great thought to the decision of a single individual. There is a passage in Simplicius that I find particularly mind-boggling. Commenting on Aristotle's *Physics*, the writer recopies several dozen verses of Parmenides' poem because, he says, it is becoming rare.[9] In fact, we have lost almost all of this didactic poem. Without Simplicius we would have no idea of the vertiginous depths of Parmenides' thought. And what would we know of Epicurus if Diogenes Laertius had not decided to copy three short treatises ("letters") which summarized his thought?

Diogenes Laertius and Simplicius after him, were perhaps not aware of what they were doing, that, like Atlas, they bore an entire world. This does not prevent each one of us from asking if we too might not be in the same situation.

Shipwreck

The consciousness of a heritage is barely born when the questions are raised, *what precisely* should be transmitted? What needs to be copied? What texts are worth the cost of reproducing (papyrus or parchment)? For which ones should we pay a scribe?

We possess seven of Aeschylus's tragedies and as many by Sophocles, while the others are only known by fragments. Why? Because these seven had found favor in the eyes of critics who considered them the best these tragedians had to offer. What these authors themselves would have preserved, or what we would have chosen if, *per impossibile*, we could have done so, we don't know and we will never know.

We have all of Plato's work, and about all of Aristotle's courses. In contrast, we only have bits and scraps of the first Stoics, the atomists,

---

9   Simplicius, *In Aristotelis Physicorum librorum [...] commentaria*, H. Diels (ed.), *CAG* IX (Berlin: 1882), 28, p. 144.

and the skeptics. Why? Because only the Neoplatonic schools remained at the end of Antiquity. Plato's work constituted the basic text and Aristotle's courses the pedagogical manuals for beginners. What we call "Greek philosophy" is hardly anything more than the library of the last Neoplatonists.

The Arabs of the ninth century, like the Eastern Christians who spoke Syriac before them, only interested themselves in Greek *learning*, in astronomy, philosophy, medicine, botany. They neglected belles-lettres, what we call literature, which only came to Europe rather late. In contrast, Europe received it directly, following the libraries of Constantinople. Without the Arab translators of Baghdad, we would be lacking entire swaths of Greek learning in medicine, mathematics, and philosophy: long passages of Galen, the mathematician Diophantus, the philosopher Themistius.[10] But if we only had the Arab intermediary, and no direct transmission of Greek to Latin, we would have had nothing of Greek literature. Neither Homer nor Plato, neither the lyric poets nor the tragedians, or the historians.

We live in the cemetery of civilizations, among the ruins of disappeared worlds that have become the objects of archeology. Earlier, I recalled Valery's oft-cited words, which suggest that civilizations would have been aware of their mortality only lately. But the fact was known for thousands of years, including the case of Rome. Other examples have been added in the last century, for example the Sanskrit brought to the knowledge of the West by William Jones, the cuneiform deciphered by Grotefend, and the hieroglyphs by Champollion. What is new, and what Valery emphasizes, is that we know that we too can join them.[11]

This is because there is no such thing as cultural inertia. Cultural realities do not advance on their own; they have no future unless someone at present maintains them. It is the same for the transmission of the classical heritage as it is for the pursuit of the human adventure. It depends on us. Not on what we say, not on our discourses, including the one you are reading right now. It depends upon what we do, on the concrete decisions we make here and now.

---

10   See Dimitri Gutas, *Greek Thought, Arabic Culture, op. cit.*
11   From memory: Paul Valéry, "La crise de l'esprit" [1919], in J. Hytier (ed.), *Oeuvres* (Paris: Gallimard, "Bibliothèque de la Pléide," 1957), t. 1, p. 988.

Two concepts of tradition

Here I need to distinguish two models of transmission or tradition. One is spontaneous, automatic. The other designates the conscious and voluntary act of transmitting.

The first model above all concerns language, which is the main medium of everything that is transmitted, and therefore should occupy a central place in hermeneutics, as was recalled by the German philosopher Hans-Georg Gadamer in his master work, *Truth and Method*.[12] Morphology, syntax, basic vocabulary, are transmitted and received by the sole fact that the parents and relatives of the child speak to it. Moreover, the speakers of a given language are very rarely conscious of the rules that govern its functioning. And rarely do they have the conscious intention of teaching them. It is the work of the student, later, to make these rules self-conscious and to enlarge his vocabulary. It is the same with eating habits and tastes, with gestures and all the signs expressed by the body, but also for customs, the elementary morality of "what is done" and "is not done," which is not yet distinguished from etiquette.

The second model is education. Knowledge here is objective. It can be put into texts, some of which are explicitly pedagogical, for example, manuals, and memorized. It can also remain at a preverbal level, as when one learns to dance, to play an instrument, or play a sport. In the two cases, it is acquired by a deliberate and chosen transmission. But not every civilization has made the choice to transmit by means of education, much less by a formal institution. Civilizations called "primitive" did not have schools.

I will take a single example, that of the transmission of the most fundamental beliefs, which are religious. In Christendom, only countries in the Latin tradition chose to have catechism classes, and today to propose courses in religion. On the contrary, the orthodox Churches trust in the family and the liturgy as an apprenticeship in doctrines and rites. Children attend the divine liturgy from their earliest years, where they also, from the time of their baptism, receive the central sacrament of the Eucharist. The West made the choice of *instruction* centuries ago. In so doing, it took a considerable risk. For the newborn finds himself less *in* the religion than

---

12   Hans-Georg Gadamer, *Wahrheit und Methode* [1960], III part.

before it, as before an object, summoned to make a decision whether to adhere or not.

As for classical languages, they present a particularly interesting case. On one hand, as languages they constitute the key example of what customarily is transmitted by tradition. On the other, their transmission is uniquely active, being the object of instruction. This is the phenomenon designated by the strange phrase "dead languages." They can become as living as the others, but they receive their life from without. A dead language can, moreover, become living, as the case of modern Hebrew shows.

Nothing automatically maintains the classical languages. All the matters taught in secondary school are fueled by some necessity. French is taught because of the obligation to communicate with one's fellow citizens; English, because it is the *lingua franca* of an increasingly globalized world; the scientific languages because of the technologies that depend upon them.

Alone the classical languages are the result of freedom, and freedom alone. That is why at this point I would associate myself with the highest praise ever given: classical languages *do not serve any merely useful purpose.* If they did, they would be—the word coins itself—servile. The slaves or even the freedmen who imagine that they make a valid criticism of classical languages by saying they do not serve the order of production and consumption, thus show that they still bear on their neck the presence, or at least the mark, of their iron collar.

Classical languages as paradigms

For a long time, classical languages were the support and the sustaining milieu of Western culture. This is no longer the case. It is not necessary to recall this fact, but nonetheless they can still constitute something of a paradigm for this culture. And the difficulties their teaching encounters today can themselves be a paradigm for the more general crisis the culture is undergoing, a crisis that nothing guarantees it will survive.

The question of reproduction has acquired an urgent relevance, as is indicated (to those who have the ears to hear it) by the deafening silence with which some hasten to surround it. It is remarkable, and very regrettable, that the term "reproduction" has become a quasi-insult since the book of that title published by Pierre Bourdieu and Jean-Claude Passeron in

1970.[13] To point out that every institution or social group seeks its own re-production, and to unmask the circuitous mechanisms by which they succeed, is a scientific result that is to sociology's credit. To reproach institutions for seeking to perpetuate themselves is a second step, a moral judgment. At present, however, there is a third fact: the survival of humanity depends upon reproduction in the most banally biological sense of the term. There is no need to invent the nightmare of a collision with a gigantic meteor. It would suffice to have a few sterile decades for the human race, which appeared millions of years ago, to disappear without any hope of return.[14] Now, the existence of humanity has a point in common with classical languages: it is "useless," it doesn't factor into a utilitarian calculus.

It depends upon us today, and upon no one else, that humanity lasts. And *a fortiori*, that a particular form of humanity lasts, this civilization that happens to be our own. Even more so, the survival of classical culture depends upon our good will, because it is the fine point where an even vaster and more wrenching problem is concentrated. Hence, the awesome responsibility of those who have received the charge of keeping it afloat. Woe to them, woe to us, if they fail.

13   Pierre Bourdieu and Jean-Claude Passeron, *La Reproduction. Éléments pour une théorie du système d'enseignement* (Paris: Minuit, 1970).
14   See my *Anchors in the Heavens, op. cit.*

15

AN EDUCATIONAL DREAM

Let us dream and imagine an ideal school, ideally medieval, ideally conscious of the culture to transmit to the modern world. In so doing, we find ourselves before a double paradox, perhaps a double challenge: a dream while we are awake, and a dream-on-command. Here, though, the dream is nothing more than what dreams normally are, a way of giving the imagination free rein.

This double character will have two consequences. Since it is a dream, I will totally abstract from the conditions of its realization, even its possibility (which seems rather remote to me). Here I will do like the author of the very first educational utopia, no one less than Plato and his *Republic*. Socrates had just sketched at the level of conversation the plan of a "Beautiful City" (*kallipolis*). He states that it does not really matter that it did or did not exist in the past, that it exists or does not exist in a far-off country, that it will be realized or not in the future. What is important is that it can serve here and now as a model for us, a model that we can always follow, anywhere on earth, no matter the time in which we live.[1]

Still, because it is a dream, we must more precisely state the specifications of the dream. There needs to be some method to its madness, which we need to make explicit, at least briefly. Happily, it owes entirely to the name we will give to the imaginary school, if only by implication. It must be a matter of *education,* not *instruction*.

Education and instruction

Education and instruction are two concepts that are traditionally distinguished, and rightly so. Instruction consists in providing the necessary

---

1   Plato, *Republic*, IX, 592a–b.

formation so that someone can efficiently perform an action he is regularly called upon to perform. This is already an achievement. The person in an unknown city who points out the way to a meeting merely informs me by communicating a discrete piece of information; he does not yet instruct me. In order to do that, it would have to be the case that he transmitted to me a competence that I could generalize and exercise at will. He would have to show me how to orient myself by the sun, or use a map of the city. The competence acquired by instruction can be of a technical nature, such as driving a car, steering a boat, piloting a plane. It can be part of a profession or career: to handle a plane, or work a machine tool. It can be a social role: to acquire the competences necessary for life in a democratic political order, what we metaphorically call "the profession of citizen," which is the goal of what is called "civic instruction."

A school that aims at giving young people the best possible instruction must teach them how to find their bearings in the world of today, how to participate in the various technical or social systems. But in my dream, to repeat, the focus is on education, not instruction. However, what one learns today in the establishments that are still called "educational" depart further and further from education and are increasingly transformed into technical instruction. This diagnosis is not original with me, but each year confirms it ever more. Education is increasingly an object of nostalgia, which one can play in various registers from one end of the spectrum of visions of the world to the other: from Leo Strauss and his writings on liberal education to the young Marx with his utopia of a society in which each individual, his or her capacities fully developed, can exercise in turn, and according to whim, all the occupations, be they productive or not.[2]

To reprise a formulation that has become banal, education ought not to form a technician, but a man, without further specification. Hence the name "humanities" which still attach to what is also called *liberal education*.

This appellation goes back to antiquity. The human race was divided into free men and slaves. The productive occupations were for slaves, and hence received the unflattering designation, "servile." They were necessary, if the elementary needs were to be satisfied, to eat, to be clothed, to lodge,

---

2   Leo Strauss, *Liberalism Ancient and Modern* (New York: Basic Books, 1968), pp. 3–25; Karl Marx, *Die deutsche Ideologie*, I (Berlin: Dietz, 1953), p. 30.

needs that do not differ essentially between men and the other animals. In contrast, free men did not have to work. They occupied themselves with governing the city and, as needed, defending it through force of arms. Their time of leisure was devoted to musical or intellectual pursuits. These activities, worthy of free men, were therefore called "liberal." Free men therefore were the only ones who truly deserved the appellation "human." Liberal studies could therefore also be called "concern for [one's] humanity" (*studium humanitatis*) or the "humanities."

Is the project of providing an education still possible today? Nothing proves that this is the case.

Mission impossible? Dangerous task?

Liberal education becomes less and less thinkable today, because to form a man presupposes that one can say with some precision what being a man means, and not as simply possessing this-or-that competence. To be sure, people deplore that we only seek to form engineers or computer experts rather than men. In fact, the complaint is rather old and goes back at least to the first German romanticism, for example when the Greek hero of the epistolary novel of the young Hölderlin said that he saw in Germany "craftsmen, but not men, thinkers, but not men, priests, but not men."[3]

But this protestation is too facile. One must be able to say what it is to be a man *simpliciter*, and not an expert in this-or-that domain. It is rather easy to say what a good computer scientist must be; but to say what a man must be, *qua* human, that is what gives us a lot more trouble.

It becomes more and more difficult to say what model of humanity it would be desirable to have. It is even difficult to have the idea accepted that there could be some general model, whatever it might be. For many, the sole ideal of humanity that we have the right to imagine rests, precisely, on the exclusion of all models. The fashionable slogans of "multiculturalism," of "cultural mixing," of "tolerance," make the idea of a model of humanity to which one should conform impossible, even unthinkable.

Suppose that by some miracle these problems were resolved. Should

---

3   Friedrich Hölderlin, *Hyperion oder der Eremit in Griechenland*, II, ii, 7, in F. Beissner (ed.), *Sämtliche Werke* (Frankfurt: Insel, 1965), p. 636.

we immediately turn to the task? Perhaps not … . We ordinarily make the distinction between instruction and education also a difference in rank; we do not content ourselves with pointing out a difference, but we classify, rank, and grant education a higher rung than simple instruction. We therefore need to be more circumspect.

The intention of educating thus presupposes the possession of a specific model of what the child or adolescent to be educated should become. The education called "liberal" therefore can run counter to the liberty of the one who is being educated. In contrast, instruction, which is more modest in its aims, contents itself with putting in the hands of the student competences that he will be able to use as he will.

There is a lot that is true in the foregoing. The most criminal political utopias of the last century all included an educative project. And those that still exist attempt to influence Western public opinion by funding public schools and by fighting against illiteracy. One hears: "Cuban children don't want bread, they prefer pencils!" This implies that they can freely choose between two abundantly available goods.

Perhaps the very project of an education is susceptible to dangerous ideological perversions. These would be rooted in a conception of man as an indifferent material to which one could impart any form that one wanted. Thus, one would be quite warranted to take a critical distance from the intention to obtain a specific human type by the appropriate means. The Enlightenment took as its point of departure the idea that man is capable of indefinite progress toward perfection, and they expressed this idea or project in the concept of "perfectibility," which was formulated by Rousseau, who saw in it what was proper to man.[4]

The French Revolution saw programs of universal education proliferate. According to the publicists of the period, all evil came from a bad education, while, conversely, it would suffice to expose children to good influences for them to become "virtuous." How those who wanted to subject them to such good influences could themselves have become their spokesmen and vehicles despite the "fanatical" education they had received, and

---

4   Jean-Jacques Rousseau, *Discours sur l'origine de l'inégalité parmi les hommes*, 1, in
     B. Gagnebin and M. Raymond (ed.), *Oeuvres complètes, op. cit.*, pp. 142, 162.

"the ridiculous prejudices of superstition" they had had to suffer, they didn't say.[5]

Thus, the ideology which grafts itself on pedagogical practice assumes two initial postulates, first, that man is a *tabula rasa*, such that education can begin from zero, and that the educator can educate himself.

From these come two temptations. On one hand, that of erasing everything that is already there in order to make room for the realization of a totally new plan. Most of the time this ends with the destruction of everything that exists, without anything new coming into existence. History shows this. Revolutions produce nothing, it is the restorations that follow that are creative. On the other hand, since the educator is supposed to be able to liberate himself from the influence of all that is called "prejudice," he who wishes to educate is tempted to place himself above ordinary morality, putting himself in a situation of absolute power, where everything will be permitted. "Everything is permitted" is not only the bold formulation that Dostoyevski placed in the mouth of Ivan Karamazov. It is also the theme of the editorial of the first issue of the *Red Sword*, the journal of the State police of the newly founded Soviet Union, the Cheka.[6]

The idea of a "new man" produced by the means of the appropriate educational policies manifested itself throughout the different revolutions. In a sense, it was already found in Plato's *Republic*. And in the last century, if the concentration camps of National Socialism sometimes sought the extermination, pure and simple, of undesirables, their Soviet and Chinese equivalents sought to "reeducate" the subjects they judged salvageable.

And there are other versions, softer, more discreet, of this idea, found in widely respected authors. For example, the psychologist B. F. Skinner (1904–1990) of the behaviorist school, a professor at Harvard, in 1948 in his scientific utopia *Walden Two* acknowledged with a laudable candor:

5   See Mona Ozouf, "La Révolution française et la formation de l'homme nouveau," in *L'Homme régénéré. Essais sur la Révolution française* (Paris: Gallimard, 1989), pp. 116–57.
6   Dostoyevski, *Les Frères Karamazov*, I, ii, 6, *op. cit.*, p. 73; *Krasnyi Metch*, n. 1, 18 August 1919, p. 1, cited in S. Courtois et al., *Le Livre noir du communisme. Crimes, terreur, répression* (Paris: Laffont, 1997), p. 117.

We haven't yet seen what man can do with man [...]. When we ask what Man can make of Man we don't mean the same thing by "Man" in both instances. We mean to ask what a few men can make of mankind. [...]. What kind of world can we build— those of us who understand the science of behavior?[7]

An education, not simply instruction

One therefore is tempted to completely reject the dream of an education which showed itself to be a nightmare, and to content oneself, quite soberly and modestly, with instruction. But let us now indicate the *sed contra* of our "disputed question." How can we do without education, without putting in danger the very idea of civilization, since civilization is the collective version of what corresponds to education for the individual?

We speak of education in connection with what is thought to be received at school or the university. In this sense, the educated man is the instructed man, learned if he is "literary," a scholar if he is "scientific," in both cases, a man with the relevant competences. But we also speak of "education" to describe the well-raised human being. This person certainly possesses a sort of knowledge, but a practical knowledge, which implies awareness of the rules that govern certain social milieus. One would say that a person displays education when she can adapt her words and behavior to each person, no matter what age, sex, origin, or occupation; one would say she lacks it, if we do not find in her this sort of versatility.

Education in this sense is not only imparted by schools. In fact, we should avoid expecting too much from an academic system, whatever it be. Education is communicated, for best and worst, directly and indirectly, voluntarily or willy-nilly, consciously or not, by a thousand channels: the example of one's parents and milieu (exhibiting "what's done" and "what's not done"), the media, etc. It comes to us through the many value-judgments contained in language. Adults, moreover, receive a kind of education long after they have left their school desks. All this leads one to believe that school and formal education of all sorts only play a rather secondary role in the formation of children.

7   B. F. Skinner, *Walden Two* (New York: Macmillan, 1948), chap. xxxiii, p. 279.

Educate for liberty

The idea that allows us to escape from the dilemma of an education that is at once necessary and impossible is the idea of liberty. It constitutes the very definition of man. Implicit in the traditional definition of man as "the living thing endowed with *logos*," its explicit statement surfaces from time to time during the history of thought, before coming fully to light with Kant.[8] Now, the free man is not a human model among others, alongside that of the worker, the intellectual, the gentleman, but man *tout court*. To propose liberty as the goal of education is not to impose a model, quite the contrary.

Let us therefore try to elaborate this idea, not however without under-lining the partial truth contained in the distrust of the idea of liberal edu-cation, which does begin from a concept of liberty that is no longer defensible. Moreover, the concept has been surpassed in practice. The Greek ideal of *paideia*, as we saw, rested implicitly on the ideal of the free man. But liberty here was reduced to its social aspect: he was free who was not a slave. As a consequence, liberty could not appear as a result to acquire by formation, but as a point of departure.

It is only in Israel that liberty appeared, no longer as the inalienable property of a dominant class, but as the quality received by a people initially reduced to slavery and liberated by an external intervention, coming from the radical exteriority which belongs to God, he who made the people leave Egypt, the house of slaves (*Exodus* XX, 2). The Hebrew word for "free man," *hofši*, testifies to this: in Canaanite it meant "slave."[9] With Christi-anity, liberty is explicitly presented not as a means, but as the goal of the salvation wrought by God in Christ: "Christ has liberated you *for liberty*" (Galatians V, 1).

---

8   See, for example: Alexander of Aphrodisias, *De anima liber cum mantissa*, I. Bruns (ed.) (Berlin: Reimer, 1887), p. 175; Gregory of Nyssa, *Discours Caté-chétique*, V, 9, L. Méridier (ed.) (Paris: Picard, 1908), pp. 30–32; Pierre de Jean Olivi, *Quaestiones in II. Sententiarum*, q. LVII, B. Jansen (ed.) (Florence: Quaracchi, 1924), t. 2, p. 338; Jean-Jacques Rousseau, *Discours sur l'origine de l'inégalité*, 1, in B. Gagnebin and M. Raymond (ed.), op. cit., p. 141.

9   See William F. Albright, *From the Stone Age to Christianity*, op. cit., p. 285; for the context, see my *The Law of God*, op. cit., p. 47.

Even today, education cannot have the means to attain its aim unless it takes cognizance, explicitly or not, of the revolution that the Bible introduced in the idea of liberty. A great English historian, Lord Acton, put it magnificently: "Liberty is not a means in view of a higher political goal. It is itself the highest political goal."[10]

If, therefore, we carefully distinguish between education and instruction, we must recognize that there is no other sort of education than liberal education. To speak of "liberal education" is in fact a tautology. And instruction, by definition, is not liberal. We still must ask, though, what concept of liberty can properly support our use of the adjective "liberal." A philosopher from antiquity, if he came back to life and visited our schools, would be surprised by what would seem to him to be a contradiction. We prize our freedom, but we only teach servile arts. Our passion for technologies and techniques of all sorts would seem to him the sign that we have become slaves, or at least slavish.

I, however, would have a more positive view of this development. The classical idea of liberal education, as we saw, assumed as "going without saying" the division of humanity into free men (in practice: free males) and slaves. We have abolished slavery, at least in law, and since the Industrial Revolution we have for the most part replaced human slaves with mechanical ones. In a short but substantial essay, the American historian of medieval technology Lynn White Jr. responded to the famous chapter of Henry Adams, "The Dynamo and the Virgin."[11] In it he pointed out the importance of the technical and intellectual revolution of the Middle Ages. According to him, it was inconceivable without the Christian conception of the dignity of every man before God. He particularly noted that the cathedrals were the first significant monuments that were not built by slave labor, but by free workers, even (with some anachronism) unionized.[12]

---

10 Lord Acton, *The History of Freedom in Antiquity* [1877], in *Selected Writings*, J. R. Fears (ed.) (Indianapolis: Liberty Press, 1985), t. 1, p. 22.

11 *The Education of Henry Adams* [1907], chap. xxv, I. B. Nadel (ed.) (Oxford: Oxford University Press, 1999), pp. 317–26.

12 Lynn J. White, "The Dynamo and the Virgin Revisited," in *Machina ex Deo. Essays in the Dynamism of Western Civilization* (Cambridge, MA/London: The MIT Press, 1968), pp. 61–73.

The freedom of men and of things

An educated man must first of all be a man, a human being. This is a platitude that means that we sometimes have to do with conceptions of man that prevent the possibility of receiving an education. Every anthropology does not permit one to conceive of man as a being capable of being educated. Therefore the question bears raising, whether we possess a concept of man that is widely shared and which would allow us to think that education is or could be possible. Some anthropologies have no problem explaining that man can be shaped at will. Human liberty is harder to think about.

Moreover, man is not the product of education. Men must exist before we attempt to educate them. Aristotle expressed this fact, which he held to be obvious, in a phrase that came from political science: the city, social life, does not produce men, but receives them from nature. The Stoics in turn contented themselves with saying that nature only provides a sketch of men, and that they must fill it in.[13]

Education consists in promoting the liberty of the person whom one educates. Now let us show that this liberty of the subject corresponds to, even calls for, what one can call the liberty of the object, which has the right to be treated in the way it presents itself.

Aristotle defined the educated man (*pepaideumenos*) as the one who knows in what case a specific approach is suited to its object and when it is not. Such a person uses the rigorous method of demonstration, as in the deduction of theorems from axioms, when he deals with a mathematical problem. In this case, he would not employ rhetorical procedures. On the other hand, it would be ridiculous to use geometric thinking in moral matters.[14] For example, we all know that returning evil for good is wrong, and those who do so elicit our disapproval. But we cannot demonstrate that in the same way we can a theorem.

It is in a similar way, as we have seen, that a well-raised person will adapt his conduct to his partner in a conversation, or social exchange

---

13 Aristotle, *Politics*, I, 10, 1258a21-3; see Cicero, *De finibus*, IV, xiii, 34, T. Schiche (ed.) (Stuttgart: Teubner, 1915), p. 135.

14 Aristotle, *Metaphysics*, X, 3, 995a6-17; *Nicomachean Ethics*, I, 3, 1094b11–1095a2.

generally. Pascal had the merit of connecting the two phenomena. The one called a generalist does not conduct himself as a mathematician or a soldier when he is with those who are neither. He will know how to adapt his method to the matter. For example, he will not seek to subject persons, and *a fortiori* God, to a kind of experimental method, even if that is perfectly suitable to discover the laws of nature.[15]

If we take this as our point of departure, we can give education a larger meaning and concept, which would contain two categories. In connection with knowledge, one would be the application of appropriate methods; the other, when it is a matter of our relations with other person, the appropriate conduct. As a whole, the concept is equivalent to *respect*. It consists in treating *what is* the way that it is; more precisely, treating what is given, the way that it offers itself. "Offer itself" has a variable meaning. Strictly speaking, the expression only pertains to persons, who can freely decide if they want to offer themselves. "Things" cannot be the adequate subject of "an offer."

To treat the given as what offers itself can imply on the part of the recipient the active decision to remain on the surface, to renounce venturing too far into the depths of the other. Thus, when it comes to a person, one will not ask what we tellingly call "personal questions" until and unless the other person asks, as is the case with a doctor or psychiatrist. As for what concerns the phenomena of nature, the educated person will remain aware of the process of abstraction required by scientific knowledge, and will abstain from thinking that what science yields is the truth *tout court*.

Of knowledge and its interest

The problem therefore is to define the type of knowledge which can promote nascent liberty and nourish it once it is there. But first, can *knowledge* as such provide what is expected of it?

If it were a question of founding a school of instruction, and giving young people the necessary equipment to orient themselves in the world of today, one would have to focus this equipment on what would give them the most effective *compass*. In our world, marked decisively by the mathematical physics inaugurated by Galileo, it is clear that this compass must be science.

---

15   Blaise Pascal, *Pensées, op. cit.*, # 557, t. 3, p. 7; $ 430, t. 2, pp. 336–37.

However, what we need to establish is not a school of instruction, but of education. In this perspective, science, and with it all sorts of knowledge, suffers from a major defect. Science instructs enormously. But can it educate? In general, science teaches us humility before what is. The science of nature teaches us to abandon an hypothesis as soon as the experiment disconfirms it. In the same way, philology teaches us to try to understand a text before venturing to take a position on its content. What one needs to reproach science does not concern the science of nature in contrast to the moral sciences, or the humanities, but any and all sorts of knowledge. Education tells us what the appropriate behavior is. This implies an entire register of "commandments," which begin at the humblest level: table manners, rules of etiquette, grammar, eating, everything we call "culture."

Now, knowledge tells us what is, but it leaves us free concerning what we ought to do. I insist on this point. The fundamental distinction is not that which separates the sciences of nature and humanistic learning. All of these enlist under the same banner.[16] To know the chemical formula of water, or that Shakespeare died in 1616, does not help us to act. This needs to be recalled: *pace* C. P. Snow, there are not "two cultures." Quite obviously, there are two domains of knowledge, but neither of them insofar as they are simply knowledge is a culture. The humanities do not acquire cultural pertinence until they teach us how to proceed, how to write a poem, how to paint a picture.

As for science, to put it in a brutally direct and willingly provocative way: it isn't *interesting*.[17] To explain, let's distinguish three senses of "interest". What is interesting can be either 1) rewarding, "profitable"; or 2) fascinating; or 3) interesting in the proper sense. We can be interested in the profits of a corporation as shareholders or as board members. We can be fascinated by a spectacle in which we are absorbed. It can be a work of art. It can also be a natural phenomenon, from the delicate structure of a flower or an insect to a constellation of stars.

I call "interesting" in the proper sense whatever teaches us something about what we are, which obliges us to reflect upon the human condition,

---

16   See above, Chapter 8, "Are There Really Two Culture?".
17   Here I summarize my *Au moyen du Moyen Âge, op. cit.*, pp. 97–118, especially pp. 98–99.

and to change something in our lives. Here one can engage in word-play. What *inter-ests* is what lies between, what we need to cross in order to arrive at what we are. Great art, Greek tragedy, for example, plays this role, but a simple conversation with someone we admire can do the same thing. In contrast, a circus act or a good detective novel can be fascinating, some sidewalk slapstick comic can rivet us to the spot, but none of that is interesting in the strong sense.

Let us apply these three concepts to the science of nature. It is always fascinating. It already was so for Aristotle.[18] In addition, ancient science was interesting, because it was deemed to permit the observer to discover his deepest nature.[19] The modern science of nature, by its technological applications, is extremely profitable. We owe our entire material civilization to it; and often we owe it our life. Moreover, its fantastic discoveries and hypotheses give it an unbelievable power of fascination, even when it is cast in a popular form. However, it is not *interesting* in the proper sense of the term.

The program of an impossible school

What therefore would be the curriculum of this imaginary school, which would have the luxury of neglecting all instruction and only aiming at education?

There, I would rehabilitate the study of classical languages. And for the very reason that they are abandoned today. They are totally useless and thus they give us an idea of the value of what is useless. More precisely, they show us that what has value is always useless. People say, "They don't serve any useful purpose!" "Oh, what magnificent praise!"

Furthermore, I would study them because they are dead. They are the native language of no one. Therefore, no one has a privileged position vis-à-vis them.

And finally, they have the advantage of making us feel small. They humble us, but in the right way. For if we had to learn the language of the

---

18 Aristotle, *Parts of animals*, I, 5.
19 See, for example: Seneca, *Quaestiones Naturales*, Preface, # 12, P. Oltramare (ed.) (Paris: Les Belles Lettres, 1929), p. 10; for the context, see my *La Sagesse du monde*, op. cit., pp. 151–53.

ruling class or nation that sets the civilizational tone (the French in the eighteenth century, English today), we would be humiliated vis-à-vis the people for whom this is their native language. To learn the language of people who have disappeared makes us aware of what remains inchoate and unpolished in us, but allows us to avoid the sentiment of resentment.

Then I would give a large place to teaching the arts. To be sure, it would not be to learn their history, but to learn how to perform them, to paint, to play an instrument. In teaching how to draw, to sculpt, to sing, we communicate the right way, the correct way, to do something. I chose that formulation deliberately. Let me explain its two elements: the *right or correct* way, and *to do* something. The presence of a result is more immediate in artistic education than in other disciplines. The picture is beautiful or not, one sings on pitch or not. The student thereby learns, and learns quickly, that acting or performing well or not has palpable consequences. On the other hand, the student acquires the ability to make, to do, or to produce, to dance or paint. She thus augments her liberty, and in the most practical way possible.

And at the same time, the classical languages and art have this advantage in common, which is also shared with every form of rigorous knowledge: they require precision and help form its capacity. To mistake a declination, to miss a half-note, lead to mistakes and worse. Above all, one learns the chief condition for respect: forgetting oneself for the sake of the object, which ought to have first place.

With this, we are at the threshold of moral education, at least by implication. Would I include moral education, one that would be explicit? I first pose a preliminary question. Does a strictly non-moral education exist? Is it conceivable? If it were a question of instruction, the question would not be raised. Instruction can exclude all references to ultimate realities, and even every value-judgment on the competence thus acquired. It even has to do that. In order to learn how to manipulate things, one has to forget why one learns to do so. A good executioner has to forbid himself from asking the question of the legitimacy of the death penalty. In contrast, one needs a moral education to know what to do with one's liberty, how to employ it, and, more radically, how not to *lose* it by enclosing it in choices that paralyze it, or which destroy its conditions of existence. This education will not go beyond the "grand platitudes" of what C. S. Lewis called the *Tao*, beyond which, moreover, no one has ever been able to go, or will.[20]

Will I include religious education? To which I again reply: Can education dispense with a response to religious questions? To say yes, is already to respond with a religious idea. And to say that God does not exist, one must already have a sort of theology if one wants to know what one is talking about. To be sure, this would be a rather impoverished theology, but it would imply an idea of God. True theology, that which is practiced by genuine theologians, is a much more discerning discipline than this minimal theology that serves to deny God's existence. It begins by posing the question of the *very existence* of its object, which is what no other domain of knowledge dares to do, and it makes progress by constantly refining the concept it constructs of this object. In my school, therefore, I would only teach the religions that have produced a theology.

In my school, though, theology would be the fundamental science. No one should be scandalized by this. Here, I make no claim of sovereignty, no return to the (legendary) situation when the sciences would have been the "handmaids of theology." To say that theology is the *fundamental* science, is only to note a postulate upon which all education rests. It is only to have the honesty to acknowledge it. Education implies a fundamental confidence in Being, a fundamental faith in the identity of Being and the Good. This is true for two reasons. The first concerns the very *movement* of education, which is to transmit something (a knowledge, competences, or "values") to the following generations. This presupposes that they exist. Thus, before transmitting anything else, one must begin by transmitting life. More and more, as I have argued, it depends upon the free, conscious, even deliberate choice of the present generation to call the next generation into being. And why would it do so, if it is not convinced, at least implicitly, that existence is, in the final analysis, whatever might happen, in itself a good?

The second reason concerns the *content* of education. For why would we be obliged to admit what is true? Because it "works," because it allows us to operate? Here we have returned to simple instruction. Why, though, prefer the truth to an agreeable illusion? Truth can be quite ugly, detestable,

---

20 C. S. Lewis, *The Abolition of Man, op. cit.*

despairing. This question is at least as old as Renan, who asked, "Is despair right, and truth sad?"[21] A distrust of the truth courses through European culture at least since Schopenhauer, of whom Renan perhaps was thinking. The German philosopher's position itself, however, was the result of a long and complicated intellectual drift of the West. The love of truth supposes that the truth is loveable. It presupposes—to borrow a technical term from scholastic thought—that the "transcendentals," the true, the good, and the beautiful, are convertible (*convertuntur*), one with the other. If this is not the case, we certainly can remain sincere; then our last virtue would be intellectual probity. But can this virtue give us life?

Why in fact should we love the truth? In the final analysis, it is an imperative of the moral order. Nietzsche was right to see that our purported "love of the truth" was the last trace of a conviction of a moral nature that was rooted in Plato and in Christianity, which he considered to be a "Platonism" for the people.[22] But is it so sure that we ought to *unmask* this faith? Would it not be better to *assume* it?

---

21 Ernest Renan, "La Métaphysique et son avenir" [1860], in H. Psichari (ed.), *Oeuvres complètes, op. cit.*, t. 1, p. 714.
22 Friedrich Nietzsche, *Die fröhliche Wissenschaft*, V, # 344, KSA, t. 3, p. 577, and the Preface to *Jenseits von Gut und Böse, ibid.*, t. 5, p. 12.

16

NOT TO BETRAY (:) THE TRADITION

"Tradition" is a dangerous word, full of pitfalls and at the origin of many confusions, mainly because of the strange ambivalence it contains. This ambiguity comes most clearly to light in the adjective "traditional." This has a pejorative cast, it even becomes something of an insult when it qualifies, e.g., morality or family, in contrast to what John Stuart Mill called new "experiments in living."[1] The vision of the world of those called "bobos,"[2] from the Bloomsbury group in London during the 1920s to our day, disdains everything that has the infamous mark of "traditional." Those whom tradition disgusts ratify, if need be by caricaturing it, the fundamental choice of Modernity against everything that is traditional.

On the other hand, the same adjective conveys an entirely positive meaning and becomes a powerful argument in advertising when it qualifies a food and the manner in which it is prepared. A baguette will taste better (and be more expensive), when it is cooked "according to a traditional recipe," and bobos line up in front of the bakeries that do so, without noticing that in this way their stomachs witness to a nostalgia characteristic of reactionaries.

With philosophers, tradition is also presented with a Janus-face. At the beginning of his cruel history of Napoleon III's accession to power, Marx wrote: "The tradition of all the dead generations weighs like an incubus or a nightmare (*Alp*) on the brain of the living."[3] Close to a century later,

---

1   John S. Mill, *On Liberty* [1859], chap. III, in A. D. Lindsay (ed.), *Utilitarianism, Liberty and Representative Government, op. cit.*, p. 115; see also p. 122, and chap. IV, p. 137.

2   David Brooks, *Bobos in Paradise. The New Upper Class and How They Got There* (New York: Simon & Shuster, 2000).

3   Karl Marx, *Der achtzehnte Brumaire von Louis Bonaparte* [1852], 1, at the beginning.

meditating on the origin of geometry, Husserl on the other hand wrote: "The world of culture, under all its forms, exists by tradition."[4] Tradition is at once a crushing weight and a gift that gives us everything of value.

Tradition as productive

Time passing, and at an ever more accelerated pace, the opposition between the two sides of the coin, the positive and the negative, has become even more accentuated.

Today, the pendulum swings in the direction of the negative. Everything occurs as if the West is plunged into a sort of all-encompassing self-hatred. It envisages its past not only as containing crimes, a trait common to all civilizations, but as an uninterrupted series of them: the conquest of the New World, the colonization of Africa, capitalist exploitation, the Holocaust. "The white man's burden" that Kipling wrote about now takes on a bitter irony. And as a counterpart, the West looks nostalgically on other civilizations, judged innocent, or at least not as guilty as it is.[5] Since the nineteenth century we have learned that the past shapes us much more profoundly than we are aware. Historical science has taught us to take more and more seriously the saying of Auguste Comte: "The living are always, and increasingly, necessarily governed by the dead: this is the fundamental law of the human order."[6] This does not only hold true for the domain of human action and its results. In biology, Darwin, in a book published in 1859, taught us that we are the heirs of a past that in the final analysis goes back to the origins of life in the "warm little pond" that he imagined.[7] Today astrophysics adds: We are the heirs of the entire past history of the universe. Our bodies are composed of atoms that appeared billions of years ago. In this way the past is not content merely to guide us, it makes us what we are.

4　Edmund Husserl, [Der Ursprung der Geometrie], Beilage III, in *Die Krisis der europäischen Wissenschaften und die transzendentale Phänomenologie*, W. Biemel (ed.) (La Haye: Nijhoff, 1961), Husserliana, t. 6, p. 366.

5　Pascal Bruckner, *Le Sanglot de l'homme blanc. Tiers-monde, culpabilité, haine de soi* (Paris: Seuil, 1986).

6　Auguste Comte, *Catéchisme positiviste* [1852], I, 2, P.-F. Pécault (ed.) (Paris: Garnier, s. d.), p. 70.

7　Darwin, *Letter to Joseph Hooker*, February 1, 1871.

Two attitudes result from these symmetrical facts: the revolutionary's and the reactionary's. Both emphasize one or another of these two dimensions, in themselves perfectly sensible, but then go on to absolutize them.

The revolutionary wants to break with the past. He refuses to admit that our past can influence our choices today. To cite the formula coined by a Frenchman on the eve of the Revolution: "Our history is not our code."[8] This history, one must not merely forget it, one must erase it. The revolutionary wants to make a *tabula rasa*, to begin again at zero. Mao Zedong declared that one cannot write a beautiful poem without a perfectly clean piece of paper; he wanted to write on the human material of China with the most magnificent social calligraphy. It is from this point of view that the adjective "traditional" took on polemical value and served to discredit whatever was so qualified.

The traditionalist is he who wants to return to the past, or at least to conserve it. His argument is not without plausibility. The past has proven itself, the state of things it represents is possible, because it was real, while the future will probably be worse than the past. And in any case, it is uncertain, both in its content and its very existence, because we do not know if there will be a future. Some natural or manmade catastrophe, a huge meteor or a nuclear war, can very well put an end to the human adventure. "Traditional" would then have the connotation of "worthy of trust."

The truth of the revolutionary: the phenomenon of birth

The revolutionary begins from a fundamental trait of the human. It is one of Hannah Arendt's great merits to have brought it to light and, in order to give it a name, to have coined the term "natality" as the counterpart to the "mortality" on which philosophers have been much more expansive. From her first book in English, she wrote: "Beginning, before it becomes a historical event, is the supreme capacity of man; politically, it is identical with man's freedom. [...] This beginning is guaranteed by

8   Jean-Paul Rabaut Saint-Étienne, *Considérations sur les intérêts du tiers-état adressées au peuple des provinces par un propriétaire foncier* [1788] (Paris: Kleffer, 1826), pp. 1–105, citation # 1, p. 11.

each new birth; it is indeed every man."[9] The idea received a more finished form in what seems to me to be a masterwork of philosophy: "[A]ction has the closest connection with the human condition of natality; the new beginning inherent in birth can make itself felt in the world only because the newcomer possesses the capacity of beginning something anew, that is, of acting. In this sense of initiative, an element of action, and therefore of natality, is inherent in all human activities."[10] Each human being in being born brings a novelty that one can call *absolute*, in the etymological sense of the term: untied, detached, liberated from what preceded.

Liberty is spontaneity, the capacity to introduce into the tissue of facts a new one, unforeseen and unforeseeable. On this, Bergson seems to me to have written the decisive pages.[11] Now, this new beginning implies that what existed already is left behind, forgotten. Forgetting is not necessarily a negative process, due to the lack of attention. It can be the "valiant forgetting" about which Hölderlin spoke: "The spirit loves the colony and the valiant forgetting."[12] In his second *Untimely Meditation*, Nietzsche meditated on the disadvantages of historical research for life. One has to forget what was already done in order to be able to create.[13] And more than a century before the German philosopher, a Frenchman wrote that "in order to be happy, men have more need of forgetting than learning."[14]

---

9 Hannah Arendt, *The Origins of Totalitarianism* [1951] (New York: Schocken Books, 2004), p. 616 (the last words of the book in the second edition of 1958).

10 Hannah Arendt, *The Human Condition* [1958] (Chicago: The University of Chicago Press, 1998), p. 9; see also, besides the references given in the index, pp. 178 & 191.

11 Henri Bergson, *Essai sur les données immédiates de la conscience* [1889], ch. III.

12 Friedrich Hölderlin, *Brot und Wein* [1801], lesson, *GSA*, II-2, p. 608.

13 Friedrich Nietzsche, *Unzeitgemäße Betrachtungen*, "II: Vom Nutzen und Nachteil der Historie für das Leben" [1877], KSA, t. 1, pp. 252–53.

14 François-Jean de Chastellux, *De la félicité publique ou Considérations sur le sort des hommes dans les différentes époques de l'histoire* [1772], "Vues ultérieures sur la félicité publique" (Bouillon: Société typographique, 1776) t. 2, p. 313; the attention of historians of ideas was drawn to this forgotten author by Carl L. Becker, *The Heavenly City of the Eighteenth-Century Philosophers, op. cit.,* pp. 93–94.

The error of the revolutionary

However, the newborn cannot develop, or even survive, without receiving from his milieu. Already at the biological level, we have need of breathing and nourishing ourselves. The experience of "feral children" shows that humanity does not develop itself completely except in an already human milieu.[15] The infant is still incapable of speaking, the *in-fans* in the Latin sense of the term, already receives language as the vehicle of the quasi-totality of the tradition. This language, the individual can use it in a personal way, each will have his style, and this individuality will be carried to the highest degree with the great writer.

Moreover, the revolutionary himself is an entirely different thing than a subject who would be capable of taking up an external and neutral position vis-à-vis the past, like a judge who considers from the outside. The present subject is himself a product of the past. Even if he wants to be an innovator, it can happen that he only repeats archaic forms. The attempt to break with the past often entails a "return of the repressed" which resurfaces under such a form. Among the protagonists of the French Revolution, this was shown by their obsessive references to Antiquity, Roman in particular, at least as they had imagined the Romans in their reading of Plutarch or Tacitus in the middle schools of the Oratorians and Jesuits.

Forgetting cannot but be unconscious and something we suffer.[16] One cannot will to forget. To be sure, we can wish to forget certain events, especially when they are traumatic. But we cannot decide to forget. An effort of this kind would end as an affectation. To decide to forget, one must know exactly what ought to be forgotten, and have a very vivid memory of what must be erased. The will to forget thus ends with an exacerbation of memory. One can call this the "Herostratus effect." Herostratus was immortalized, not by his idiotic crime (which was to burn the temple of Diana at Ephesus, one of the seven marvels of the world), but by the even more

---

15   Roger Shattuck, *The Forbidden Experiment. The Story of the Wild Boy of Aveyron* (New York: Farrar, Strauss & Giroux, 1980).

16   Umberto Eco and Marilyn Migiel, "An Ars Oblivionalis? Forget It!," *Publications of the Modern Language Association*, CIII, 3, 1988. Pp. 254–61.

stupid order of the local sovereign who commanded that his name was never to be pronounced.[17]

To make a *tabula rasa* of the past by imagining that that would make the place clear for the novelty to come—unfortunately, this experiment has been tried in recent history. These attempts ended with the destruction of a thousand traces of what existed before, including the human brains that were the bearers of these memories. But nothing came in its place. During the few years that he spent at the head of the newly created Soviet Union, Lenin was able to destroy many things. His successor, Stalin, put into execution plans on an even grander scale, as did Mao, then Pol Pot, and others. But nothing was created. Where is the "socialist society"? There remains only the desert, and charnel-houses.

As for the necessity of a forgetting prior to creation, of a destruction that would be at the same time a creation, one could reverse the perspective and risk saying that one must first create in order to be able to forget. Let us begin with creating, and then see if the new is up to the measure of the old, even to the point of causing it to be forgotten. The Polish poet Czesław Miłosz, Noble Prize winner for Literature in 1980, put it magnificently: "It is not critique, nor theoretical manifestos, but a fuller existence that overcomes faded existences."[18]

The error of the traditionalist: the invention of tradition

The traditionalist is mistaken in his tendency to exaggerate the distance that separates him from the past. He neglects the common elements that subsist, which often are the overwhelming majority of what goes into the composition of our world. Conversely, he attributes more weight to the ruptures in the historical continuum than they actually possess. This makes him an unwittingly companion of the revolutionary.

The traditionalist seeks, if not to return to the past, which is impossible, at least to maintain it. But this past is the result of a selection operated by the present subject, individual or collective, which gives itself the past it imagines. What we take for a tradition is in large part invented. The

---

17 Valerius Maximus, *Memorable deeds and sayings*, VIII, 14: "Strange examples," 5; Lucian, *The Passing of Peregrinus*, 22.
18 Czeslaw Milosz, *La Terre d'Ulro*, # 19, end.

English historian Eric Hobsbawn, who died recently, in 1983 published a book that very quickly became a classic, which he entitled *The Invention of Tradition*.[19] He succeeded in showing the great number of folkloric elements believed to be traditional that were invented when nations sought to ground their identities on a purported ancient history, which happened many times in the nineteenth century. The book was followed by a flood of books entitled *The invention of . . .* or *The Making of . . .* , when it wasn't *The Social Construction of . . .*, a title whose origin is perfectly legitimate, but which was so overused that people could make fun of it.[20]

We retain from the past what seems to us pertinent for today, in function of our present interests. It is not the past that dictates to us what we ought to do. On the contrary, it is we who, at least in some measure, decide what the past was by constantly recapitulating it. We decide in view of projects that we form for the future. In our personal lives, we constantly reread and review our own past and reinterpret it in connection with our present decisions. This is the truth contained in Jean-Paul Sartre's analyses of human existence as a project.[21]

This observation leads us to a more radical conclusion, which obliges us to nuance something that seems obvious, and was expressed in Aristotle's teaching. The Greek philosopher suggested a parallel between the three temporal dimensions and three faculties of the soul. The present would be the object of perception, the past, of memory, the future, of "anticipation" (*elpis*).[22] That memory has access to the past, nothing seems clearer. But Heidegger observed, orally at least, that paradoxically the attitude in which the past is given as such is not memory, but forgetfulness.[23] In fact, memory

19 Eric Hobsbawn and Terence Ranger (dir.), *The Invention of Tradition* (Cambridge: Cambridge University Press, 1983).

20 See Ian Hacking, *The Social Construction of What?* (Cambridge, MA: Harvard University Press, 2000). The serious work in this vein was by Peter L. Berger and Thomas Luckmann, *The Social Construction of Reality. A Treatise in the Sociology of Knowledge* (New York: Doubleday, 1967).

21 Jean-Paul Sartre, *L'Être et le Néant* [1943] (Paris: Gallimard, 1968), p. 508 ff.

22 Aristotle, *De memoria*, I, 449b27–8; *Rhetoric*, I, 11, 1369b34–5; see also *Nicomachean Ethics*, IX, 7, 1168a13–14. *Elpis* does not only mean "hope."

23 Cited by Hans-Georg Gadamer, "Die Kontinuität der Geschichte und der Augenblick der Existenz" [1965], *Wahrheit und Methode. Ergänzungen*, in *Gesammelte Werke* (Tübingen: Mohr, 1986), t. 2, p. 145.

makes the past present, it "re-presents" it, and thus lacks the essential characteristic that makes the past the past.

The truth of traditionalism

The person who respects tradition is often styled a "conservative," an adjective that is also a technical term in medicine. A surgical intervention is said to be "conservative" when it tries to remove the least amount of the impaired organ.

The contemporary German philosopher Odo Marquard (1928–2015), from whom I borrowed the previous observation, provides an argument in favor of conservatism. Everything else being equal, the scales tip in favor of conservatism because we are temporal and finite beings. Descartes told us to put everything in doubt.[24] But we will never have the time to reexamine everything before having to make decisions necessary for life. It is therefore prudent not to depart from what has been done up until the present.[25] Even before Marquard, the English philosopher George E. Moore, even though he renewed ethical reflection in a very original way, argued in the concrete for a wholly traditional morality: "The individual can therefore be confidently recommended *always* to conform to rules which are both generally useful and generally practiced."[26]

The just attitude toward the past consists in letting it be what it is, and allowing it to produce its effects. The question "What to do?" is no doubt as old as humanity, but it has taken a sinister turn ever since Lenin, very consciously employing the title of a novel by Chernyshevsky, made it the title of a pamphlet he published in 1902: *What is to be done?* The consequences of the Leninist solutions showed themselves much more "painful" than the "problems" to which the subtitle alludes. As for me, the answer I would give would be, "But nothing at all!"; or very specific reforms to put an end to injustices; and in no case, global efforts "to change society," even less to create "a new man" by first liquidating the old.

24   Descartes, *Discours de la Méthode*, II, *AT*, t. 6, pp. 13–14.
25   Odo Marquard, "Abschied vom Prinzipiellen. Auch eine autobiographische Einleitung," in *Abschied vom Prinzipiellen* (Stuttgart: Reclam, 1981), p. 16.
26   G. E. Moore, *Principia Ethica* [1903], V, # 99, T. Baldwin (ed.) (Cambridge: Cambridge University Press, 1993), p. 213.

The most important point consists in noting that respect for the past in no way inhibits preparing the future. On the contrary, it is what permits there to be a future. Why so? Because we must know that we have been the future of our past, in order to become the past of our future. This abstract rule has for an example an entirely concrete fact, an example that is more than an example, but the foundation of all history. We have to recognize that we are the children of our parents, in order to have children and to become their parents.

> [T]radition is only democracy extended through time. [...] Tradition means giving votes to the most obscure of all classes, our ancestors. It is the democracy of the dead. Tradition refuses to submit to the small and arrogant oligarchy of those who merely happen to be walking about; tradition objects to their being disqualified by the accident of death. Democracy tells us not to neglect a good man's opinion, even if he is our groom; tradition asks us not to neglect a good man's opinion, even if he is our father. I, at any rate, cannot separate the two ideas of democracy and tradition; it seems evident to me that they are the same idea.[27]

Pietas *as the virtue of temporal existence*

If one must give a name to the proper attitude, the virtue, that bears upon temporal existence as such, I propose the almost untranslatable Latin term, pietas.[28] Here I am inspired by a book by Richard Weaver that has become a classic; the last chapter develops this idea.[29]

On the root of the substantive, *pietas*, which is obviously the Latin adjective *pius*, our best guides fail us somewhat.[30] The Latin word seems to

27   G. K. Chesterton, *Orthodoxy*, chap. IV (San Francisco: Ignatius Press, s.d.), pp. 52–53.

28   Here I reprise a passage from my preface to the French translation of Theodor Haecker's book, *Virgile, Père de l'Occident* (Genève: Ad Solem, 2007), pp. XI–XII.

29   Richard M. Weaver, *Ideas Have Consequences* (Chicago and London: The University of Chicago Press, 1948), pp. 170–87.

30   The word is not found in the index of Émile Benveniste, *Le Vocabulaire des institutions indo-européennes, II. Pouvoir, droit, religion* (Paris: Minuit, 1969).

have some relation to the ideas of purity and purification, hence the verb "expiate." In any case, in most cases it refers to the duties of children toward their parents, and even more to the parent of each citizen, the *patria*, to which even filial piety must yield.[31]

Piety is far from reducing itself to a clutching on to the past, whose inexorable disappearance one wants to slow. Aeneas bears witness to this, the paradigmatic hero of Roman experience, whom Virgil constantly calls *pius Aeneas*, and not merely for metrical reasons. He never shows himself to be more pious than when he *transfers* the penates of Troy going down in flames to Latium, according to the legend of the origins of the *gens Julia* and, subsequently, the Roman Empire. To be sure, he has to bear his wounded father on his shoulders, a scene that has inspired many artists. But this is not a crushing burden, contrary to what Jean-Paul Sartre thought in a passage of his childhood memories.[32] The piety of Aeneas toward his own origins culminates when he *buries* the old Anchises. The final result of his piety is not conservation, but, to the contrary, a new foundation, the opening of a new space of possibilities.

The Latin *pietas* survives in the Romance languages and in English words of French origin as the root not only of "piety," but also "pity." The two words in fact were separated rather late in the history of the French language. The kinship between the two reveals a proximity in their meanings. One must display a certain indulgence towards the past to be able to receive its influence. Not indulgence towards the errors and misdeeds that the past almost always contains, which need to be acknowledged and can be forgiven, but rather the much deeper pardon of the fact that the past is past, and irreversibly so. This is what Nietzsche called resentment toward the past and its "it was," which feeds the "spirit of vengeance," the latter being "the ill will of the will towards time and its 'it was.'"[33] The German philosopher proposes his vision of the world as the remedy to this spirit, and in particular the eternal return of the same. I would suggest that *pietas* could be just as efficacious.

---

31 See, for example: Cicero, *De officiis*, III, xxiii, 90, C. Atzert (ed.) (Leipzig: Teubner, 1963), p. 113.

32 Jean-Paul Sartre, *Les Mots* (Paris: Gallimard, 1964), p. 11.

33 Friedrich Nietzsche, *Also sprach Zarathustra*, II, "Von der Erlösung," *KSA*, t. 4, p. 180.

Of all this, we have a negative proof. A civilization that, like ours, wishes to be *impious* no longer can *expiate*. To be sure, we are the opposite of "men without public avowals." Don't we spend our time accusing, and in particular accusing our ancestors of all sorts of crimes, both real and imagined? A good part of the historical production of the West today is nourished by self-hatred. Distinguished authors show that the past is an arbitrary construct, hence the proliferation of titles noted earlier, which imply that what was "made" or "constructed" can be unmade or "deconstructed." The more vulgar popularizers reduce our past to a long chain of crimes and injustices. This analysis is certainly not entirely false, for what civilization, what group of human beings that could use force against others, ever abstained from doing so?

It is a fact that it was Europe that discovered the rest of the world and colonized and ruled it. It did so because of its technological advances. It is the only culture that had the physical *possibility* of intervening in the others. The other cultures, were they innocent victims? Looked at more closely, the purported innocence comes from the denial and expunging of the past. In any case, this innocence would be that of the one-armed man, innocent of all theft, mute, therefore innocent of all calumny, or, finally, the eunuch, guiltless of any rape. Here I recall the parable of the elephant and the mouse that I recounted earlier. And what good do these perverse confessions do that never result in absolution? They can only inoculate us with a paralyzing poison.

Two relations to tradition

Now, I would like to return to the ambivalence I indicated at the beginning and show it in another light. We imagine that what we don't like in tradition is the connection with the past, and that to it we prefer the future. In this way we consider ourselves "progressive." In truth, however, the line that separates the tradition that we love, for example in the case of the baguette, and that which we do not like, for example "the traditional family," should be placed elsewhere. And the distinction does us much less honor, because here too applies the distinction made by St. Augustine between two aspects of the truth, *lucens* and *redarguens*, which I developed above.

The tradition that we love is the one that makes the past appear to culminate with us, and which we can enjoy. Thus the baguette that we eat, and therefore destroy by that very fact. What we do not like is what permits the very passage from the past to the future and requires that we give it free passage. We love tradition as reception; we do not like it as transmission.[34]

In this light a very important characteristic of the past appears. The past, our past, perhaps has many somber aspects. It has been the place of many crimes and many stupidities. But at the very least, it had a two-fold merit. On one hand, it existed, while no one knows if the future will exist; and on the other, which is more important, *it produced us*, we who place ourselves as judges vis-à-vis it.

Retrospectively, we can say that the past was pregnant with what for it was the future, and which is today our present. In contrast, nothing guarantees that our present contains anything other than itself, that it in fact opens to a future. The future will not come of its own, one must make it come. There are decisions that prevent the future from coming. Those that will render it possible ought to be taken starting today.

34 Here, I develop a few lines of my *Anchors in the Heavens, op. cit.*